Implementing the
Project Management
Balanced Scorecard

Implementing the Project Management Balanced Scorecard

Jessica Keyes

CRC Press
Taylor & Francis Group
Boca Raton London New York

CRC Press is an imprint of the
Taylor & Francis Group, an **informa** business

AN AUERBACH BOOK

CRC Press
Taylor & Francis Group
6000 Broken Sound Parkway NW, Suite 300
Boca Raton, FL 33487-2742

First issued in paperback 2019

© 2011 by Taylor and Francis Group, LLC
CRC Press is an imprint of Taylor & Francis Group, an Informa business

No claim to original U.S. Government works

ISBN-13: 978-1-4398-2718-5 (hbk)
ISBN-13: 978-1-138-37432-4 (pbk)

Library of Congress Cataloging-in-Publication Data

Keyes, Jessica, 1950-
    Implementing the project management balanced scorecard / Jessica Keyes.
        p. cm.
    Includes bibliographical references and index.
    ISBN 978-1-4398-2718-5 (hbk. : alk. paper)
    1. Project management--Evaluation. 2. Performance--Evaluation. 3. Business planning--Evaluation. I. Title.

HD69.P75K5115 2011
658.4'04--dc22   2010021875

**Visit the Taylor & Francis Web site at
http://www.taylorandfrancis.com**

**and the CRC Press Web site at
http://www.crcpress.com**

This book is dedicated to my family and friends.

Contents

Foreword

The goals of a project-based balanced scorecard include the alignment of the project plan with business objectives, the establishment of measures of the project's effectiveness, the directing of employee efforts toward project objectives, and the achievement of balanced results across the various stakeholder groups. Project managers can achieve these goals by considering multiple perspectives, long- and short-term objectives, and how the project-based scorecard is linked to other scorecards throughout their organizations. *Implementing the Project Management Balanced Scorecard* provides both a strategic overview of the corporate balanced scorecard, as well as a tactical discussion for implementing the scorecard approach at the project level.

This volume thoroughly explains the concept of the scorecard framework from the corporate, departmental, and project perspectives. It provides examples, case histories, and current research for critical issues such as performance measurement and management, continuous process improvement, benchmarking, metrics selection, and people management. The book also discusses how to integrate these issues with the four perspectives of the balanced scorecard: customer, business processes, learning and innovation, and financial. Finally, the book directly relates the scorecard concept to the major project management steps of determining scope, scheduling, estimation, risk management, procurement, and project termination.

Implementing the Project Management Balanced Scorecard also provides a plethora of resources in its appendices, and on the accompanying CD, including detailed instructions for developing a measurement program, a full metrics guide, a sample project plan, and a set of project management fill-in forms.

Preface

Quite a few things can go wrong with a typical project. For the most part, there are three classes of problems: people, process, and product. These can be categorized, as shown in Table P.1

Hyvari (2006) provides a different spin on this, as shown in Table P.2. There are also a wide variety of management considerations (e.g., project scope, scheduling, risk, tracking, estimation, etc.) that can make or break a project. We usually call these considerations critical success factors (CSF). They include

- *Executive Support:* The executive sponsor must have a global view of the project, set the agenda, arrange the funding, articulate the project's overall objectives, be an ardent supporter, be responsive, and finally, and ultimately, be accountable for the project's success.
- *User Involvement:* Primary users must have good communication skills allowing them to clearly explain business processes in detail to the project team. Primary users should also be trained to follow project management protocols. Finally, users must be realists and aware of the limitations of the projects.
- *Experienced Project Manager:* Project managers must possess technology and business knowledge, judgment, negotiation, and good communication and organization skills. The primary focus is on softer skills, such as diplomacy and time management.
- *Clear Business Objectives:* The project objectives must be clearly defined and understood throughout the organization. Projects must be measured against these objectives regularly to provide an opportunity for early recognition and correction of problems, justification for resources and funding, and preventive planning on future projects.
- *Minimized Scope:* Scope must be realistic and able to be accomplished within the identified project duration and measured regularly to eliminate scope creep.

Table P.1 Classic Project Mistakes

People-Related Mistakes	Process-Related Mistakes	Product-Related Mistakes
Undermined motivation	Overly optimistic schedules	Requirements gold-plating (i.e., too many product features)
Weak personnel	Insufficient risk management	Feature creep
Uncontrolled problem employees	Contractor failure	Tools don't fit the problem
Heroics	Insufficient planning	Push me, pull me negotiation (i.e., constantly changing schedule)
Adding people to a late project	Abandonment of planning under pressure	Overly research-oriented (i.e., stretching the limits of technology)
Noisy crowded offices	Wasted time before project actually starts (i.e., the approval and budgeting process)	
Friction between developers and customers	Shortchanged upstream activities (e.g., requirements analysis, etc.)	
Unrealistic expectations	Inadequate design	
Lack of effective project sponsorship	Shortchanged quality assurance	
Lack of stakeholder buy-in	Insufficient management controls	
Lack of user input	Premature or too frequent convergence (i.e., releasing the product too early)	
Politics over substance	Omitting necessary tasks from estimates	
Wishful thinking	Planning to catch up later	

Table P.2 Success/Failure Factors	
Factors Related to Project	**Size and Value**
	Having a clear boundary
	Urgency
	Uniqueness of project activities
	Density of the project network (in dependencies between activities)
	Project life cycle
	End-user commitment
	Adequate funds/resources
	Realistic schedule
	Clear goals/objectives
Factors Related to the Project Manager/Leadership	**Ability to Delegate Authority**
	Ability to trade off
	Ability to coordinate
	Perception of his or her role and responsibilities
	Effective leadership
	Effective conflict resolution
	Having relevant past experience
	Management of changes
	Contract management
	Situational management
	Competence
	Commitment
	Trust
	Other communication

(continued)

Table P.2 Success/Failure Factors (Continued)

Factors Related to Project Team Members	Technical Background
	Communication
	Troubleshooting
	Effective monitoring and feedback
	Commitment
Factors Related to the Organization	**Steering Committee**
	Clear organization/job descriptions
	Top management support
	Project organization structure
	Functional manager's support
	Project champion
Factors Related to the Environment	**Competitors**
	Political environment
	Economic environment
	Social environment
	Technological environment
	Nature
	Client
	Subcontractors

- *Agile Business Requirements Process:* Requirements management is the process of identifying, documenting, communicating, tracking, and managing project requirements, as well as changes to those requirements. Agile requirements process is the ability to perform requirements management quickly and without major conflicts. This is an ongoing process and must stay in lockstep with the development process.
- *Formal Methodology:* Following formal methodology provides a realistic picture of the project and the resource commitment. Certain steps and procedures are reproduceable and reusable, maximizing projectwide consistency.
- *Reliable Estimates:* Be realistic.

- *Skilled Staff:* Properly identify the required competencies, the required level of experience and expertise for each identified skill, the number of resources needed within the given skill, and when these will be needed. Soft skills are equally important when identifying competencies.
- *Contract Negotiation and Management:* Properly managing a contract for external services and products can make or break a project's deadline or budget.
- *Implementation:* Project plans often overlook the implementation phase of the effort. Many project managers seem to end the project once the code has been developed and delivered. Implementing that system is as important as developing it.

Measurement is the gauge by which we determine whether the desired level of critical success has been achieved. Time and motion studies performed in the 1920s and 1930s used quantitative performance data that had been collected internally within the organization to identify exactly what each worker should do to achieve maximum production efficiency. Nowadays we use more sophisticated measurement methodologies to make sure our organizations, departments, projects, and people are all on track.

Most modern business-oriented measurement approaches focus on five categories of metrics: profitability, productivity, external quality, internal quality, and those that measure intangibles such as innovation, safety, and organizational culture.

A family of metrics is needed at every step in the process, not just at the strategic level. Some metrics are used at the lowest levels and others are rolled up into organizationwide metrics. This family-of-measures approach provides a framework in terms of categories of metrics. Balanced scorecard, the subject of this book, and other approaches use the framework approach.

The Balanced Scorecard and the Project

Most business units have implemented measures of their own levels of productivity (e.g., number of transactions processed, number of calls answered, etc.). However, these are unitary metrics and do not effectively measure the linkage between corporate strategy and the business unit at large, and the projects within the business unit, although recent dashboard approaches, as shown in Table P.3, are definitely moving in the right direction.

The goals of a project-based balanced scorecard are simplistic in scope but complex to execute. Some rules of thumb for successful execution include

1. Align departmental (business unit) strategy with business goals and needs.
2. Align discrete projects with departmental strategy (which is itself aligned with business strategy, as per step 1).
3. Establish appropriate measures for evaluating the effectiveness of the project.

Table P.3 A Dashboard Approach to Project Measurement

Dashboard Area	Green	Yellow	Red
Scope	Project satisfies at least 95 percent of all business objectives, and All major components are implemented as planned	Project satisfies at least 90 percent of all business objectives, and No more than one major component is deferred to later phase	Project satisfies less than 90 percent of all business objectives, or At least one major component is not implemented
Schedule	Project completion no later than 10 percent of original schedule duration	Project completion no later than 20 percent of original schedule duration	Project completion later than 20 percent of original duration
Budget	Budget variance is less than 5 percent of total budget	Budget variance is less than 10 percent of total budget	Budget variance is at least 10 percent of total budget
Success Factors	Weighted score is at least 90 percent	Weighted score is at least 80 percent	Weighted score is less than 80 percent

4. Align employees' efforts toward achieving objectives.
5. Stimulate and improve performance.
6. Achieve balanced results across stakeholder groups.

The key word here is "balanced." It reflects the balance between the six goals listed above, the four balanced scorecard perspectives (customer, business processes, learning and innovation, and financial), and long- and short-term objectives, as well as between qualitative and quantitative performance measures.

The remainder of this book provides detailed explanations on how to implement the project balanced scorecard. We review more than a few sample scorecards, metrics, and techniques, while providing insight, experience, and research into the project management process as a whole. However, as Kaplan and Norton (2001) themselves readily admit, the balanced scorecard is only a template that must be customized for the specific elements of an organization or industry.

For it to work effectively at the project level, the balanced scorecard approach must be adopted by the organization as a whole. In other words, discrete business units crafting balanced scorecards for projects in isolation are doomed to failure. It's only when the organization develops an organizationwide set of linked, or cascading, scorecards can there be any hope of success.

References

Hyvari, I. 2006. Success of projects in different organizational conditions. *Project Management Journal* 37(4, September). pp. 31–41.

Kaplan, R.S., and D.P. Norton (2001, February). On Balance. (Interview). *CFO, Magazine for Senior Financial Executives.* pp. 72–78.

Acknowledgments

I would especially like to thank those who assisted me in putting this book together. As always, my editor, John Wyzalek, was instrumental in getting my project approved and providing great encouragement.

About the Author

Jessica Keyes is president of New Art Technologies, Inc., a high-technology and management consultancy and development firm started in New York in 1989.

Keyes has given seminars for such prestigious universities as Carnegie Mellon, Boston University, University of Illinois, James Madison University, and San Francisco State University. She is a frequent keynote speaker on the topics of competitive strategy and productivity and quality. She is former advisor for DataPro, McGraw-Hill's computer research arm, as well as a member of the Sprint Business Council. Keyes is also a founding Board of Director member of the New York Software Industry Association. She completed a two-year term on the Mayor of New York City's Small Business Advisory Council. She currently facilitates doctoral and other courses for the University of Phoenix, and is a member of the Faculty Council for the College of Information Systems & Technology. She has been the editor for WGL's *Handbook of eBusiness* and CRC Press' *Systems Development Management* and *Information Management*.

Prior to founding New Art, Keyes was managing director of R&D for the New York Stock Exchange and has been an officer with Swiss Bank Co. and Banker's Trust, both in New York City. She holds a Masters of Business Administration from New York University, and a doctorate in management.

A noted columnist and correspondent with over 200 articles published, Keyes is the author of the following books:

The New Intelligence: AI in Financial Services, HarperBusiness, 1990
The Handbook of Expert Systems in Manufacturing, McGraw-Hill, 1991
Infotrends: The Competitive Use of Information, McGraw-Hill, 1992
The Software Engineering Productivity Handbook, McGraw-Hill, 1993
The Handbook of Multimedia, McGraw-Hill, 1994
The Productivity Paradox, McGraw-Hill, 1994
Technology Trendlines, Van Nostrand Reinhold, 1995
How to Be a Successful Internet Consultant, McGraw-Hill, 1997
Webcasting, McGraw-Hill, 1997
Datacasting, McGraw-Hill, 1997

The Handbook of Technology in Financial Services, Auerbach, 1998
The Handbook of Internet Management, Auerbach, 1999
The Handbook of eBusiness, Warren, Gorham & Lamont, 2000
The Ultimate Internet Sourcebook, Amacom, 2001
How to Be a Successful Internet Consultant, 2nd ed., Amacom, 2002
Software Engineering Handbook, Auerbach, 2002
Real World Configuration Management, Auerbach, 2003
Balanced Scorecard, Auerbach, 2005
Knowledge Management, Business Intelligence, and Content Management: The IT Practitioner's Guide, Auerbach, 2006
X Internet: The Executable and Extendable Internet, Auerbach, 2007
Leading IT Projects: The IT Manager's Guide, Auerbach, 2008
Marketing IT Products and Services, Auerbach, 2009

Chapter 1

Balanced Scorecard and the Project Manager

A study of 179 project managers and project management office managers found that although most organizations understood the importance of effective project management, they simply do not do a good job of managing their project management (PM) process. This translates to project outcomes less stellar than expected.

There are many different stakeholder groups involved in a typical project (e.g., business process users, owners, users, business managers, clients, etc.) so it is understandable that each of these stakeholder groups has different goals and objectives for assessing project outcomes. At the most basic level, the triple constraint methodology (time, cost, quality) is most often used to assess project success. However, many now believe that triple constraint does not account for the varied dimensions of projects that need to be considered in their assessments. Current research in this area finds that there is a real lack of agreement on not only what constitutes project success, but on methods for more comprehensive assessment of project outcomes (Barclay, 2008).

Given the varied dimensionality of a typical project, some have argued that there needs to be a distinction between PM success, in terms of the traditional triple constraints of time, cost, and quality, and project success, which is aligned with the product outcome of the project, and discerned through the stakeholders. Thus, it is quite possible to experience product success, but not PM success.

It is by now obvious that the traditional project measures of time, cost, and quality need to be enhanced by adding some additional project measurement dimensions, such as stakeholder benefits (e.g., customer satisfaction), product benefits (competitive advantage, financial rewards), and preparing for the future (e.g., value, personal growth, etc.; Barclay, 2008).

Quite a few studies (Barclay, 2008; Lynn, 2006) suggest that an adaptation of the balanced scorecard business approach to performance management measurement provides just this sort of vehicle. Robert S. Kaplan and David P. Norton developed the balanced scorecard approach in the early 1990s to compensate for shortcomings they perceived in using only financial metrics to judge corporate performance. They recognized that in this new economy it was also necessary to value intangible assets. Because of this, they urged companies to measure such esoteric factors as quality and customer satisfaction. By the middle 1990s, balanced scorecard became the hallmark of a well-run company. Kaplan and Norton often compare their approach for managing a company to that of pilots viewing assorted instrument panels in an airplane cockpit: both have a need to monitor multiple aspects of their working environment.

In the scorecard scenario, as shown in Figure 1.1, a company organizes its business goals into discrete, all-encompassing perspectives: Financial, Customer, Internal Process, and Learning/Growth. The company then determines cause–effect relationships: for example, satisfied customers buy more goods, which increases revenue. Next, the company lists measures for each goal, pinpoints targets, and identifies projects and other initiatives to help reach those targets.

Departments create scorecards tied to the company's targets, and employees and projects have scorecards tied to their department's targets. This cascading nature provides a line of sight among the individuals, the projects they are working

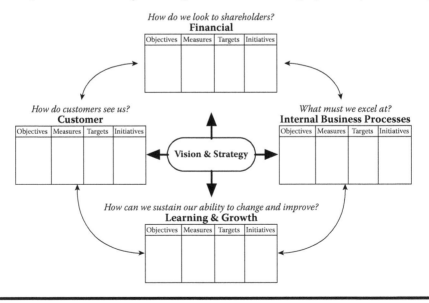

Figure 1.1 The balanced scorecard.

on, the units they support, and how that affects the strategy of the enterprise as a whole.

For project managers, the balanced scorecard is an invaluable tool that permits the project manager to link a project to the business side of the organization using a "cause and effect" approach. Some have likened balanced scorecard to a new language, which enables the project manager and business line managers to think together about what can be done to support or improve business performance.

A beneficial side effect of the use of the balanced scorecard is that, when all measures are reported, one can calculate the strength of relations among the various value drivers. For example, if the relation between high implementation costs and high profit levels is consistently weak, it can be inferred that the project, as implemented, does not sufficiently contribute to results as expressed by the other (e.g., financial) performance measures.

This first chapter examines the fundamentals of balanced scorecard as it relates to the precepts of project management. Balanced scorecard is examined in relationship to the organization and the people, processes, technologies, and products that are components of the organization's discrete projects, programs, and collaborative efforts.

Adopting the Balanced Scorecard

Kaplan and Norton (2001) provide a good overview of how a typical company adapts to the balanced scorecard approach:

> Each organization we studied did it a different way, but you could see that, first, they all had strong leadership from the top. Second, they translated their strategy into a balanced scorecard. Third, they cascaded the high-level strategy down to the operating business units and the support departments. Fourth, they were able to make strategy everybody's everyday job, and to reinforce that by setting up personal goals and objectives and then linking variable compensation to the achievement of those target objectives. Finally, they integrated the balanced scorecard into the organization's processes, built it into the planning and budgeting process, and developed new reporting frameworks as well as a new structure for the management meeting.

The key, then, is to develop a scorecard that naturally builds in cause-and-effect relationships, includes sufficient performance drivers, and, finally, provides a linkage to appropriate measures, as shown in Table 1.1.

At the very lowest level, a discrete project can also be evaluated using balanced scorecard. The key here is the connectivity between the project and the objectives of the organization as a whole, as shown in Table 1.2.

Table 1.1 Typical Departmental Sample Scorecard

Objective	Measure/Metrics	End of FY 2010 (Projected)
Financial		
Long-term corporate profitability	Percentage change in stock price attributable to	+25 percent per year for next 10 years
	Earnings growth	+20 percent per year for next 10 years
Short-term corporate profitability	Revenue growth	+20 percent related revenue growth
1. New products	Percentage cost reduction	Cut departmental costs by 35 percent
2. Enhance existing products		
3. Expand client-base		
4. Improve efficiency and cost-effectiveness		
Customer		
Customer satisfaction	Quarterly and annual customer surveys, satisfaction index	+35 percent, raise satisfaction level from current 60 to 95 percent
1. Customer-focused products		
2. Improve response time	Satisfaction ratio based on customer surveys	+20 percent
3. Improve security		
Customer retention	Percentage of customer attrition	–7 percent, reduce from current 12 to 5 percent
Customer acquisition	Percentage of increase in number of customers	+10 percent
Internal		
Complete M&A transitional processes	Percentage of work completed	100 percent
Establish connectivity	Percentage of workforce full access to corporate resources	100 percent

Table 1.1 Typical Departmental Sample Scorecard (Continued)

Objective	Measure/Metrics	End of FY 2010 (Projected)
Improve quality	Percentage saved on reduced work	+35 percent
Eliminate errors and system failures	Percentage reduction of customer complaints	+25 percent
	Percentage saved on better quality	+25 percent
Increase ROI	Percentage increase in ROI	+20–40 percent
Reduce TCO	Percentage reduction of TCO	–10–20 percent
Increase productivity	Percentage increase in customer orders	+25 percent
	Percentage increase in production/employee	+15 percent
Product and services enhancements	Number of new products and services introduced	5 new products
Improve response time	Average number of hours to respond to customer	–20 minutes, reduce from current level of 30–60 minutes to only 10 minutes or less
Learning and innovations		
Development of skills	Percentage amount spent on training	+10 percent
	Percentage staff with professional certificates	+20 percent
Leadership development and training	Number of staff attending colleges	18
Innovative products	Percentage increase in revenue	+20 percent

(continued)

Table 1.1 Typical Departmental Sample Scorecard (Continued)

Objective	Measure/Metrics	End of FY 2010 (Projected)
Improved process	Number of new products	+5
R&D	Percentage decrease in failure, complaints	−10 percent
Performance measurement	Percentage increase in customer satisfaction, survey results	+20 percent
	Percentage projects to pass ROI test	+25 percent
	Percentage staff receiving bonuses on performance enhancement	+25 percent
	Percentage increase in documentation	+20 percent

Table 1.2 A Simple Project Scorecard Approach

Perspective	Goals
Customer	Fulfill project requirements
	Control cost of the project
	Satisfy project end users
Financial	Provide business value (e.g., ROI, ROA, etc.)
	Project contributing to organization as a whole
Internal processes	Adhere to triple constraint: time, cost, quality
Learning and growth	Maintain currency
	Anticipate changes
	Acquire skillsets

The internal processes perspective maps neatly to the traditional triple constraint of project management, using many of the same measures traditionally used (as discussed in this book). For example, we can articulate the quality constraint using the ISO 10006:2003 standard. This standard provides guidance on the application of quality management in projects. It is applicable to projects of varying complexity, small or large, of short or long duration, in different environments, and irrespective of the kind of product or process involved.

Quality management of projects in this International Standard is based on eight quality management principles:

1. Customer focus
2. Leadership
3. Involvement of people
4. Process approach
5. System approach to management
6. Continual improvement
7. Factual approach to decision making
8. Mutually beneficial supplier relationships

Sample characteristics of these can be seen in Table 1.3.

Characteristics of a variable (e.g., quality, time, etc.) are used to create the key performance indicators (KPIs), or metrics, used to measure the success of the project. Thus, as you can see from Tables 1.1 through 1.3, we've got quite a few choices in terms of measuring the quality dimension of any particular project.

Example: FedEx

There are three key measurement indicators applied at FedEx. The goal of the *customer-value creation indicator* is to define a customer value that is not currently being met and then use technology to meet that need. Ultimately, the information produced by the system should be stored for analysis.

A hallmark of the "FedEx way" is that they really listen to their customers and create services to fulfill core needs. When FedEx initiated its overnight services in the 1970s, customers told them that their "peace of mind" required access to more extensive delivery information. The original tracking service was a tedious manual process requiring numerous telephone calls to a centralized customer service center. In turn, customer service had to call one or more of 1,400 operations centers to track a single package. This process was expensive and slow. Today's rapid online tracking capability was conceived to meet this need.

FedEx's tracking system also fulfills another important company requirement. The system automatically calculates whether the commitment to the customer was met by comparing ship date and service type to delivery date and

Table 1.3   ISO 10006 Definition of Quality Management for Projects

Quality Characteristic	Subcharacteristic
Customer focus	Understanding future customer needs
	Meet or exceed customer requirements
Leadership	Setting the quality policy and identifying the objectives (including the quality objectives) for the project
	Empowering and motivating all project personnel to improve the project processes and product
Involvement of people	Personnel in the project organization have well-defined responsibility and authority
	Competent personnel are assigned to the project organization
Process approach	Appropriate processes are identified for the project
	Interrelations and interactions among the processes are clearly identified
System approach to management	Clear division of responsibility and authority between the project organization and other relevant interested parties
	Appropriate communication processes are defined
Continual improvement	Projects should be treated as a process rather than as an isolated task
	Provision should be made for self-assessments
Factual approach to decision making	Effective decisions are based on the analysis of data and information
	Information about the project's progress and performance are recorded
Mutually beneficial supplier relationships	The possibility of a number of projects using a common supplier is investigated

time. This information forms the basis of FedEx's money-back guarantee, and appears on customer invoices. More important, this statistic is aggregated for the internal index on service quality that is the focal point for corporate improvement activities.

Another key FedEx indicator is *performance support*. The goal here is to create appropriate tools that enable front-line employees to improve their personal performance using the information in FedEx's vast databases. Individual performance is then aggregated to location and geographic unit, and ultimately makes its way into the corporatewide statistics. These stats are available on every desktop in the company.

An example of performance support indicators, from the perspective of a courier, include:

1. Does the count of packages delivered equal the Enhanced Tracker's count of deliverables?
2. Does the count of revenue forms equal the Enhanced Tracker's count of shipments picked up?

As the courier is closing out the day's activities he or she uses a handheld device, the Enhanced Tracker, as a guide through this series of performance measurements. During the day, the Tracker records activity information and timer per activity as the courier does the job. Information from the handheld Tracker gets ported to the corporate database with the aggregated historical information ultimately used for manpower tracking, or comparison of actual achievements to performance standards.

Perhaps the most important indicator is *business goal alignment*. This is used to align the incentives of employees and management with corporate and customer objectives.

These indicators, then, form the basis for FedEx's balanced scorecard. The FedEx corporate philosophy, called "People, Service, Profit," guides all decisions.

Attributes of Successful Project Management Measurement Systems

There are certain attributes that set apart successful performance measurement and management systems, including:

1. *A conceptual framework is needed for the performance measurement and management system.* A clear and cohesive performance measurement framework that is understood by all project managers and staff and that supports objectives and the collection of results is needed.
2. *Effective internal and external communications are the keys to successful performance measurement.* Effective communication with employees, process owners, end users, and stakeholders is vital to the successful development and deployment of project management-oriented performance measurement and management systems.
3. *Accountability for results must be clearly assigned and well understood.* Project managers must clearly identify what it takes to determine success and make

sure that staff understand what they are responsible for in achieving these goals.

4. *Performance measurement systems must provide intelligence for decision makers, not just compile data.* Performance measures should relate to strategic goals and objectives, and provide timely, relevant, and concise information for use by decision makers at all levels to assess progress toward achieving predetermined goals. These measures should produce information on the efficiency with which resources (i.e., people, hardware, software, etc.) are transformed into goods and services, on how well results compare to a program's intended purpose, and on the effectiveness of activities and operations in terms of their specific contribution to program objectives.

5. *Compensation, rewards, and recognition should be linked to performance measurements.* Performance evaluations and rewards need to be tied to specific measures of success by linking financial and nonfinancial incentives directly to performance. Such a linkage sends a clear and unambiguous message as to what's important.

6. *Performance measurement systems should be positive, not punitive.* The most successful performance measurement systems are not "gotcha" systems, but learning systems that help identify what works—and what does not—so as to continue with and improve on what is working and repair or replace what is not.

7. *Results and progress toward program commitments should be openly shared with employees, customers, and stakeholders.* Performance measurement system information should be openly and widely shared with employees, end users, stakeholders, vendors, and suppliers.

If used *properly*, the balanced scorecard approach provides a framework to accomplish these ends. Notice the emphasis on the word "properly." Balanced scorecard is not a panacea for all project management problems. Just implementing it willy-nilly is not going to solve performance problems, nor will it enhance alignment among the project, the business units, and corporate strategy. For balanced scorecard to work, it has to be carefully planned and executed.

Project Management Office

Project management is actually a set of discrete steps that sees a project from inception to closure, as shown in Figure 1.2.

A particular project is just one of many projects that will be implemented at any given time within a typical organization. A particular project might be one out of many projects for a specific program. A program is related to a corporate strategy, for example, "become an e-book publisher." In our e-book example, there might be multiple projects related to this goal. One project might be to develop a Web site

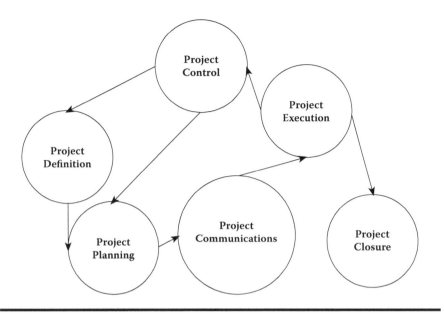

Figure 1.2 Project management perspectives.

where e-books could be sold. Another project might be to develop the software that converts print books into e-books.

Most organizations will have several ongoing programs all in play at once, all related to one or more business strategies. It is conceivable that hundreds of projects are ongoing, all in various stages of execution. Portfolio management is needed to provide the business and technical stewardship of all of these programs and their projects, as shown in Figure 1.3.

Portfolio management requires the organization to manage multiple projects at one time creating several thorny issues (Dooley, Lupton, and O'Sullivan, 2005); the most salient ones are shown in Table 1.4.

Not only does each project need to be measured, but the portfolio as a whole should be assessed, sample internal business process metrics for which can be seen in Table 1.5. The baseline indicates that the metric is informational, for example, only the raw value will be displayed (i.e., aggregated by the specified period: weekly, monthly, etc.). The targets should be set to default (or 0 in the case of baselined targets).

Portfolio management is usually performed by a project management office (PMO). This is the department or group that defines and maintains the standards of process within the organization. The PMO strives to standardize and introduce economies of repetition in the execution of projects. The PMO is the source of documentation, guidance, and metrics in the practice of project management and execution.

A good PMO will base project management principles on accepted industry standard methodologies. Increasingly, influential industry certification programs such as ISO9000 and the Malcolm Baldrige National Quality Award (see appendices),

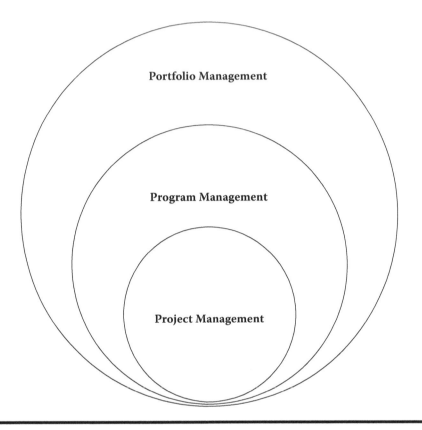

Figure 1.3 Portfolio management.

Table 1.4 Multiple Project Management Issues

Responsibility	*Issue*
Alignment management	Balancing individual project objectives with the organization's objectives
Control and communication	Maintaining effective communications within a project and across multiple projects
	Maintaining motivation across project teams
	Resource allocation
Learning and knowledge management	Inability to learn from past projects
	Failure to record lessons learned for each project
	Lack of timely information

Table 1.5   Sample Portfolio-Related Metrics for the Internal Business Process Perspective

Objective	Measure	Target
Enhance applications portfolio	Age distribution of applications	Baseline
	Technical performance of applications portfolio	Baseline
	Rate of product acceptance	>=95 percent

government regulatory requirements such as Sarbanes–Oxley, and business process management techniques such as balanced scorecard have propelled organizations to standardize processes.

If companies manage projects from an investment perspective—with a continuing focus on value, risk, cost, and benefits—costs should be reduced with an attendant increase in value. This is the driving principle of portfolio management.

By now it should be obvious that a major emphasis of PMO is standardization. To achieve this end, the PMO employs robust measurement systems. For example, the following metrics might be reported to provide an indicator of process responsiveness:

1. Total number of project requests submitted, approved, deferred, and rejected
2. Total number of project requests approved by the portfolio management group through the first project request approval cycle (providing an indicator of quality of project requests)
3. Total number of project requests and profiles approved by the portfolio management group through secondary and tertiary prioritization approval cycles (to provide a baseline of effort versus ROI for detailed project planning time)
4. Time and cost through the process
5. Changes to the project allocation after portfolio rebalancing (total projects, projects canceled, projects postponed, projects approved)
6. Utilization of resources: percentage utilization per staff resource (over 100 percent, 80 to 100 percent, under 80 percent, projects understaffed, staff-related risks)
7. Projects canceled after initiation (project performance, reduced portfolio funding, reduced priority, and increased risk)

Interestingly, PMOs are not all that pervasive in industry. However, they are recommended if the organization is serious about enhancing performance and standardizing project management performance measurement. Implementation of a PMO is a project unto itself, consisting of three steps: take inventory, analyze, and manage:

1. A complete inventory of all initiatives should be developed. Information such as the project's sponsors and champion, stakeholder list, strategic alignment with corporate objectives, estimated costs, and project benefits should be collected.
2. Once the inventory is completed and validated, all projects on the list should be analyzed. A steering committee should be formed that has enough insight into the organization's strategic goals and priorities to place projects in the overall strategic landscape. The output of the analysis step is a prioritized project list. The order of prioritization is based on criteria that the steering committee selects. This is different for different organizations. Some companies might consider strategic alignment to be the most important, whereas other companies might decide that cost–benefit ratio is the better criterion for prioritization.
3. Portfolio management is not a one-time event. It is a constant process that must be managed. Projects must be continually evaluated based on changing priorities and market conditions.

It is the analyze step where the balanced scorecard should be created. The scorecard should be fine-tuned in the prioritize phase and actually used in the manage step.

In all likelihood the PMO will standardize on a particular project management methodology. There are two major project management methodologies. The Project Management Body of Knowledge (PMBOK), which is most popular in the United States, recognizes five basic process groups typical of almost all projects: initiating, planning, executing, controlling and monitoring, and closing. Projects in Controlled Environments, PRINCE2, which is the de facto standard for project management in the United Kingdom and is popular in more than 50 other countries, defines a wide variety of subprocesses, but organizes these into eight major processes: starting a project, planning, initiating a project, directing a project, controlling a stage, managing product delivery, managing stage boundaries, and closing a project.

Both PRINCE2 and PMBOK consist of a set of processes and associated subprocesses. These can be used to craft relevant metrics, as shown in Table 1.6.

Inasmuch as the PMO is the single focal point for all things related to project management, it is natural that the project management balanced scorecard should be within the purview of this department.

Table 1.6   Sample PRINCE2 Related Metrics

Process	Subprocess	Associated Sample Metric
Initiating a project (IP)	IP1 Planning quality	Requirement error rate
	IP2 Planning a project	Percentage resources devoted to planning and review of activities
	IP3 Refining the business case and risks	Percentage definitional uncertainty risk

Project Management Process Maturity Model (PM)² and Collaboration

The PM² model determines and positions an organization's relative project management level with other organizations (Kwak and Ibbs, 2002). There are a variety of project management process maturity models, and they are all based on work done by the Software Engineering Institute at Carnegie Mellon on improving the quality of the software development process.

The PM² model defines five steps, as shown in Figure 1.4.

Unfortunately, quite a good number of organizations are still hovering somewhere between the ad hoc and planned levels. Here, some very basic project management techniques are being utilized, usually limited to use of some project management tool (e.g., Microsoft Project). Even then, what and how things are done is usually subject to the whims of a particular project manager and is not often standardized across the company as a whole. Introduction of a PMO goes a long way toward moving up the ladder, particularly if performance measurement and management are thrown into the mix (level 4).

Companies that are serious about improving performance strive to achieve level 5, continuous learning. To do this requires a company to compare itself to others in its peer grouping, the goal of a model such as PM².

In the PM² model, key processes, organizational characteristics, and key focus areas are defined, as shown in Table 1.7. Each maturity level is associated with a set of key project management processes, characteristics of those processes, and key areas on which to focus. When mapped to the four balanced scorecard perspectives, PM² becomes a reference point or yardstick for PM best practices and processes.

Although the PM² model determines and positions an organization's relative project management level with other organizations, it is worthwhile to note that there has been a shift toward more decentralized and distributed project teams, with some teams going all virtual and many teams working in partnership with teams in other companies. Thus, measurement across collaborative distributed partners must be considered in any measurement program. Several interest groups and partnerships

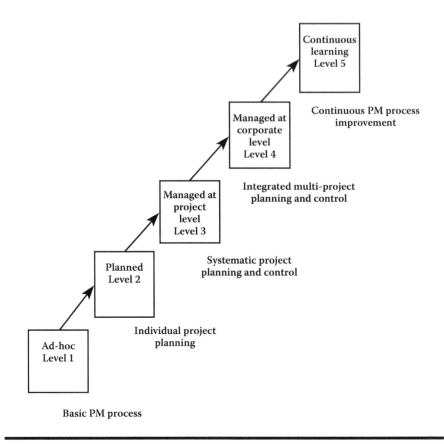

Figure 1.4   The PM² model.

in the automotive industry were formed to develop new project management methods and processes that worked effectively in a collaborative environment (Niebecker, Eager, and Kubitza, 2008). The German Organization for Project Management (GPM e.V.), the PMI automotive special interest group, the Automotive Industry Action Group (AIAG), and others have embarked on projects to develop methods, models, and frameworks for collaborative product development, data exchange, quality standards, and project management. One recent output from this effort was the ProSTEP-iViP reference model to manage time, tasks, and communications in cross-company automotive product development projects (http://www.prostep.org/en/).

A set of drivers and KPIs for a typical stand-alone project can be seen in Table 1.8.

Using guidelines from the ProSTEP reference model, Niebecker, Eager, and Kubitza (2008) have reoriented the drivers and KPIs in Table 1.8 to account for the extra levels of complexity found in a project worked on by two or more companies in a networked collaborative environment, as shown in Table 1.9.

Table 1.7   Key Components of the PM2 Model

Maturity Level	Key PM Processes	Major Organizational Characteristics	Key Focus Areas
Level 5 (Continuous learning)	PM processes are continuously improved	Project-driven organization	Innovative ideas to improve PM processes and practices
	PM processes are fully understood	Dynamic, energetic, and fluid organization	
	PM data is optimized and sustained	Continuous improvement of PM processes and practices	
Level 4 (Managed at corporate level)	Multiple PM (program management)	Strong teamwork	Planning and controlling multiple projects in a professional manner
	PM data and processes are integrated	Formal PM training for project team	
	PM data is quantitatively analyzed, measured, and stored		
Level 3 (Managed at project level)	Formal project planning and control systems are managed	Team oriented (medium)	Systematic and structured project planning and control for individual projects
	Formal PM data is managed	Informal training of PM skills and practices	

(continued)

Table 1.7 Key Components of the PM2 Model (Continued)

Maturity Level	Key PM Processes	Major Organizational Characteristics	Key Focus Areas
Level 2 (Planned)	Informal PM processes are defined	Team oriented (weak)	Individual project planning
	Informal PM problems are identified	Organizations possess strengths in doing similar work	
	Informal PM data is collected		
Level 1 (Ad hoc)	No PM processes or practices are consistently available	Functionally isolated	Understand and establish basic PM processes
	No PM data is consistently collected or analyzed	Lack of senior management support	
		Project success depends on individual efforts	

Niebecker, Eager, and Kubitza's (2008) recommendations expand the traditional balanced scorecard methodology, providing an approach for monitoring and controlling cross-company projects by aligning collaborative project objectives with the business strategies and project portfolio of each company.

We've Reached the End of Chapter 1

Projects operate in an environment much broader than the project itself. This means that the project manager needs to understand not only the intricacies of the particular project, but the greater organizational context in which its stakeholders exist. Project managers must identify and understand the needs of all the stakeholders (i.e., project team, management, end users, inter- and extra-company partners, etc.) while delivering a quality product on time and within budget. The only way to

Table 1.8   Representative Drivers and KPIs for a Standard Project

Balanced Scorecard Perspective	Drivers	KPIs
Finances	Project budget	Human resources
	Increase of business value	Share of sales
		Profit margin
	Multiproject categorization	Savings
		ROI Expenditure
	Project management	
Customer	Customer satisfaction	Cost overrun
		Number of customer audits
		Change management
		Process stability
Process	Adherence to schedules	Adherence to delivery dates
	Innovation enhancement	Lessons learned
	Minimizing risks	Number of patent applications
	Optimization of project structure	External labor
	Quality	Quality indices
		Duration of change management
		Product maturity
		Percentage of overhead
		Number of internal audits
		Project risk analysis
Development	Employee satisfaction	Rate of employee fluctuation
	Employee qualification enhancement	Travel costs
		Overtime
		Index of professional experience
		Continuing education costs

achieve this end is to standardize and measure the performance of the process of project management. One way to do this is through adoption of the project-based balanced scorecard.

Table 1.9 Drivers and KPIs for a Collaborative Project (CP)

Balanced Scorecard Perspective	Drivers	KPIs
Finances/Project	Project cost Increase of business value Categorization into CP management Project maturity	Product costs Production costs Cost overruns Savings Productivity index Turnover Risk distribution Profit margin Feature stability Product maturity index
Process	Adherence to schedules Innovation enhancement Minimizing risks Adherence to collaboration process Quality	Variance to schedule Changes before and after design freeze Duration until defects removed Number and duration of product changes Number of postprocessing changes Continuous improvement process Project risk analysis Maturity of collaboration process Frequency of product tests Defect frequency Quality indices

Table 1.9   Drivers and KPIs for a Collaborative Project (CP) (Continued)

Balanced Scorecard Perspective	Drivers	KPIs
Collaboration	Communication Collaboration	Number of team workshops Checklists Degree of communication efficiency Collaborative lessons learned Maturity of collaboration Degree of lessons learned realization
Development	Team satisfaction Team qualification enhancement Trust between team members	Employee fluctuation Project-focused continuing education Employee qualification

References

Barclay, C. 2008. Towards an integrated measurement of IS project performance: The project performance scorecard. *Information Systems Frontiers*, 10(May): 331–345.

Dooley, L., G. Lupton, and D. O'Sullivan, 2005. Multiple project management: A modern competitive necessity. *Journal of Manufacturing Technology Management*, 16(5): 466–482.

Kaplan, R.S. and D.P. Norton, 2001. On balance. (Interview). *CFO, Magazine for Senior Financial Executives*, February, pp. 72–78.

Kwak, Y.H. and C.W. Ibbs, 2002. Project management process maturity (PM2) model. *Journal of Management in Engineering*, 18(3, July): 150–155.

Lynn, S.C. 2006. "Project Management Methodologies and Strategic Execution." Retrieved from *www.asapm.org/asapmag/articles/Lynn12-06.pdf*

Niebecker, K., D. Eager, and K. Kubitza, 2008. Improving cross-company management performance with a collaborative project scorecard. *International Journal of Managing Projects in Business,* 1(3): 368–386.

Chapter 2

Aligning the Project to Meet Strategic Objectives

From an organizational perspective, the concepts of performance management are very much the base that supports the balanced scorecard (BSC) framework. Indeed, the balanced scorecard approach becomes very understandable when one realizes that, instead of being a radical new approach to performance management and measurement, it merely brings together and organizes tried and true performance-enhancing "best practices" that companies have been utilizing for decades. The project balanced scorecard is commonly used to align a project-based strategy to a business strategy (see the appendices for more information on crafting business strategy). The format of scorecards varies from company to company, but they do share some common characteristics.

The very best scorecards are limited to a single page of from 10 to 20 metrics written in nontechnical language. The scorecard should be tightly coupled to the strategic planning process and assist in tracking progress against key goals and objectives. Project managers as well as senior business managers should be involved in the scorecard process, both during creation and ongoing. Consensus should be quickly achieved on metrics definitions. The review meetings should focus on decisions rather than debate over metrics. The scorecard should allow for detailed review of trends or variance by providing more granularity on component elements. Finally, individual manager compensation should be linked to scorecard performance.

Progressive scorecard practitioners often track metrics in five key categories:

1. *Financial performance.* Spending in the content of service levels, project progress, and so on. Example metric: Spending per portfolio category.

2. *Project performance.* Example metric: Percentage of new product investment resulting in new revenue streams.
3. *Operational performance.* Instead of concentrating measurement efforts on day-to-day measures, best-in-class practitioners seek to provide an aggregate, customer-focused view of operations. Example metric: Include peak time availability.
4. *Talent management.* This category of metrics seeks to manage human capital. Measures include staff satisfaction and retention, as well as attractiveness of the department to external job seekers. Example metric: Retention of high-potential staff.
5. *User satisfaction.* Example metric: User perspective.

Bowne & Co. (www.bowne.com), a New York City-based documents management company, used the following steps to implement their scorecard:

1. Kick-off training for staff.
2. Ongoing strategy mapping. Metrics selection. A team creates a list of metrics. The list is refined using analysis of each potential metric's strengths and weaknesses.
3. Metrics definition. A set of standard definitions is created for each metric. It defines the measurement technique as well as data collection process. It outlines initiatives that must be completed to allow tracking of the metrics.
4. Assigning metric ownership. Owners are assigned to each metric. These people are responsible for scorecard completion. Their bonuses are related to their scorecard-related duties.
5. Data collection and quality assurance. Data frequency varies by metric based on cost of collection, the corporate financial reporting cycle, and volatility of the business climate.
6. Senior managers review the scorecard every six months. Metrics are revisited annually.

Bowne is a good example of a departmentwide scorecard but this process can also be used to develop a scorecard for a particular project. The Central Intelligence Agency (Hagood and Friedman, 2002) did this for a human resource information system (HRIS). The program director developed six criteria for success that would drive the balanced scorecard development effort:

1. Delivering each new program segment on time and within budget
2. Delivering each functionality as promised
3. Maintaining high system performance standards
4. Reducing reliance on legacy systems
5. Increasing customer satisfaction
6. Employee satisfaction

The resulting scorecard can be seen in Table 2.1.

Table 2.1	CIA's HRIS Balanced Scorecard		
Goals	*Objectives*	*Measures*	*Sources*
Customer Perspective			
Provide HR information systems that meet Agency needs	• Incorporate stakeholder feedback into strategic planning • Provide timely and accurate responses to customer service requests	• HR officer survey • HRIS help desk performance • Level of participation in CIA forums percentage with collaboration	• HR front office • Help desk • Personnel
Deliver all projects for customers in conformance with an acceptable plan	• All projects have plans negotiated with customers and baselined	• Percentage of baselined projects with a plan	• Chief of operations
Manage HRIS work in conformity with published strategic and tactical plans	• Maintain HR roadmap as basis for resource allocation • Communicate HRIS strategic direction to stakeholders	• Roadmap reviewed every two weeks and updated • Number of projects performed for direct customers • Level of participation in CIA forums with collaborations	• Personnel • Chief of operations

(continued)

Table 2.1   CIA's HRIS Balanced Scorecard (Continued)

Goals	Objectives	Measures	Sources
Internal Process Perspective			
HRIS data is available for users to conduct their business	• Improve accuracy of data entry • Maintain data accurately within the HRIS • Make HRIS available to users for input 97 percent of the time • Ensure retrievable data is no older than 24 hours	• Data entry error rates • HRIS hourly availability data • Payroll processing time • Age of data	• Compensation group • System engineer
Achieve the optimal balance between technical and strategic activities	• Maintain balance between repair and new work • Reduce demand for customer service needing intervention	• Rework cost/ unit of service • Percentage of time devoted to ad hoc work	• Budget officer
Achieve the minimum architecture effective for HRIS	• Implement an HRIS integration strategy • Maintain alignment with CIA IS direction/ initiatives	• Number of non-Lawson apps in HRIS • Total number of interfaces	• System architect

Table 2.1   CIA's HRIS Balanced Scorecard (Continued)

Goals	Objectives	Measures	Sources
Resource Perspective (Financial)			
Maximize the cost efficiency of operating and evolving the HRIS	• Execute the budget consistent with strategic plan • Understand and manage the cost drivers of HRIS	• Percentage of employees who have up-to-date information • Cost/unit of service • HRIS overhead as percentage of total • Total number of direct labor hours	• Budget officer
Each project delivers its product as advertised	• Scope, budget, and schedule are baselined at project initial review for 100 percent of projects • Project performance meets or exceeds baseline expectations	• Schedule data • Budget data • Scope performance data	• Chief of operations

(continued)

Table 2.1   CIA's HRIS Balanced Scorecard (Continued)

Goals	Objectives	Measures	Sources
Learning and Growth Perspective			
Maintain a skilled and productive workforce to operate and evolve the HRIS	• Implement an effective strategic workforce plan • Recruit skilled workers who have initiative, innovation, and flexibility • Retain employees by giving opportunities and incentives • Enhance employees' knowledge and skills	• Number of employees with certification • Project management training levels • Percentage of technical training goals met	• Personnel
Maintain a high degree of HRIS employee satisfaction	• Enhance employees' knowledge and skills • Provide opportunities for individual career growth	• Project management training levels • Percentage of technical training goals met • Job description index (JDI) scores • Percentage of voluntary separations	• Personnel

Table 2.1   CIA's HRIS Balanced Scorecard (Continued)

Goals	Objectives	Measures	Sources
Ensure that HRIS learns from past for better future performance	• Record, analyze, and use lessons learned • Develop best practices for HRIS	• Percentage of leaders' time devoted to mentoring • Percentage of projects with lessons learned in database	• Personnel

Altering the Balanced Scorecard to Be Project Specific

Some suggest that the four balanced scorecard perspectives might require some modification to be effective as a project-based scorecard. Projects are commonly carried out for the benefit of both the end users and the organization as a whole, rather than individual customers within a large market.

Because scorecards are most successful when cascaded through the organization, one must first start at the corporate level, narrow the focus to the departmental level, and then finally end up with an even narrower focus at the project level. At the departmental level, the narrowed view might include:

1. User orientation (end-user view).
   a. Mission: Deliver value-adding products and services to end users.
   b. Objectives: Establish and maintain a good image and reputation with end users; exploit opportunities; establish good relationships with the user community, satisfy end-user requirements, and be perceived as the preferred supplier of products and services
2. Business value (management view).
   a. Mission: Contribute to the value of the business.
   b. Objectives: Establish and maintain a good image and reputation with management; ensure that projects provide business value; control project costs; and sell appropriate products and services to third party.
3. Internal processes (operations-based view).
   a. Mission: Deliver products and services in an efficient and effective manner.
   b. Objectives: Anticipate and influence requests from end users and management; be efficient in planning and developing new processes; be efficient in operations and maintenance; and provide cost-effective training that satisfies end users.

4. Future readiness (innovation and learning view).
   a. Mission: Deliver continuous improvement and prepare for future challenges.
   b. Objectives: Anticipate and prepare for problems that could arise; continuously upgrade skills through training and development; and conduct cost-effective research into emerging technologies and their suitability for the business.

It is then possible to drill down to provide measures for each of these four perspectives. Most of the metrics have been derived from mainstream literature and include (Table 2.2) the three key balanced scorecard principles of:

1. Cause-and-effect relationships
2. Sufficient performance drivers
3. Linkage to financial measures

which should be built into a project-based scorecard. Cause-and-effect relationships can involve one or more of the four perspectives. For example, better staff skills (future readiness perspective) will reduce the frequency of problems in a process (internal operations perspective).

It doesn't take much extrapolation to translate this to a scorecard for a particular project, as shown in Table 2.3, which is an extrapolation of Table 2.2.

Case Study: ERP

Figure 2.1 graphically depicts the three levels of scorecards we have addressed so far. Those at the project level are sometimes referred to as micro-level scorecards.

A good example of a micro-level scorecard is one that can be built for the implementation of an enterprise resource planning (ERP) system. Enterprise resource planning is one of the most sophisticated and complex of all software systems. It is a customizable software package that includes integrated business solutions for core business processes such as production planning and control and warehouse management. It is probably the highest priority project being implemented by most modern organizations and cuts across organizational boundaries, affecting all departments and all processes. Rosemann and Wiese (1999) use a modified balanced scorecard approach to:

1. Evaluate the implementation of ERP software.
2. Evaluate the continuous operation of the ERP installation.

Table 2.2 Departmental-Specific Scorecard Metrics

Perspective	Metric
User orientation	Customer satisfaction
Business Value	
Cost control	Percentage over/under budget
	Allocation to different budget items
	Budget as a percentage of revenue
	Expenses per employee
Sales to third parties	Revenue from products/services
Business value of a project	Traditional measures (e.g., ROI, payback)
	Business evaluation based on information economics: value linking, value acceleration, value restructuring, technological innovation
	Strategic match with business contribution to: product/service quality, customer responsiveness, management information, process flexibility
Risks	Unsuccessful strategy risk, definitional uncertainty (e.g., low degree of project specification), technological risk (e.g., bleeding edge hardware or software), development risk (e.g., inability to put things together), operational risk (e.g., resistance to change), service delivery risk (e.g., human/computer interface difficulties)
Business value of the department/functional area	Percentage resources devoted to strategic projects
	Percentage time spent by manager in meetings with corporate executives
	Perceived relationship between departmental management and top management

(continued)

Table 2.2 Departmental-Specific Scorecard Metrics (Continued)

Perspective	Metric
Internal Processes	
Planning	Percentage resources devoted to planning and review of activities
Development	Percentage resources devoted to development
Operations	Number of end-user queries handled
	Average time required to address an end-user problem
Future Readiness	
Specialist capabilities	Training and development budget as a percentage of overall budget
	Expertise with specific technologies
	Expertise with emerging technologies
	Age distribution of staff
Satisfaction of staff	Turnover/retention of employees
	Productivity of employees
Research into emerging technologies	Research budget as percentage of budget
	Perceived satisfaction of top management with the reporting on how specific emerging technologies may or may not be applicable to the company

Along with the four balanced scorecard perspectives of financial, customer, internal processes, and innovation and learning, they've added a fifth for the purposes of ERP installation: the project perspective. The individual project requirements, such as identification of critical path, milestones, and so on, are covered by this fifth perspective which represents all the project management tasks. Figure 2.2 represents the Rosemann–Wiese approach.

Rosemann and Wiese (1999) contend that most ERP implementers concentrate on the financial and business process aspects of ERP implementation. Using the ERP balanced

Table 2.3   Project Scorecard Metrics

Perspective	Metric
User orientation	End-user satisfaction
Business Value	
Cost control	Percentage over/under project budget
	Project budget as a percentage of revenue
	Project expenses per employee
Business value of the project	Traditional measures (e.g., ROI, payback)
	Business evaluation based on information economics: value linking, value acceleration, value restructuring, technological innovation
	Strategic match with business contribution to: product/service quality, customer responsiveness, management information, process flexibility
Risks	Unsuccessful project strategy risk, Improper linkage to business strategy, project strategy risk, definitional uncertainty (e.g., low degree of project specification), technological risk (e.g., bleeding- edge hardware or software), development risk (e.g., inability to put things together), operational risk (e.g., resistance to change), service delivery risk (e.g., human/computer interface difficulties)
Business value of the project	Percentage resources devoted to project
	Percentage time spent by project staff in meetings with end users
	Perceived relationship between project management and end-user management

(continued)

Table 2.3 Project Scorecard Metrics (Continued)

Perspective	Metric
Internal Processes	
Planning	Percentage resources devoted to planning and review of project
Development	Percentage resources devoted to development
Operations	Number of end-user queries handled related to project
	Average time required to address an end-user problem related to project
Future Readiness	
Project specialist capabilities	Training and development budget as a percentage of overall project budget
	Expertise with technologies relevant to project
	Expertise with emerging technologies
Satisfaction of project staff	Turnover/retention of project staff
	Productivity of project staff
Research into emerging technologies	Research budget as percentage of project budget
	Perceived satisfaction of top management with the reporting on how specific emerging technologies may or may not be applicable to the project and company

scorecard would enable them also to focus on the customer as well as innovation and learning perspectives. The latter is particularly important as it enables the development of alternative values for the many conceivable development paths that support a flexible system implementation.

Implementation measures might include:

1. *Financial:* Total cost of ownership, which would enable identification of modules where overcustomization took place

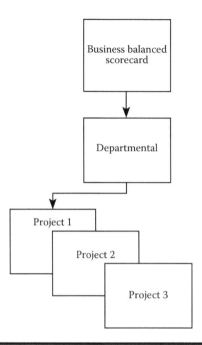

Figure 2.1   Three levels of organizational scorecards.

2. *Project*: Processing time along the critical path, remaining time to the next milestone, time delays that would affect the financial perspective
3. *Internal processes:* Processing time before and after ERP implementation, coverage of individual requirements for a process
4. *Customer:* Linkage of customers to particular business processes automated, resource allocation per customer
5. *Innovation and learning:* Number of alternative process paths to support a flexible system implementation, number of parameters representing unused customizing potential, number of documents describing customizing decisions

As in all well-designed balanced scorecards, this one demonstrates a very high degree of linkage in terms of cause-and-effect relationships. For example, "customer satisfaction" within the Customer perspective might affect "total cost of ownership" in the Financial perspective, "total project time" in the Project perspective, "fit with ERP solution" in the Internal process perspective and "user suggestions" in the Innovation and learning perspective.

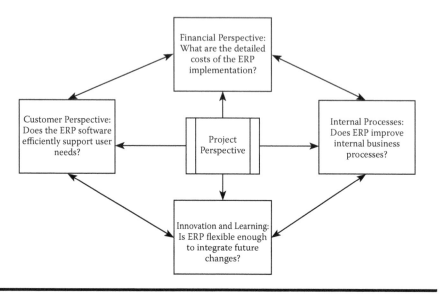

Figure 2.2   The ERP balanced scorecard.

Rosemann and Wiese (1999) do not require the Project perspective in the balanced scorecard for evaluating the continuous operation of the ERP installation. Here the implementation follows a straightforward balanced scorecard approach. Measures include:

1. Financial: Compliance with budget for hardware, software, consulting
2. Customer:
   a. Coverage of business processes: Percentage of covered process types, percentage of covered business transactions, percentage of covered transactions valued good or fair
   b. Reduction of bottlenecks: Percentage of transactions not finished on schedule, percentage of canceled telephone order processes due to noncompetitive system response time
3. Internal process:
   a. Reduction of operational problems: Number of problems with customer order processing system, percentage of problems with customer order processing system, number of problems with warehouse processes, number of problems with standard reports, number of problems with reports on demand

      b. Availability of the ERP system: Average system availability, average downtime, maximum downtime

      c. Avoidance of operational bottlenecks: Average response time in order processing, average response time in order processing at peak time, average number of OLTP-transactions, maximum number of OLTP-transactions

      d. Actuality of the system: Average time to upgrade the system, release levels behind the actual level

      e. Improvement in system development: Punctuality index of system delivery, quality index

      f. Avoidance of developer bottlenecks: Average workload per developer, rate of sick leave per developer, percentage of modules covered by more than two developers

4. Innovation and learning:

      a. Qualification: Number of training hours per user, number of training hours per developer, qualification index of developer (i.e., how qualified is this developer to do what he or she is doing)

      b. Independency of consultants: Number of consultant days per module in use >2 years, number of consultant days per module in use <2 years

      c. Reliability of software vendor: Number of releases per year, number of functional additions, number of new customers

Validating the Project Scorecard

Validation is the process of determining the degree of accuracy and completeness of the measurement techniques and the resulting data. Balanced scorecard assessment practices and results should be periodically validated. The success of the self-assessment will depend largely on the mutually agreed and understood performance objectives, measures, and expectations; the scope, depth, and effectiveness of the self-assessment; and the integrity of the self-assessment.

Verification is the process of substantiating a set of data results by such means as checking stated facts, citations, measurements, or attendant circumstances. Verification of data resulting, for example, from the self-assessment and other operational awareness activities will, in part, formulate the basis of the approval of the business system. The data should be analyzed to determine its accuracy and to ensure that comparisons or benchmarks are valid.

Verification of narrative or statistical data should be tailored by data type. For example, reports and documentation could substantiate the self-assessment results of measures designed to demonstrate efficiency. Likewise, interviews with selected internal and external customers and the organization's employees may also verify reported survey results. Trend analysis of the self-assessment results should reflect the factual information provided by the interviews with staff.

The following suggestions can assist in the validation and verification of the self-assessment process and results:

1. Mutually understand what and how the organization will measure performance.
2. Be familiar with the data sources and methods that will be used in the calculations.
3. Confirm that the collection methodology is accurate, complete, and timely.
4. Confirm that the data is properly controlled.
5. Become familiar with the trend analysis techniques to be used and gain assurances that the organization's personnel are qualified in this area.

Establishing Performance Measures

Balanced scorecard is wrapped around metrics. We've already provided quite a few examples of these, and you can expect to come across more in the remainder of the book. However, it is reasonable to assume that you might need to develop your own set of performance measures over and above what you might pull from this book. Several steps need to be undertaken to establish performance measures that make sense and are workable for your organization, department, and specific project (see the appendices for a guide to establishing a measurement program).

Define Organizational Vision, Mission, and Strategy

The balanced scorecard methodology requires the creation of a vision, mission statement, and strategy for the organization. This ensures that the performance measures developed in each perspective support accomplishment of the organization's strategic objectives. It also helps employees visualize and understand the links between the performance measures and successful accomplishment of strategic goals.

The key is first to identify where you want the organization to be in the near future, and then set a vision that seems somewhat out of reach. In this way, as Kaplan and Norton (2001) contend, managers have the instrumentation they need to navigate to future competitive success. It is nearly impossible to implement a successful balanced scorecard program for a project, or within a department, without the organization first defining theirs.

Develop Performance Objectives, Measures, and Goals

Next, it is essential to identify what the organization must do well (i.e., the performance objectives) in order to attain the identified vision. For each objective that must be performed well, it is necessary to identify measures and set goals covering a reasonable period of time (e.g., three to five years). Although this sounds simple, many variables actually affect how long this exercise will take. The first, and most significant, variable is how many people are employed in this process and the extent to which they will be involved in setting the measures and goals.

The balanced scorecard translates the project's vision into a set of performance objectives distributed among four perspectives: financial, customer, internal business processes, and learning and growth, although, as you have seen, some do modify or add to these perspectives. Some objectives are maintained to measure progress toward achieving this vision. Other objectives are maintained to measure the long-term drivers of success.

When creating performance measures, it is important to ensure that they link directly to the strategic vision of the organization. The measures must focus on the outcomes necessary to achieve the organizational vision and the objectives of the strategic plan. When drafting measures and setting goals, ask whether achievement of the identified goals will help achieve the organizational vision.

Each objective within a perspective should be supported by at least one measure that will indicate an organization's performance against that objective. Define measures precisely, including the population to be measured, the method of measurement, the data source, and the time period for the measurement. If a quantitative measure is feasible and realistic, then its use should be encouraged.

When developing measures, it is important to include a mix of quantitative and qualitative measures. Quantitative measures provide more objectivity than qualitative measures. They may help to justify critical decisions on resource allocation (e.g., budget and staffing) or systems improvement. The project manager should first identify any available quantitative data and consider how it can support the objectives and measures incorporated in the balanced scorecard. Qualitative measures involve matters of perception, and therefore of subjectivity. Nevertheless, they are an integral part of the BSC methodology. Judgments based on the experience of end users, employees, managers, and contractors offer important insights into acquisition performance and results.

Establish Measures

It's important to recognize that measures might not be perfect the first time out of the gate. Performance management is an evolutionary process that requires adjustments as experience is gained in the use of performance measures.

In order to establish goals and be able to evaluate performance against them, input measures must be developed and regularly monitored. Input measures describe the resources, time, and staff utilized for a program. Financial resources can be identified as current dollars, or discounted, based on economic or accounting practices. Nonfinancial measures can be described in proxy measures. These measures are not described in terms of ratios. They are often used as one element of other measures such as efficiency and effectiveness.

Examples

1. Total project funding
2. Actual number of labor hours

Output measures describe goods or services produced. Outputs can be characterized by a discrete definition of the service or by a proxy measure that represents the product. Highly dissimilar products can be rolled up into a metric. As with input measures, these measures are not described in terms of ratios. They are often used as one element of other measures such as efficiency and effectiveness measures.

Examples

1. Reports generated
2. Number of end-user requirements satisfied

Efficiency is the measure of the relationship of outputs to inputs and is usually expressed as a ratio. These measures can be expressed in terms of actual expenditure of resources as compared to expected expenditure of resources. They can also be expressed as the expenditure of resources for a given output.

Examples

1.	Unit cost per output	$\dfrac{\text{Total cost of project development}}{\text{Number of end users}}$
2.	Labor productivity	$\dfrac{\text{Number of completed transactions}}{\text{Actual number labor hours}}$
3.	Cycle time	$\dfrac{\text{Number days to complete development effort}}{\text{Number programs}}$

Effectiveness measures are measures of output conformance to specified characteristics.

Examples

1.	Quantity	<u>Number tasks completed</u> Number tasks required to be developed
2.	Timeliness	<u>Number tasks completed by target time</u> Total number tasks required
3.	Quality	<u>Number defect-free processes used by end users</u> Number processes received by end users
4.	Customer satisfaction	a. Customer satisfaction survey results b. Complaint rates

The creation of sound metrics requires a great deal of thought and an adequate measure of testing and validation.

Developing Benchmarks

So, how do you come up with the perfect metric? One just doesn't pull a key performance indicator out of a hat or a book. The normal methodology is benchmarking. The dictionary definition of benchmark is "a point of reference from which measurements may be made." It is something that serves as a standard by which others may be measured. The purpose of benchmarking is to assist in the performance improvement process. Specifically, benchmarking can:

1. Identify opportunities
2. Set realistic but aggressive goals
3. Challenge internal paradigms on what is possible
4. Understand methods for improved processes
5. Uncover strengths within your organization
6. Learn from the leaders' experiences
7. Better prioritize and allocate resources

Table 2.4 describes the ramifications of not using benchmarking.

Many organizations use a four-phase model to implement benchmarking:

1. Plan
2. Collect
3. Analyze
4. Adapt

Table 2.4 Benchmarking Versus Not Benchmarking

	Without Benchmarking	*With Benchmarking*
Defining customer requirements	• Based on history/gut feel • Acting on perception	• Based on market reality • Acting on objective evaluation
Establishing effective goals	• Lack external focus • Reactive • Lagging industry	• Credible, customer-focused • Proactive • Industry leadership
Developing true measures of productivity	• Pursuing pet projects • Strengths and weaknesses not understood	• Solving real problems • Performance outputs known, based on best in class
Becoming competitive	• Internally focused • Evolutionary change • Low commitment	• Understand the competition • Revolutionary ideas with proven performance • High commitment
Industry practices	• Not invented here • Few solutions	• Proactive search for change • Many options • Breakthroughs

When planning a benchmarking effort considerable thought should be given to who is on the benchmarking team. In some cases, team members will need to be trained in the different tools and techniques of the benchmarking process.

The creation of a benchmarking plan is similar to the creation of a project, with a few twists:

1. The scope of the benchmarking study needs to be established. All projects must have boundaries. In this case, you will need to determine which departmental units or processes will be studied.
2. A purpose statement should be developed. This should state the mission and goals of the plan.
3. If benchmarking partners (i.e., other companies in your peer grouping who agree to be part of your effort) are to be used, specific criteria for their involvement should be noted. In addition, a list of any benchmarking

partners should be provided. Characteristics of benchmarking partners important to note include: policies and procedures, organizational structure, financials, locations, quality, productivity, competitive environment, and products/services.

4. Define a data collection plan and determine how the data will be used, managed, and ultimately distributed.
5. Finally, your plan should discuss how implementation of any improvements resulting from the benchmarking effort will be accomplished.

The collection phase of a benchmarking effort is very similar to the requirements elicitation phase of software engineering. The goal is to collect data and turn it into knowledge. During the collection phase the focus is on developing data collection instruments. The most widely used is the questionnaire, with follow-up telephone interviews and site visits. Other methods include interviewing, observation, participation, documentation, and research.

Once the data has been collected it should be analyzed. It is hoped that you've managed to secure the cooperation of one or more benchmarking partners so that your analysis will be comparative rather than introspective. The goal of data analysis is to identify any gaps in performance. Once you find these you will need to:

1. Identify the operational best practices and enables. In other words, what are your partners doing right that you're not? Then you need to find out exactly how they're doing it.
2. Formulate a strategy to close these gaps by identifying opportunities for improvement.
3. Develop an implementation plan for these improvements.

The analysis phase uses the outputs of the data collection phase, that is, the questionnaires, interviews, observations, and the like. It is during this phase that process mapping and the development of requisite process performance measurements are performed.

Once the plan has been formulated it will be implemented in this phase. Traditional project management techniques should be used to control, monitor, and report on the project. It is also during this phase that the continuous improvement plan is developed. In this plan, new benchmarking opportunities should be identified and pursued.

We've Reached the End of Chapter 2

In this chapter we discussed the unique concepts of the departmental and project scorecards and discovered that some researchers and many organizations have fine-tuned the idea of the balanced scorecard to suit their own particular purposes.

We also discussed a variety of project-specific scorecard examples, along with their associated metrics. It Is hoped that by now you're becoming far more comfortable with the topic—as well as the process—and are getting ready to embark on a balanced scorecard project of your own.

References

Hagood, W. and L. Friedman, 2002. Using the balanced scorecard to measure the performance of your HR information system. *Public Personnel Management*, 31(4 Winter).

Kaplan, R.S., and D.P. Norton (2001, February). On Balance. (Interview). *CFO, Magazine for Senior Financial Executives*, pp. 72–78.

Parker, M., R. Benson, and H. Trainor, 1988. *Information Economics: Linking Business Performance to Information Technology*. Englewood Cliffs, NJ: Prentice-Hall.

Rosemann, M. and J. Wiese, 1999. Measuring the performance of ERP software – A balanced scorecard approach. *Proceedings of the 10th Australasian Conference on Information Systems*. http://www2.vuw.ac.nz/acis99/Papers/PaperRosemannWiese-089.pdf

Chapter 3

Aligning the Project to Meet Financial Objectives

The end result of a project is either a product or a service. It is quite possible to measure this end result from a financial perspective. A study by Utunen (2003) determined the following priorities for financially based measurement: commercialization, customer focus, stock, protection, acquisition, competence of personnel, and management focus. For each indicator one or more metrics was established, as shown in Table 3.1.

This chapter summarizes a variety of financially based methodologies, indicators, and metrics that can be used within the financial perspective of the project balanced scorecard.

Cost–Benefit Analysis

Cost–benefit analysis is quite easy to understand (see the appendices for more detailed information on feasibility studies and cost–benefit analysis). The process compares the costs to the benefits of the product or service. We all do this on a daily basis. For example, if we go out to buy a new $1,000 personal computer we weigh the cost of expending that $1,000 against the benefits of owning the personal computer. For example, these benefits might be:

1. No longer have to rent a computer. Cost savings are $75 per month.
2. Possible to earn extra money by typing term papers for students. Potential earnings are $300 per month.

Table 3.1 **Financially Based Measurement**

Indicator	Metric
Commercialization	
Product/service cost savings	Total product/services costs
	Costs of acquired products/services
	Total R&D expenditure
Sales of new or improved product/service	Total sales
Customer Focus	
Customer complaints	Number of problems solved
Customer intelligence expenditure	Amount of R&D invested in researching R&D ideas among customers
Number of projects aligned with customers	Number of projects performed in cooperation with customer
Stock	
Stock amount	Number of products/services owned or possessed by the company
Stock competitiveness	Qualitative evaluation of products/services compared to competitors
Protection	
Patenting activity	Number of new patents generated by R&D
Patentable innovations	Number of patentable innovations that are not yet patented
Importance of patents	Number of patents protecting the core of a specific business area
Acquisition	
Allocation of R&D	Total R&D expenditure
R&D efficiency and effectiveness	Amount of R&D expenditure spent on successfully commercialized products/ services
New projects	Total number of new R&D projects started

Table 3.1 Financially Based Measurement (Continued)

Indicator	Metric
Merger and acquisition	Amount of new products/services acquired through mergers and acquisitions
Personnel Competence	
Personnel competence level	Qualitative evaluation of the level of personnel competencies
Management Focus	
Top management focus	Total number of working hours
Top management reaction time	Top management reaction time to strategic or environmental changes
R&D link to strategy	Percentage of R&D directly in line with business strategy

We can summarize this as follows:

Costs/One Time	Benefits/Year
$1,000	1. Rental computer savings: $75 × 12 = $900
	2. Typing income: $300 × 12 = $3,600
$1,000/one time	$4,500/year
Potential savings/earnings	$3,500/first year; $4,500 subsequent years

One-time capital costs such as computers are usually amortized over a certain period of time. For example, a computer costing $1,000 can be amortized over five years, which means that instead of comparing a one-time cost of $1,000 to the benefits of purchasing the PC, we can compare a monthly cost instead.

Not all cost–benefit analyses are so clear cut, however. In our example above the benefits were both financially based. Not all benefits are so easily quantifiable. We call benefits that can't be quantified intangible benefits. Examples are:

1. Reduced turnaround time
2. Improved customer satisfaction
3. Compliance with mandates
4. Enhanced interagency communication

Aside from having to deal with both tangible and intangible benefits, most cost–benefit analyses also need to deal with several alternatives. For example, let's say that a bank uses a loan processing system that is old and often has problems. There might be several alternative solutions:

1. Rewrite the system from scratch.
2. Modify the existing system.
3. Outsource the system.

In each case a spreadsheet should be created that details one-time as well as continuing costs. These should then be compared to the benefits of each alternative, both tangible as well as intangible.

An associated formula is the benefit-to-cost ratio (BCR). The computation of the financial benefit/cost ratio is done within the construct of the following formula: Benefits/Cost.

Break-Even Analysis

All projects have associated costs. All projects will also have associated benefits. At the outset of a project, costs will far exceed benefits. However, at some point the benefits will start outweighing the costs. This is called the *break-even point*. The analysis that is done to figure out when this break-even point will occur is called *break-even analysis*. In the following table we see that the break-even point comes during the first year.

Costs/One-Time	Benefits/Year
$1,000	1. Rental computer savings: $75 × 12 = $900
	2. Typing income: $300 × 12 = $3,600
$1,000/one time	$4,500/year
Potential savings/earnings	$3,500/first year; $4,500 subsequent years

Calculating the break-even point in a project with multiple alternatives enables the project manager to select the optimum solution. The project manager will generally select the alternative with the shortest break-even point.

Estimating ROI for a Project

Most organizations want to select projects that have a positive return on investment. The return on investment, or ROI as it is most commonly known, is the additional amount earned after costs are earned back. In our "buy versus not buy" PC decision discussed above we can see that the ROI is quite positive during the first, and especially during subsequent years of ownership.

The project manager and the finance department need to be joint owners of the ROI process. The International Data Group (IOMA, 2002), a technology research firm, provides two examples of where this failed and where it succeeded. Lanier International is a copy machine manufacturer. Unfortunately, all discussions between finance and project managers were more like confrontations. The finance department battled every facet of the project manager's methodology for arriving at his numbers. On the other hand, Owens-Corning, a building materials company, assigned a finance department person to each project. The finance person tracked the progress of benefits during and after the project. In this way, the project manager owned the ROI numbers jointly with the business.

The basic formula for ROI is:

$$\text{ROI} = \frac{(\text{Benefit} - \text{Cost})}{\text{Cost}}$$

ROI calculations require the availability of large amounts of accurate data, which is sometimes unavailable to the project manager. Many variables need to be considered and decisions made regarding which factors to calculate and which to ignore.

Before starting an ROI calculation, identify the following factors:

1. Know what you're measuring: Successful ROI calculators isolate their true data from other factors, including the work environment and the level of management support.
2. Don't saturate: Instead of analyzing every factor involved, pick a few. Start with the most obvious factors that can be identified immediately.
3. Convert to money: Converting data into hard monetary values is essential in any successful ROI study. Translating intangible benefits into dollars is challenging and might require some assistance from the accounting or finance departments. The goal is to demonstrate the impact on the bottom line.
4. Compare apples to apples: Measure the same factors before and after the project.

There are a variety of ROI techniques:

1. Treetop: Treetop metrics investigate the impact on profitability for the entire company. Profitability can take the form of cost reductions due to project implementation.
2. Pure cost: There are several varieties of pure cost ROI techniques. Total cost of ownership (TCO) details the hidden support and maintenance costs over time that provide a more concise picture of the total cost. The Gartner Group's NOW, or normalized cost of work produced, index measures the cost of one's conducting a work task versus the cost to others doing similar work.
3. Financial: Aside from ROI, economic value added tries to optimize a company's shareholder wealth.

There are also a variety of ways of actually calculating ROI:

1. Productivity: Output per unit of input
2. Processes: Systems, workflow
3. Human resources: Costs and benefits for a specific initiative
4. Employee factors: Retention, morale, commitment, and skills

ROI calculation is not complete until the results are converted to dollars. This includes looking at combinations of hard and soft data. Hard data include such traditional measures as output, time, quality, and costs. In general, hard data are readily available and relatively easy to calculate. Soft data are hard to calculate and includes morale, turnover rate, absenteeism, loyalty, conflicts avoided, new skills learned, new ideas, successful completion of projects, and so on, as shown in Table 3.2.

After the hard or soft data have been determined, they need to be converted to monetary values:

Step 1: Focus on a single unit.
Step 2: Determine a value for each unit.
Step 3: Calculate the change in performance. Determine the performance change after factoring out other potential influences on the results.
Step 4: Obtain an annual amount. The industry standard for an annual performance change is equal to the total change in performance data during one year.
Step 5: Determine the annual value. The annual value of improvement equals the annual performance change, multiplied by the unit value. Compare the product of this equation to the cost of the program using this formula: ROI = net annual value of improvement – program.

Table 3.2   Hard Data versus Soft Data

Hard Data	
Output	Units produced
	Items assembled or sold
	Forms processed
	Tasks completed
Quality	Scrap
	Waste
	Rework
	Product defects or rejects
Time	Equipment downtime
	Employee overtime
	Time to complete projects
	Training time
Cost	Overhead
	Variable costs
	Accident costs
	Sales expenses
Soft Data	
Work habits	Employee absenteeism
	Tardiness
	Visits to nurse
	Safety-rule violations
Work climate	Employee grievances
	Employee turnover
	Discrimination charges
	Job satisfaction

(continued)

Table 3.2   Hard Data versus Soft Data (Continued)

Attitudes	Employee loyalty
	Employee self-confidence
	Employee perception of job responsibility
	Perceived changes in performance
New skills	Decisions made
	Problems solved
	Conflicts avoided
	Frequency of use of new skills
Development and advancement	Number of promotions or pay increases
	Number of training programs attended
	Requests for transfer
	Performance appraisal ratings
Initiative	Implementation of new ideas
	Successful completion of projects
	Number of employee suggestions

The U.S. Department of Veterans Affairs uses spreadsheets to calculate ROI at various stages of a project.

Initial Benefits Worksheet

Calculation: hours/person average × cost/hour × number of people = total $ saved

1. Reduced time to learn system/job (worker hours)
2. Reduced supervision (supervision hours)
3. Reduced help from co-workers (worker hours)
4. Reduced calls to help line
5. Reduced downtime (waiting for help, consulting manuals, etc.)
6. Fewer or no calls from help line to supervisor about overuse of help service

Continuing Benefits Worksheet

Calculation: hours/person average × cost/hour × number of people = total $ saved

1. Reduced time to perform operation (worker time)
2. Reduced overtime

3. Reduced supervision (supervisor hours)
4. Reduced help from co-workers (worker hours)
5. Reduced calls to help line
6. Reduced downtime (waiting for help, consulting manuals, etc.)
7. Fewer or no calls from help line to supervisor about overuse of help service
8. Fewer mistakes (e.g., rejected transactions)
9. Fewer employees needed
10. Total savings in one year
11. Expected life of system in years

Quality Benefits Worksheet

Calculation: unit cost × number of units = total $ saved

1. Fewer mistakes (e.g., rejected transactions)
2. Fewer rejects, ancillary costs
3. Total savings in one year
4. Expected life of system/process in years

Other Benefits Worksheet

Calculation: = $ saved per year

1. Reduced employee turnover
2. Reduced grievances
3. Reduced absenteeism/tardiness (morale improvements)

ROI Spreadsheet Calculation

Calculation: ROI = (Benefits – Costs/Costs)

1. Initial time saved total over life of system/process
2. Continuing worker hours saved total over life of system/process
3. Quality improvements with fixed costs total over life of system/process
4. Other possible benefits total over life of system/process
5. Total benefits
6. Total costs

ROI evaluates an investment's potential by comparing the magnitude and timing of expected gains with the investment costs. For example, a new initiative costs $500,000 and will deliver an additional $700,000 in increased profits. Simple ROI = gains – investment costs/investment costs. ($700,000 – $500,000 = $200,000. $200,000/$500,000 = 40%.) This calculation works well in situations where benefits and costs are easily known, and is usually expressed as an annual percentage return.

However, some investments involve financial consequences that extend over several years. In this case, the metric has meaning only when the time period is clearly stated. Net present value (NPV) recognizes the time value of money by discounting costs and benefits over a period of time, and focuses on the impact on cash flow rather than net profit, or savings.

A meaningful NPV requires sound estimates of the costs and benefits and use of the appropriate discount rate. An investment is acceptable if the NPV is positive. For example, an investment costing $1M has a NPV of savings of $1.5M. Therefore, ROI = (NPV of savings – initial investment cost)/initial investment cost. ($1,500,000 – $1,000,000 = $500,000. $500,000/$1,000,000 = 50%.) This may also be expressed as ROI = $1.5M (NPV of savings)/$1M (initial investment) × 100 = 150%.

The internal rate of return (IRR) is the discount rate that sets the net present value of the program or project to zero. Although the internal rate of return does not generally provide an acceptable decision criterion, it does provide useful information, particularly when budgets are constrained or there is uncertainty about the appropriate discount rate.

The U.S. CIO Council developed (see the appendices) the value-measuring methodology (VMM) to define, capture, and measure value associated with electronic services unaccounted for in traditional return-on-investment calculations, to fully account for costs and to identify and consider risk.

Earned-Value Management

Most companies track the cost of a project using only two dimensions: planned costs versus actual costs. Using this particular metric, if managers spend all of the money that has been allocated to a particular project, they are right on target. If they spend less money, they have a cost underrun; a greater expenditure results in a cost overrun. Fleming (2003) contends that this method ignores a key third dimension: the value of work performed.

Earned-value management—or EVM—enables you to measure the true cost of performance of long-term capital projects. Even though EVM has been in use for many years, government contractors are the major practitioners of this method.

The key tracking EVM metric is the cost performance index or CPI, which has proven remarkably stable over the scope of most projects according to Fleming (2003). The CPI shows the relationship between the value of work accomplished ("earned value") and the actual costs. Fleming provides the following example to show how it works:

If the project is budgeted to have a final value of $1 billion, but the CPI is running at 0.8 when the project is, say, one-fifth complete, the actual cost at completion can be expected to be around $1.25 billion ($1 billion/0.8). You're earning only

80 cents of value for every dollar you're spending. Management can take advantage of this early warning by reducing costs while there's still time.

Several software tools, including Microsoft Project, have the capability of working with EVM. PMPlan (http://www.pmplan.com) was written specifically to handle EVM, as shown in Figures 3.1 as well as 3.1a and 3.1b. (Note: the screen shot was so large it had to be split into two for readability.)

Governance One also offers an interesting Flash-driven demo of its EVM offering at http://www.governanceone.com/flash/governance_demo.swf.

Rapid Economic Justification

Microsoft developed the Rapid Economic Justification (REJ) framework (http://www.microsoft.com/windows/windowsmedia/Enterprise/AboutWM/BusinessValue/default.aspx) as an assessment and justification process that helps organizations align projects with business requirements and then quantify the direct financial benefits of the proposed solution. This approach combines the total cost of ownership (TCO) with project substantiation.

Freedman (2003) describes the five-step REJ process:

1. Understand the business. Managers should first evaluate the company's overall strategic direction and goals along with any tactical problems and opportunities. This is done to ensure that the initiatives being considered actually do fit with the organization's overall objectives.
2. Understand the solutions. Both project and business leaders need to work together to design possible alternative solutions to the identified problems.
3. Understand the cost–benefit equation. This step calculates the summation of costs found under traditional TCO models. It incorporates hard financial benefits as well as intangible benefits (e.g., enhanced responsiveness).
4. Understand the risks. Standard risk analysis and development of risk mitigation strategies are performed.
5. Understand the financial metrics. Finally, the team projects the impact of the proposed investment in financial terms (i.e., payback, NPV, etc.) used by the specific company.

Calculating the Net Worth of Organizational Information

Calculating the value of information or VOI (Keyes, 1993), is a useful exercise that assists an organization in determining the true worth of its investment in information.

Report Date	4/30/2003 ▼	New Status Date		Threshold	0 ▼		Print CSSR		Print GPR		Import Actuals			
WBS No.	Description	Work Package	Total Budget	Planned Value	Percent Complete	Earned Value	Actual Cost	Open Commitment	Schedule Variance	Cost Variance	Estimate at Completion	Variance at Completion	SPI	CPI
1	Sample Project Plan	WP	$40,000.00	$35,000.00	73.00	$29,000.00	$32,000	$0	($6,000)	($3,000)	$44,138	($4,138)	0.829	0.906
2	1 Literature Search		$5,000.00	$5,000.00	100.00	$5,000.00	—	—	—	—	—	—	—	—
3	2 Concepts Development		$2,000.00	$2,000.00	100.00	$2,000.00	—	—	—	—	—	—	—	—
4	3 Lab Models		$8,000.00	$8,000.00	100.00	$8,000.00	—	—	—	—	—	—	—	—
5	4 Design		$10,000.00	$10,000.00	80.00	$8,000.00	—	—	—	—	—	—	—	—
6	5 Prototype		$15,000.00	$10,000.00	40.00	$6,000.00	—	—	—	—	—	—	—	—

Figure 3.1   EVM calculation.

Report Date	4/30/2003 ▼	New Status Date		Threshold	0 ▼		Print CSSR		Print GPR	
WBS No.	Description	Work Package	Total Budget	Planned Value	Percent Complete	Earned Value	Actual Cost	Open Commitment	Schedule Variance	
1	Sample Project Plan	WP	$40,000.00	$35,000.00	73.00	$29,000.00	$32,000	$0	($6,000)	
2	1 Literature Search		$5,000.00	$5,000.00	100.00	$5,000.00	—	—	—	
3	2 Concepts Development		$2,000.00	$2,000.00	100.00	$2,000.00	—	—	—	
4	3 Lab Models		$8,000.00	$8,000.00	100.00	$8,000.00	—	—	—	
5	4 Design		$10,000.00	$10,000.00	80.00	$8,000.00	—	—	—	
6	5 Prototype		$15,000.00	$10,000.00	40.00	$6,000.00	—	—	—	

Figure 3.1a   EVM calculation first part.

Import Actuals				
Cost Variance	Estimate at Completion	Variance at Completion	SPI	CPI
($3,000)	$44,138	($4,138)	0.829	0.906
—	—	—	—	—
—	—	—	—	—
—	—	—	—	—
—	—	—	—	—

Figure 3.1b   EVM calculation second part (note the CPI).

The following exercise is not meant to be performed by the technology group in a vacuum. Calculating the worth of the company's data is very much a group exercise that cuts across the organization. This is also not an exercise that can be rushed through and, in fact, can even harm the organization if hastily prepared.

Before any meetings are held to debate the relative worth of data, a data dictionary should be prepared that describes all automated systems as well as systems to be automated but still on the drawing board. This task is not as onerous as it sounds if the technology department employs an automated data dictionary. In those shops where an automated dictionary is not employed, a bit of work will have to be done to uncover this information and organize it logically. One of the key tasks of this assignment is to track all data elements that are being used by more than one system. The reason for this becomes clearer as we proceed with this exercise.

At a minimum, a chart is to be prepared that looks similar to the one in Table 3.3. Although it is common, from a data definition perspective, to break down each data element into its component parts, that should not be done in this

Table 3.3   Creating the Data Dictionary for the VOI Process

Custfile	*Customer File*
Cust_name	Customer name
Cust_addr	Customer address
Cust_phone	Customer phone
Cust_credit	Customer credit score
Cust_line	Customer credit line
Cust_last	Customer last order number
Cust_date	Customer date of entry

case. For example, a customer address may be composed of four individual data elements: street address, city, state, and zip code. For the purposes of the VOI exercise, we are interested in customer addresses as a single entity only. A corresponding document should be made available that carries complete explanations of the rather cryptic system names contained within the chart.

The ultimate goal of this exercise is to assign a monetary value to each unitary piece of information. In this way, an organization used to calculating relative worth based on bottom-line statistics can instantly recognize the value of information in terms that it understands.

With this in mind, a team should be assembled that is composed of representatives from the technology and user groups. Bear in mind that because this task is somewhat subjectively judgmental, a senior manager who is in the position to act as a corporate tiebreaker should be in attendance at the assignment of relative worth to any individual data element.

The team is now ready to evaluate each data element and apply a weighting algorithm that will ultimately tie the data element back to the organization in a monetary sense. The steps that should be taken for this assessment are as follows:

1. Assign each system a weighting relative to the importance to the organization. Permissible weights for the entirety of this exercise are one for a low relative value, two for a middle relative value, and three for a high relative value.
2. For each data element within the system, assign a weighting that indicates that data element's importance relative to that system. Again, use the weightings one through three.
3. Multiply these two numbers together to get the total weighting of the data element relative to all data in the organization.
4. Each data element should have an annotation next to it indicating the number of systems in which this data element is cross-referenced. For example, it is possible that customer name is used in the sales system, the inventory system, and the marketing system. This will give us a total of three systems. The product calculated in instruction three is now multiplied by the number determined in this instruction.
5. Convert this number to a percentage.
6. Using the last audited net income amount for the organization, calculate the VOI by multiplying the percentage calculated in instruction six by the net income amount. A completed chart in shown in Table 3.4.

Table 3.4   VOI Calculation Based on Net Income of $5 Million

Custfile	Customer File	Corp. Weighting	System Weighting	Cross References	VOI
Cust_name	Customer name	2	3 = 6	5 = 30	$1.5M
Cust_addr	Customer address	2	2 = 4	2 = 8	$.4M
Cust_phone	Customer phone	2	3 = 6	1 = 6	$.3M
Cust_credit	Credit score	3	3 = 9	3 = 27	$1.35M
Cust_line	Credit line	3	3 = 9	1 = 9	$.45M
Cust_last	Last order	2	2 = 4	3 = 12	$.6M
Cust_date	Date of entry	1	1 = 1	2 = 2	$.1M
			= Total weighting		In millions

IAM: Intangible Assets Monitor

Karl-Erik Sveiby (1997) developed a scorecard-like measure to monitor the value of intangible assets. The value of IAM is that it depends on the addition of intangible and tangible assets such as the ones listed in Table 3.5. IAM is based on very simplistic accounting but enables a powerful demonstration of the value of intangible assets.

We've Reached the End of Chapter 3

In this chapter we put on our finance caps and learned a great deal about how to assign metrics to project assets. Our discussions included cost–benefit analysis, return on investment, net present value, rapid economic justification, portfolio management, and value of information. These standard financial metrics form the basis of the financial perspective of the project scorecard.

Table 3.5   IAM Table of Metrics

| Intangible Assets Monitor | | |
External Structure Indicators	Internal Structure Indicators	Competence Indicators
Indicators of growth/renewal	Indicators of growth/renewal	Indicators of growth/renewal
Profitability per customer	Investment in the project	Number of years in the profession
Organic growth	Structure-enhancing customers	Level of education
Image-enhancing customers		Training and education costs
		Marketing
		Competence turnover
		Competence-enhancing customers
Indicators of efficiency	Indicators of efficiency	Indicators of efficiency
Satisfied customers index	Proportion of support staff	Proportion of professionals
Sales per customer	Values/attitudes index	Leverage effect
Win/loss index		Value added per employee
		Value added per professional
		Profit per employee
		Profit per professional
Indicators of stability	Indicators of stability	Indicators of stability
Proportion of big customers	Age of the organization	Professionals turnover
Age structure	Support staff turnover	Relative pay
Devoted customers ratio	Rookie ratio	Seniority
Frequency of repeat orders	Security	

References

Fleming, Q. 2003. What's your project's real price tag? *Harvard Business Review.* 81(9, September): 20, 2p, 1c.

Freedman, R. 2003. Helping clients value IT investments. *Consulting to Management.* 14(3, September).

IOMA. 2002. How to develop a repeatable & accurate ROI process for IT. *IOMA's Report on Financial Analysis and Reporting.* 02-10, October.

Keyes, J. 1993. *Infotrends: The competitive use of information.* New York: McGraw-Hill.

Sveiby, K. 1997. *"The Value of Intangible Assets."* http://www.sveiby.com/articles/IntangAss/CompanyMonitor.html (December).

Utunen, P. 2003. Identify, measure, visualize your technology assets. *Research Technology Management.* May/June: 31–39.

Chapter 4

Aligning the Project to Meet Customer Objectives

There are three primary sources of differentiation vis-à-vis the balanced scorecard customer perspective:

1. Product innovation: Create new products and services that keep you ahead of competitors.
2. Customer intimacy: Develop intimate knowledge of customer needs and ways of satisfying these needs.
3. Operational excellence: Deliver acceptable quality and product characteristics at the lowest possible cost.

The three sources of differentiation should be kept in mind when dealing with internal and external customers.

Customer Intimacy and Operational Excellence

The Marketing Science Institute found that customers want their products and services delivered with the following four characteristics:

1. Reliability: Customers want dependability, accuracy, and consistency.
2. Responsiveness: Customers want prompt delivery and continuous communication.

3. Assurance: The customer wants to be assured that the project team will deliver its project on time, with quality, within budget, and within scope.
4. Empathy: Customers want the project team to listen to and understand them. The customer really wants to be treated like a team member.

In all cases, customers also want a responsive project development and support team. The goal is to select or develop and then deploy initiatives and accompanying metrics that fulfill these requirements.

An eight percent drop in quarterly profits accompanied by a ten percent rise in service costs does not tell a customer service team what its service technicians should do differently on their service calls. However, knowing that several new technician hires dropped the average skill level such that the average time spent per service call rose fifteen percent—and that, as a result, the number of late calls rose ten percent—would explain why service costs had gone up and customer satisfaction and profits had gone down. The key, then, is to select metrics wisely.

The U.S. government uses an interesting variety of customer-centric measures as part of their e-services initiative:

1. Customer satisfaction index
2. Click count
3. Attrition rate
4. Complaints
5. Customer frustration (abandoned transactions divided by total completed transactions)
6. Visibility into the government process
7. Efficient use of taxpayer dollars
8. Effective sharing of information
9. Trust
10. Consistent quality of services
11. Compliance with Section 508 (handicapped access)
12. Compliance with security and privacy policies
13. Partner satisfaction
14. Political image
15. Community awareness
16. Negative/positive publicity

Project managers might want to think about replacing the "customer" perspective with the "user" perspective. This more aptly broadens the customer perspective to include the internal as well as external customers who are using the project or services developed as a result of the implementation of the project. From an end user's perspective, the value of a "project" is based largely on the extent to which it helps the user do the job more efficiently and productively. Indicators might include utilization rate, availability of training and support, and satisfaction with the project deliverables. Table 4.1 summarizes user-based indicators and metrics for a construction industry project.

The Customer Satisfaction Survey

The easiest and most typical way to find out what your customers think about your product or service is to ask them. The instrument that performs this task is the *customer satisfaction survey*. Those doing business on the Internet will find it rather easy to deploy a customer survey, such as the one shown in Figure 4.1. There are quite a few survey hosting services available on a pay-per-use basis. KeySurvey (keysurvey. com) and Zoomerang (zoomerang.com) are just two.

If a Web or e-mail-based survey is not practical, then you can opt for doing your survey either via traditional mail or phone. Because traditional mail surveys suffer from a comparatively low return rate (one to three percent) it is recommended that you utilize the telephone approach.

The steps to a successful customer/end-user survey include:

1. Assemble the survey team: The makeup of the survey team depends upon the type of survey and the target customer base. If you are going to be calling external customers, then the best people for the job are to be found in the marketing, sales, or customer services departments.
2. Develop the survey: The appendices contain some relevant information on benchmarking data collection techniques, including information on interviewing and surveying.
3. Collect contact data: Name, company, address, and phone number are the minimum pieces of information you will need for this process if you are surveying external customers. Name, extension, and e-mail address are sufficient for internal end users.
4. Select a random sample of customers/end users for the survey: You can't, and shouldn't, survey all of your customers unless your customer base is very small. Random sampling is the most popular approach to reducing the number of surveys you will be sending out. Alternatively, you can use a systematic sampling approach. Using this method you select every Nth customer to include in your survey population.
5. Conduct interviewer training for staff.
6. Call customers/end users: Complete a customer satisfaction survey instrument for each person.
7. Send the completed surveys and call sheets to the designated survey analysis team: This might be someone in the marketing department or, in the case of an internal survey, the project manager designated for this task.

Table 4.1   Customer-Driven Indicators and Metrics for a Construction Industry Project

Performance Indicator	Key Aspects	Performance Measure
Facilitate document transfer and handling	Staff are proficient with the use of the revised procedures	• Percent user proficient with procedures • Percent documents transferred using new procedures
Enhance coordination among staff	Improved coordination More efficient utilization of contractors and subcontractors	• Number of conflicts resulting from lack of coordination reduced by a percentage • Time spent on rework arising from lack of coordination reduced by a percentage
Reduce response time to answer queries	Facilitate quicker response to project queries	• Response time to answer design queries reduced by a percentage
Empower staff to make decisions	Better and faster decision making	• Time taken to provide information needed to arrive at decision reduced by a percentage
Enable immediate reporting and receive feedback	Information is made available to the project team as soon as it is ready	• Time taken to report changes to management • Time spent on reporting to total time at work reduced by a percentage
Identify errors or inconsistencies	Reduced number of QA nonconformances	• The ratio of the number of QA nonconformances for new systems to QA nonconformances for the traditional system

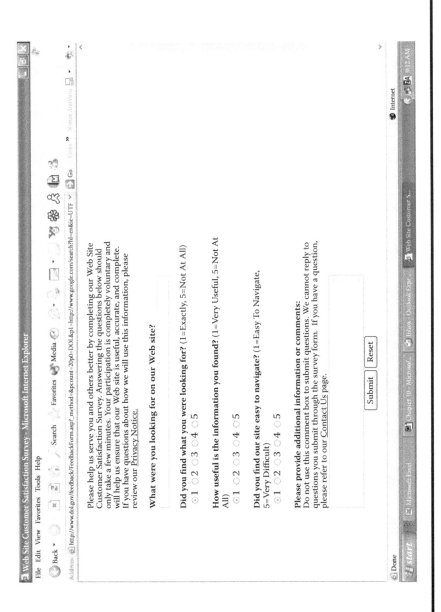

Figure 4.1 Brief customer satisfaction survey.

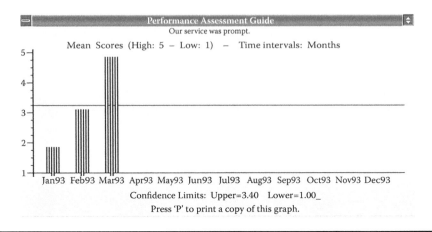

Figure 4.2 The DoD created their own performance assessment software for this purpose.

8. Summarize survey results and prepare a report: If you are using a Web-based or other automated surveying tool you will be provided with analytical capabilities (see Figure 4.2). If you are doing this manually, then it is advisable to use Excel or another spreadsheet package for analysis.

Using Force Field Analysis to Listen to End Users

One of the most common problems a project manager has when dealing with end users is haggling about the product's feature list. Force field analysis can be used to brainstorm more quickly and effectively and prioritize ideas with a group of end users.

The power of this technique, usable in small as well as in large groups, is in uncovering the driving as well as restraining forces for your projects. Driving forces can be: features, services, a Web site, and so on—anything that helps end users drive to success. Restraining forces can be quality issues, complex implementation, convoluted processes, support, or unclear procedures—anything that prevents your customers from being successful.

The procedure is simple to follow:

1. State the problem, goal, or situation where you want feedback.
2. Divide your end user feedback group into smaller groups of eight to ten. Sit them around a table and elect a scribe. A facilitator should also be appointed for each table.
3. Each discussion should take no longer than 30 minutes.
4. The table facilitator goes around the table asking each person to contribute one driving force. The table scribe records each new force.

5. Go around the table one or two more times until everyone is in agreement that their top three forces have been listed.
6. Review the list with the group.
7. Each person gets three votes for his or her top three forces.
8. The scribe will tally the votes for each force.
9. A meeting moderator should go around the room soliciting the top three driving forces from each table.
10. A meeting scribe should document the forces in a spreadsheet projected at the front of the room.
11. Each person in the room gets three votes for his or her top three forces.
12. The meeting scribe should enter the number of votes for each driving force.
13. When done, sort the list by votes to rank them.

The process is then repeated for the restraining forces. A sample list follows:

Driving forces:

1. Integration across modules   50 votes
2. Excellent tech support   45 votes
3. Standards-based technology   38 votes

Restraining forces:

1. Product quality not always consistent   70 votes
2. Difficult to migrate from release to release   60 votes
3. User security is inadequate   30 votes

Force field analysis enables you to really listen to your end users, which should lead to increased customer satisfaction and, perhaps, an improvement in the quality and competitiveness of your product.

The Customer Economy

In a *customer economy* model the customer (i.e., the end user) is firmly in control. The key indicator in this economy is ETDBW or "easy to do business with." In this economy, the customary metrics of profit and loss and return on assets are much less important than customer loyalty. The new customer-friendly manager focuses on the following metrics:

1. Retention
2. Satisfaction
3. Growth

4. Increases in customer spending
5. Rate of defection or predicted rate of defection

It's really necessary to go to the source to maintain customer loyalty. One way to do this is to create a Customer Advisory Council. I am sure that this is all very familiar to you. Most projects do employ either end user committees (new projects) or change control (or priority) boards for existing implementations where there are numerous change requests.

The Patricia Seybold Group has developed two customer-focused metrics that are useful for the project scorecard. The quality of experience (QoE) affects employee productivity and channel revenue as well as customer satisfaction. The metric assesses the user's experience in terms of responsiveness and availability. It looks at a project team's offering from the standpoint of the customer or end user, and asks, "What mix of goods, services, and support do you think will provide you with the perception that the total product is providing you with the experience you desired or expected?" It then asks, "Is this what the vendor/purveyor has actually provided?" If not, "What changes need to be made to enhance your total experience?"

The Quality of Customer Experience (QCE) is a set of metrics that allows the organization to assess, monitor, and manage the customer experience. The customer experience, according to this definition, is far more expansive than just accessing the company Web site. It also might include:

1. Phone interactions
2. E-mails
3. Visits to your offices
4. Direct-mail marketing
5. Advertising
6. Employee behavior
7. How the product actually performs
8. How the service is performed
9. How the company is perceived by the community; alternatively, how the department is perceived by the rest of the company

The heart of QCE is the *customer outcomes* and resulting *moments of truth*. A customer measures the success of his experience in terms of reaching his desired outcome. Moments of truth are those points in the customer's experience where the quality of your company's execution substantially affects his loyalty to your company and its products or services. In other words, moments of truth signify key points in the customer's experience where he is judging the quality of the experience. Therefore, the heart of the QCE assessment is measuring the customer's success in the use of your product or service to achieve his desired outcomes.

For QCE to work properly these moments of truth (or key success metrics) have to be determined. They can be different for different people, so the best way to tackle this exercise is to develop a case study or scenario and run through it pinpointing the moments of truth for each stakeholder involved in the scenario. Seybold calls this process customer scenario mapping (sm).

Consider the scenario of a company that needs a replacement motor, fast. The maintenance engineer needs to get production back up by 6 a.m. the next morning. His moments of truth are: (1) the motor is right for the job; (2) he has all the parts and tools he needs; and (3) he finishes before the shift supervisor shows up to bug him. The maintenance engineer must order his motor through his company's purchasing agent, who uses a computer system. The purchasing agent has her own moments of truth: (1) find and order a motor in 15 minutes, delivery confirmed; (2) best choice for motor was in first page of search results; (3) enough information was offered to enable a decision; (4) order department quickly confirmed delivery without making the purchasing agent wait or repeat herself; and (5) invoicing is correct.

Some of the metrics derived from this mapping include those shown in Table 4.2.

End Users Want Innovative Systems

Citibank understands innovation and how to measure it. The company long had an Innovation Index (Tucker, 2002). This index measured revenues derived from new products, but Citibank deemed this index insufficient to meet their needs. They created an Innovation Initiative, staffed by a special taskforce. This group was challenged to come up with more meaningful metrics that could be used to track progress and be easily integrated into Citibank's balanced scorecard. What a great idea to keep track of innovation in projects!

There are two types of innovation:

1. *Sustaining:* Advances that give end users something better, in ways that *they* define as "better." There is often a disconnect between what customers think is better and what project managers think is better.
2. *Disruptive:* Advances that impair or "disrupt" the traditional fashion in which a company has gone to market and made money, because the innovation offers something end user customers don't want. This is related to resistance to change. When enterprise resource management is first introduced to a company, there is often some major resistance from end users, because mostly everything they have done before, and with which they are familiar, is tossed out the window.

Table 4.2 Representative QCE Metrics

	Navigation	Performance	Operations	Environment
Using computer system, customers find and purchase in 15 minutes	• Average number of searches per order line item • Average number of support calls per order • Average elapsed time to select product and place the order	• Average elapsed time to search • Average elapsed time to select and purchase • Number of steps required to select and purchase • Average time to answer incoming phone call	• Number of seconds average response time experienced by customers • Number of seconds average response time experienced by employees who are interacting with customers • Percent availability of customer-facing applications • Number of customers on hold waiting for customer service	• Internet performance index

Most software companies continually enhance their line of software products to provide their customers with the features that they have stated they truly desired. This is *sustaining* innovation. These companies might also strive to come up with products that are radically different from what their customers want in order to expand their base of customers, compete with the competition, or even jump into a completely new line of business. This is *disruptive* innovation.

Most people equate innovation with a new invention, but it can also refer to a process improvement, continuous improvement, or even new ways to use existing things. Innovation can, and should, occur at the outset of every project development effort.

Good project managers are constantly reviewing the internal and external landscape for clues and suggestions about what might come next. Techniques include:

1. Research results from R&D. One of the challenges is being alert to market opportunities that might be very different than the inventor's original vision.
2. Competitors' innovations. Microsoft leveraged Apple's breakthrough graphical user interface and ultimately became far more dominant and commercially successful than Apple.
3. Breakthroughs outside industry.
4. Customer requests. A "customer-focused" organization's products and services will reflect a coherent understanding of customer needs.
5. Employee suggestions.
6. Newsgroups and trade journals.
7. Trade shows and networking.

Some experts argue that a company's product architecture mirrors and is based on their organizational structure This is because companies attack that first project or customer opportunity a certain way. If it works, they look to repeat the process and this repetition evolves into a company's "culture." So when we say a company is "bureaucratic," what we are really saying is that it is incapable of organizing differently to address different customer challenges because it has been so successful at the original model.

This sort of bureaucracy is disseminated right down to the project level. Many companies require that all projects use standard companywide ways of doing things. Although it is understandable that a standardized centralized method of controlling resources makes life easier for top management, it can diminish the innovation and creativity needed to create a system that just might create a competitive advantage.

There are a variety of workplace structures that promote innovation:

1. Cross-functional teams: Selecting representatives from the various functional areas and assigning them to solve a particular problem can be an effective way to quickly meld a variety of relevant perspectives and also efficiently pass the implementation stress test, avoiding, for example, the possibility that a particular functional group will later try to block a new initiative. Some variations include:
    a. "Lightweight project manager" system: Each functional area chooses a person to represent it on the project team. The project manager serves primarily as a coordinator. This function is "lightweight" in that the project manager does not have the power to reassign people or reallocate resources.
    b. "Tiger team": Individuals from various areas are assigned and completely dedicated to the project team, often physically moving into shared office

space together. This does not necessarily require permanent reassignment, but is obviously better suited for longer-term projects with a high level of urgency within the organization.

2. Cross-company teams or industry coalitions: Some companies have developed innovative partnership models to share the costs and risks of these high-profile investments, such as:
   a. Customer advisory boards
   b. Executive retreats
   c. Joint ventures
   d. Industry associations

There are several managerial techniques that can be utilized to spur department and project team innovation, as shown in Table 4.3.

Managing for Innovation

When I was at the New York Stock Exchange we had a research and development department that investigated and experimented with newfangled tools that could possibly give the Exchange a leg up or make our customers more productive. If the tool worked effectively, we threw it out to our project teams to see what they could do with it. At a very high level, every R&D process will consist of:

1. Generation of ideas: From the broadest visioning exercises to specific functionality requirements, the first step is to list the potential options.
2. Evaluation of ideas: Having documented everything from the most practical to the farfetched, the team can then coolly and rationally analyze and prioritize the components, using agreed-upon metrics.
3. Product/service design: These "ideas" are then converted into "requirements," often with very specific technical parameters.

There are two core elements of this longer-term competency-enhancing work. The first is the generation of ideas. Most companies utilize a standard process to make sure that everyone has time and motivation to contribute. The second element is to promote an environment conductive to innovation. This includes:

1. Cultural values and institutional commitment
2. Allocation of resources
3. Linkage with company's business strategy

Creating an innovation-friendly environment is time-consuming and will require the manager to forgo focusing on the here and now. However, when there is constant pressure to hit the numbers or make something happen, it is difficult to be farsighted and build in time for you and your team to create an environment.

Table 4.3 Promoting Innovation

Technique	Definition/Examples
Commitment to problem solving	• Ability to ask the "right questions" • Build in time for research and analysis
Commitment to openness	• Analytical and cultural flexibility
Acceptance of "out-of-box" thinking	• Seek out and encourage different viewpoints, even radical ones
Willingness to reinvent products and processes that are already in place	• Create a "blank slate" opportunity map, even for processes that appear to be battle-tested and comfortable
Willingness to listen to everyone (employees, customers, vendors)	• "Open door" • Respect for data and perspective without regard to seniority or insider status
Keeping informed of industry trends	• Constantly scanning business publications/trade journals, and clipping articles of interest • "FYI" participation with fellow managers
Promotion of diversity, cross-pollination	• Forward-thinking team formation, which also attempts to foster diversity • Sensitive to needs of gender, race, even work style
Change of management policies	• Instill energy and "fresh start" by revising established rules
Provision of incentives for all employees, not just researchers/ engineers	• Compensation schemes to align individual performance with realization of company goals
Use of project management	• Clear goals and milestones • Tracking tools • Expanded communication
Transfer of knowledge within an organization	• Commitment to aggregating and reformatting key data for "intelligence" purposes

(continued)

Table 4.3 Promoting Innovation (Continued)

Technique	Definition/Examples
Provision for off-site teaming	• Structured meetings and socialization outside the office to reinforce bonds between key team members
Provision for off-site training	• Development of individuals through education and experiential learning to master new competencies
Use of simple visual models	• Simple but compelling frameworks and schematics to clarify core beliefs
Use of the Internet for research	• Fluency and access to web sites (e.g., competitor home pages)
Development of processes for implementing new products and ideas	• Structured ideation and productization process • Clear release criteria • Senior management buy-in
Champion products	• Identify and prioritize those products representing the best possible chance for commercial success • Personally engage and encourage contributors to strategic initiatives

Managing innovation is a bit different than creating an environment that promotes innovation. This refers to the service or product-specific initiative, whether it is a new car or a streamlined manufacturing process. The big question is, "How do we make this process come together on time and under budget?" There are two main phases to the successful management of innovation.

The first phase seeks to stress-test the proposal with a variety of operational and financial benchmarks, such as:

1. Is the innovation "real"? Is this "next great thing" dramatic enough to justify the costs, financial and otherwise? Does it clearly and demonstrably distance you from your competitors? And, can it be easily duplicated once it becomes public knowledge?
2. Can the innovation actually be done? Does the organization have the resources? This is where you figure out whether the rubber meets the road. You need to ask whether you have the capabilities and functional expertise to realize this vision. Many organizations come up with a multitude of ideas. Upon further examination, they often find that they simply do not have the

resources to do the vast majority of them. This might lead them to become innovative in a different way as they search for partners. In other words, some organizations try to couple their brains with someone else's brawn!

3. Is the innovation worth it? Does the innovation fit into the organization's mission and strategic plan? ROI (return-on-investment) is the most frequently used quantitative measure to help us plan and assess new initiatives. Probably more useful, however, is ROM (return-on-management), which poses a fundamental question: on what should the CEO and her management team focus? Research extending over a period of 10 years led to the concept of return-on-management (Strassman, 1996). This ratio is calculated by first isolating the management value-added of a company, and then dividing it by the company's total management costs:

Return-on-Management = Management-Value-Added/Management Costs

Management value-added is that which remains after every contributor to a firm's inputs gets paid. If management value-added is greater than management costs, you can say that managerial efforts are productive because the managerial outputs exceed managerial inputs. Another way of looking at the return-on-management ratio (R-O-M™ Productivity Index) is to view it as a measure of productivity. It answers the question of how many surplus dollars you get for every dollar paid for management.

4. The second phase, design, is something we examine in greater detail later. However, for now, we are talking about the process by which these ideas and concepts get distilled into an actual product design, such as a web site map or a prototype. Many mistakes are made by delegating this process to lower-level functional experts, when in fact some of these decisions go a long way toward determining the product's ultimate acceptance in the marketplace!

Most of the outward signs of excellence and creativity we associate with the most innovative companies are a result of a culture and related values that encourage and support managers who also use their specific initiatives to reinforce and strengthen the company's processes. When these processes become repeatable, they become the rule instead of the exception, which of course makes it easier for the next manager to be innovative.

Capital One is a company that uses a model based on continuous innovation. They utilize a patented information-based strategy (IBS) that enables the company to expand its mature credit card business by tailoring more than 16,000 different product combinations to customers' needs. They are able to embrace high degrees of risk because they base their innovations on customer needs. The company tests new ideas against existing customers or possibly a separate grouping of prospects. Is it really so hard to extrapolate all of this to the customer-focused (or end-user-focused) perspective of the balanced scorecard?

We've Reached the End of Chapter 4

In this chapter we discussed the customer perspective of the balanced scorecard. Essentially, our goal here is to get and keep customers. Whether these customers are internal or external is of little importance, as the techniques are the same. Toward this end we discussed a variety of techniques for measuring customer satisfaction as well as the importance of innovation for attracting and retaining those customers.

References

Strassmann, P. 1996. "Introduction to ROM Analysis: Linking Management Productivity and Information Technology." http://www.strassmann.com/consulting/ROM-intro/Intro_to_ROM.html.

Tucker, R. 2002. *Driving Growth Through Innovation*. Berkeley, CA: Pub Group West.

Chapter 5

Aligning the Project to Meet Business Process Objectives

There are literally hundreds of processes taking place simultaneously in a typical department, each creating value in some way. In this context, a process is actually just a euphemism for some sort of developmental or supportive project. Some of these are development projects, some maintenance. Others are support services, and still others are infrastructure-related projects. The art of strategy is to identify and excel at the critical few processes that are the most important to the end-user value proposition (Kaplan and Norton, 2004).

Quite a few companies have outsourced some, or all of their infrastructure-related processes to third parties. Processes historically outsourced include asset management, customer support, infrastructure maintenance, and network management.

These outsourced services are usually referred to as "utilities" or "commodities," separate and distinct from those products and services that provide a distinct competitive advantage to the company. However, the advent of globalization, cheap offshore labor, the shift toward software-as-a-service (SaaS), and, more recently cloud computing, has expanded the definition of the service utility to encompass the bread and butter applications of many organizations, for example, enterprise resource planning (ERP), customer relationship management (CRM), supply chain management (SCM), and even activities such as research and content creation.

Measuring the Utility

Whether service or application, these utility processes should be measured. Traditional project metrics can be seen in Table 5.1.

Although all great measures, this list is too brief to adequately control a particular project. Table 5.2 provides an enhanced version which is even better, but this list of metrics is also inadequate, as most of them are internal to the project and do not adequately reflect the project's importance to and impact on the organization.

Unisys (2003) recommends the following metrics, which are far more inclusive of the business process perspective's requirements:

1. Customer satisfaction
2. Standardization
3. Incident rates
4. Security audit
5. Incident prevention rates
6. Security awareness
7. Availability
8. Reliability/quality of service
9. Call volume
10. First pass yields

Table 5.1 Traditional Project Metrics		
Project Management		
Category	*Measurement (How)*	*Metric (What)*
Costs	Actual versus budget	• Labor (costs) • Materials (hardware/software) • Other (office space, telcom)
Schedule	Actual versus planned	• Key deliverables completed • Key deliverables not completed • Milestones met • Milestones not met
Risks	Anticipated versus actual	• Event (actual occurrence) • Impact (effect on project)
Quality	Actual versus planned activities	• Number of reviews • Number of defects • Type and origin of defect

11. Cycle times
12. Architecture accuracy
13. Employee satisfaction
14. Root cause analysis
15. Change modification cycle times
16. Change modification volume by type
17. R&D presentation/information flow rate
18. Volume of technology pilots
19. Business opportunity generate rate
20. Strategic project counts

Unisys uses these metrics to establish the foundation for management review, trend analysis, and causal analysis. Management review provides insight into current performance and forms the basis for taking corrective action. Trend and root cause analysis identify opportunities for continuous improvement.

Based on its analysis and industry experience, Unisys states that a performance-based environment is anywhere from 10 to 40 percent more cost effective than a non-performance-based environment. Although customer satisfaction is usually touted as the key metric for improvement, it is actually an outcome metric dependent upon several lower-level activities as shown in Figure 5.1. Understanding the relationship between these co-dependent performance metrics is important in effecting sustainable positive performance.

Sustainable performance is Hewlett-Packard's goal as it tries to hang on to its number one position as a computer manufacturer. From a balanced scorecard perspective, HP has a number of business process objectives.

Operations cycle:

1. Optimized distribution model
2. JIT manufacturing
3. Outsourcing
4. Build-to-order
5. Reduced cycle times
6. Order process linked to production, supplies
7. Global production optimization

Innovation cycle:

1. Low-cost PCs
2. Products preconfigured with SAP and other business software
3. Pricing innovations
4. Design to market requirements: workstations, laptops
5. High-performance desktops

Table 5.2   An Enhanced List of Project Metrics

Category	Focus	Purpose	Measure of Success
Schedule performance	Tasks completed versus tasks planned at a point in time	Assess project progress Apply project resources	100 percent completion of tasks on critical path; 90 percent all others
	Major milestones met versus planned	Measure time efficiency	90 percent of major milestones met
	Revisions to approved plan	Understand and control project "churn"	All revisions reviewed and approved
	Changes to customer requirements	Understand and manage scope and schedule	All changes managed through approved change process
	Project completion date	Award or penalize (depending on contract type)	Project completed on schedule (per approved plan)
Budget performance	Revisions to cost estimates	Assess and manage project cost	100 percent of revisions are reviewed and approved
	Dollars spent versus dollars budgeted	Measure cost efficiency	Project completed within approved cost parameters
	Return on investment (ROI)	Track and assess performance of project investment portfolio	ROI (positive cash flow) begins according to plan
	Acquisition cost control	Assess and manage acquisition dollars	All applicable acquisition guidelines followed

Table 5.2 An Enhanced List of Project Metrics (Continued)

Category	Focus	Purpose	Measure of Success
Product quality	Defects identified through quality activities	Track progress in, and effectiveness of, defect removal	90 percent of expected defects identified (e.g., via peer reviews, inspections)
	Test case failures versus number of cases planned	Assess product functionality and absence of defects	100 percent of planned test cases execute successfully
	Number of service calls	Track customer problems	75 percent reduction after three months of operation
	Customer satisfaction index	Identify trends	95 percent positive rating
	Customer satisfaction trend	Improve customer satisfaction	5 percent improvement each quarter
	Number of repeat customers	Determine if customers are using the product multiple times (could indicate satisfaction with the product)	"X" percent of customers use the product "X" times during a specified time period
	Number of problems reported by customers	Assess quality of project deliverables	100 percent of reported problems addressed within 72 hours
Customer satisfaction	System availability (uptime)	Measure system availability	100 percent of requirement is met (e.g., 99 percent M–F, 8 a.m. to 6 p.m., and 90 percent S, S, 8 a.m. to 5 p.m.)

(continued)

Table 5.2   An Enhanced List of Project Metrics (Continued)

Category	Focus	Purpose	Measure of Success
	Functionality (meets customer's/user's needs)	Measure how well customer needs are being met.	Positive trend in customer satisfaction survey(s)
	Absence of defects (that affect customer)	Number of defects removed during project life cycle	90 percent of expected defects were removed
	Ease of learning and use	Measure time to becoming productive	Positive trend in training survey(s)
	Time it takes to answer calls for help	Manage/reduce response times	95 percent of severity one calls answered within three hours
	Rating of training course	Assess effectiveness and quality of training	90 percent of responses of "good" or better
Business goals/mission	Functionality tracks reportable inventory.	Validate system supports program mission	All reportable inventory is tracked in system
	Turnaround time in responding to queries	Improve customer satisfaction and national interests	Improve turnaround time from two days to four hours
	Maintenance costs	Track reduction of costs to maintain system	Reduce maintenance costs by 2/3 over three-year period
Productivity	Time taken to complete tasks	Evaluate estimates	Completions are within 90 percent of estimates
	Number of deliverables produced	Assess capability to deliver products	Improve product delivery 10 percent in each of the next three years

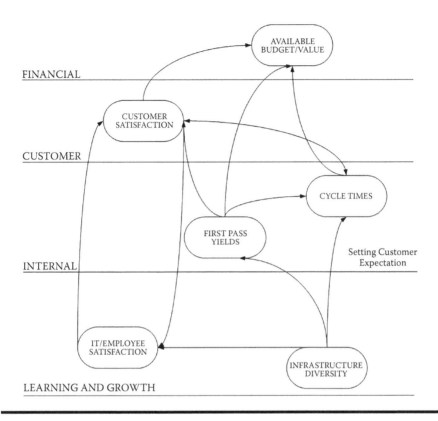

Figure 5.1   Cause and effect in the utility.

The business process perspective is linked downward to the learning and growth perspective by quality improvements, improved coordination, and integrated information. The business process perspective is linked upward to the customer and financial perspectives by lower operating costs, improved use of resources, reduced waste, new product capabilities, and better service programs.

For HP the chief component of the business process perspective is its operations cycle. This encompasses sourcing parts, components, manufacturing, marketing, distributing, and servicing products after sale. This cycle had been the major focus of a re-engineering effort, the goal of which was to bring HP to a higher level of customer focus.

The newly enhanced processes and accompanying systems allowed HP to achieve the following process efficiencies:

1. Linking orders electronically to suppliers. This improved cycle time and facilitated just-in-time manufacturing. It also provided production status information to be made available to customers so they could track their own orders.

2. Sharing information with suppliers enabled HP to anticipate changes in demand and ultimately improve HP's efficiency. This reduced cost of supplies and improved on-time delivery.
3. Integrating orders with SAP's (HP and SAP are now engaged in a business alliance) financial management and production planning modules enabled HP to reduce time and cost of orders.
4. Capturing customer information after a sale enabled HP to provide individualized service and additional marketing opportunities.

Implementation of a balanced scorecard enabled the company to improve its sales volume. This resulted from delivering value, increasing customer service, innovating new products, and reducing time-to-market. This sales spurt more than made up for the decreasing prices of PCs and ultimately generated higher revenue. Improved cycle times and decreasing costs enabled the company to operate far more efficiently, resulting in higher net income levels and, ultimately, higher revenue per employee.

Each of the enhancements HP made (e.g., linking orders with suppliers) is obviously a project, the performance measurement of which can be integrated into both a project-level scorecard as well as the departmentwide scorecard. All three scorecards must be linked (i.e., project scorecard to departmental scorecard to organizational scorecard).

Integrating CMM into Business Process Objectives

The capability maturity model (CMMI or CMM, which was the first iteration of this model) devised by the Software Engineering Institute of Carnegie Mellon has been used by a wide variety of organizations to increase the maturity level of their software engineering practices. However, it can be adapted to focus on any business process, not just an IT-based process. We briefly discussed the PM^2 model, a derivative of CMM, in Chapter 1.

Studies (Zwikael and Globerson, 2006) have found that engineering and construction organizations have high maturity levels and capabilities of performing project processes. The main reasons for this were found to be leadership, information sharing, and degree of authorization. High-tech manufacturing and telecommunications companies also score high in project management capabilities, with the telecoms particularly good at managing multiple projects at one time. The criteria used most often to assess project planning maturity, which are reflected in the CMM discussion below, are cost and schedule overruns, performance and customer satisfaction, quality of planning, project manager expertise, and organizational support.

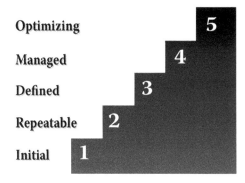

Figure 5.2   The capability maturity model.

CMM Explained

The original CMM model, as shown in Figure 5.2, consists of five levels of maturity that a department goes through on its way to becoming completely optimized and productive:

Level 1: Initial (i.e., performed). Ad hoc and chaotic.

Level 2: Repeatable (i.e., managed). Basic project management processes are established to track cost, schedule, and functionality.

Level 3: Defined. Management activities are documented, standardized, and integrated into the organization.

Level 4: Quantitatively managed. Uses detailed measures.

Level 5: Optimized. Continuous process improvement is enabled by quantitative feedback and from testing innovative ideas and technologies.

Level 1: Initial

The initial level of CMM is characterized as follows:

1. Ad hoc
2. Little formalization
3. Tools informally applied

The key actions to get to the next step include:

1. Initiate rigorous project management
2. Management oversight
3. Quality assurance

This level is characterized by an ad hoc approach to software development. Inputs to the process are not well defined but the outputs are as expected. Preliminary baseline project metrics should be gathered at this level to form a basis for comparison as improvements are made and maturity increases. This can be accomplished by comparing new project measurements with the baseline ones.

Level 2: Repeatable

The repeatable level of the CMM is characterized as follows:

Achieve a stable process with a repeatable level of statistical control.

Key actions to get to the next step include:

1. Establish a process group
2. Establish a software development process architecture
3. Introduce software engineering methods and tools

At this level the process is repeatable in much the same way that a subroutine is repeatable. The requirements act as input, the code as output, and constraints are such things as budget and schedule. Even though proper inputs produce proper outputs, there is no means to discern easily how the outputs are actually produced. Only project-related metrics make sense at this level because the activities within the actual transitions from input to output are not available to be measured. Measures are this level can include:

1. Amount of effort needed toward project implementation
2. Overall project cost
3. Personnel effort: actual person-months of effort, report person-months of effort
4. Requirements volatility: requirements changes

Level 3: Defined

The defined level of CMM is characterized as follows:

Achieve foundation for major and continuing progress.

Key actions to get to the next step include:

1. Establish a basic set of process managements to identify quality and cost parameters
2. Establish a process database

3. Gather and maintain process data
4. Assess relative quality of each product and inform management

At this level the activities of the process are clearly defined. This additional structure means that the input to and output from each well-defined functional activity can be examined, which permits a measurement of the intermediate products. Measures include:

1. Requirements complexity: Number of distinct objects and actions addressed in requirements
2. Complexity: Number of tasks to execute procedure
3. Quality metrics: Defects discovered, defects discovered per unit size (defect density), requirements faults discovered, design faults discovered

Level 4: Managed

The managed level of CMM is characterized as follows:

1. Substantial quality improvements
2. Comprehensive process measurement

Key actions to get to the next step include:

1. Support automatic gathering of process data.
2. Use data to analyze and modify the process.

At this level, feedback from early project activities is used to set priorities for later project activities. At this level, activities are readily compared and contrasted; the effects of changes in one activity can be tracked in the others. Measurements can be made across activities and are used to control and stabilize the process so that productivity and quality can match expectation. Metrics at this stage, although derived from the following data, are tailored to the individual organization.

1. Process type: What process model is used and how does it correlate to positive or negative consequences?
2. Defect identification: How and when are defects discovered?
3. Use of configuration management: Is a configuration management scheme imposed on the development process? This permits traceability which can be used to assess the impact of alterations.

Level 5: Optimized

The optimized level of CMM is characterized as follows:

Major quality and quantity improvements

Key actions to get to the next step:

Continue improvement and optimization of the process systematically.

Table 5.3 redefines the five levels in terms of continuous improvement.

CMM tailored specifically for projects was developed by the Project Management Institute. The Organizational Project Management Maturity Model, or OPM3, is a best-practice standard for assessing and developing capabilities in portfolio management, program management, and project management.

OPM3 provides a method for organizations to understand their organizational project management processes and measure their capabilities in preparation for improvement. OPM3 then helps organizations develop the roadmap that the company will follow to improve performance. OPM3 offers the key to organizational project management maturity with three interlocking elements: knowledge, assessment, and improvement.

The Washington Savannah River Co. (WSRC), a wholly owned subsidiary of Washington Group International, served as one of the first pilot OPM3 volunteers (http://www.pmi.org/PDF/cs_savannah_final_eversion.pdf). Headquartered in Boise, Idaho, with more than $3 billion (U.S.) in annual revenue, Washington Group has approximately 24,000 people at work around the world. Washington Group and its partners operate the 310-square-mile Savannah River site in South Carolina, approximately 25 miles southeast of Augusta, Georgia, for the U.S. Department of Energy (DOE). The site is home to the Defense Waste Processing Facility, the largest high-level radioactive-liquid stabilization plant in the world. More than 8000 site employees engage in environmental remediation, surplus material and facility disposition, waste management, and ongoing support of the U.S. nuclear defense mission.

The assessment team employed OPM3 methodologies to provide an analysis of the Savannah River site's organizational project management maturity; that is, how well an organization applies project, program, and portfolio knowledge, skills, tools and techniques, and best practices to achieve its goals.

To analyze how well the Savannah River site employed the hundreds of best practices in the OPM3 standard, team members interviewed more than 20 site staff members and looked for evidence that they were—or were not—achieving the outcomes expected from the best practices in their project work. The assessment team also looked at documents such as project execution plans and schedules through the Savannah River site intranet to ensure interviewee answers corresponded with actual work products.

The overall relative maturity achieved by WSRC at the Savannah River site in the traditional project arena was very high. The maturity level of the site's organizational enablers—which includes benchmarking, executive sponsorship, knowledge management, resource allocation, strategic alignment, project management training and metrics, and many others—ranked at 97 percent. Likewise, the project management domain in general had a 97 percent maturity level.

Table 5.3   CMM Using a Continuous Improvement Framework

Capability Level	Definition	Critical Distinctions
5 – Optimized	A quantitatively managed process that is improved based on an understanding of the common causes of variation inherent in the process. A process that focuses on continually improving the range of process performance through both incremental and innovative improvements.	The process is continuously improved by addressing common causes of process variation.
4 – Quantitatively Managed	A defined process that is controlled using statistical and other quantitative techniques. The product quality, service quality, and process performance attributes are measurable and controlled throughout the project.	Uses appropriate statistical and other quantitative techniques to manage the performance of one or more critical subprocesses of a process so that future performance of the process can be predicted. Addresses special causes of variation.
3 – Defined	A managed process that is tailored from the organization's set of standard processes according to the organization's tailoring guidelines, and contributes work products, measures, and other process-improvement information to the organizational process assets.	The scope of application of the process descriptions, standards, and procedures (organizational rather than project-specific). Described in more detail and performed more rigorously. Understands interrelationships of process activities and details measures of the process, its work products, and its services.
		(continued)

Table 5.3 CMM Using a Continuous Improvement Framework (Continued)

Capability Level	Definition	Critical Distinctions
2 – Repeatable	A performed process that is also planned and executed in accordance with policy; employs skilled people having adequate resources to produce controlled outputs; involves relevant stakeholders; is monitored, controlled, and reviewed; and is evaluated for adherence to its process description.	The extent to which the process is managed. The process is planned and the performance of the process is managed against the plan. Corrective actions are taken when the actual results and performance deviate significantly from the plan. The process achieves the objectives of the plan and is institutionalized for consistent performance.
1 – Initial	A process that accomplishes the needed work to produce identified output work products using identified input work products. The specific goals of the process area are satisfied.	All of the specific goals of the process area are satisfied.
0 – Incomplete	A process that is not performed or is only performed partially. One or more of the specific goals of the process area are not satisfied.	One or more of the specific goals of the process area are not satisfied.

Source: Systems Engineering Process Office. SPAWAR Systems Center. Navy.

Quality and the Balanced Scorecard

Solano et al. (2003) have developed a model for integrating systematic quality (i.e., a balance between product and process effectiveness and efficiency) through the balanced scorecard. Table 5.4 shows the four balanced scorecard perspectives oriented toward systemic quality integration.

This quality-oriented strategy is a daily, ongoing process that needs to be "bought into" by staff members. It is possible to do this by relating organizational goals to employee remuneration. Table 5.5 shows employee incentives based on the balanced scorecard. Each perspective and indicator was given a weight that depended

Table 5.4   Integrating Quality with the Balanced Scorecard

Perspective	*Strategic Topics*	*Strategic Objectives*	*Strategic Indicators*
Financial	Growth	F1 Increase shareholder value	Shareholder value
		F2 New sources of revenue from outstanding quality products and services	Growth rate of volume compared with growth rate of sector
		F3 Increase customer value through improvements to products and services	Rate of product renewal compared with total customers
	Productivity	F4 Cost leader in the sector	Comparing expenses with the sectors:
		F5 Maximize utilization of existing assets	Free cash flow Operating margin
Customer	Charm the customers	C1 Continually satisfy the customer chosen as the objective	Share of selected key markets
		C2 Value for money	Comparing value for money with the sector
		C3 Reliable operations	Percentage of errors with customers
		C4 Quality service	
Internal Process	Growth	I1 Create and develop innovative products and services	Profitability of new product investment Rate of new product acceptance
		I2 Implement a systems product quality model with a systemic approach	Rate or product quality

(continued)

Table 5.4   Integrating Quality with the Balanced Scorecard (Continued)

Perspective	Strategic Topics	Strategic Objectives	Strategic Indicators
	Increase customer value	I3 Technological improvements to products	Timeliness
			Product availability
		I4 Apply flexible development methodologies	
		I5 Advisory services	
	Operational excellence	I6 Provide a flexible global infrastructure	Cost reduction
		I7 Meet specifications on time	Fixed asset production
		I8 Cost leader in the sector	Improved yield
		I9 Implement a quality system development model process	Rate of compliance with specifications Rate of process quality
		I10 Develop outstanding relationship with suppliers	
	Good neighborliness	I11 Improve health, safety, and environment	Number of safety incidents
			Rate of absenteeism
Learning and growth	Motivated and well-prepared staff	L1 Climate for action	Employee survey
		L2 Fundamental skills and competencies	Staff hierarchy table (percent)
		L3 Technology	Availability of strategic information

on the organization's mission. Yearly bonuses depended on the goals being totally or partially attained.

How is the process (or product) quality index calculated? One of the goals of engineering is to produce a defect-free product. A product's quality profile is the metric used to predict if a module will be defect-free. It can suggest potential quality issues and thus mechanisms to redress those issues. Quality profiles adhere to

Table 5.5   Balanced Scorecard Related Incentives

Category	Indicators	Weighting (%)
Financial (60 percent)	Shareholder value	18
	Return on capital employed (ROCE)	13
	Economic value added (EVA)	13
	Free cash flow	10
	Operating costs	6
Client (10 percent)	Client satisfaction index	7
	Rate of growth of market	3
Internal processes (10 percent)	Process quality index	3
	Product quality index	3
	Productivity	4
Training and growth (20 percent)	Employee quality index	20

Table 5.6   A Software Quality Profile

Quality Profile Dimension	Criteria
Design/code time	Design time should be greater than coding time
Design review time	Design review time should be at least half of design time
Code review time	Code review time should be at least half of coding time
Compile defect density	Compile defects should be less than ten defects per thousand lines of code
Unit test defect density	Unit test defects should be less than five defects per thousand lines of code

engineering dogmas that design is good, technical reviews are necessary for quality, and high-defect density in a test phase is predictive of high-defect density in later test phases. An example of a quality profile for a software project is shown in Table 5.6. The profile is composed of five dimensions. The process quality index (PQI) is calculated by multiplying the five dimensions together.

Philips Electronics (Gumbus and Lyons, 2002) implemented a balanced scorecard predicated on the belief that quality should be a central focus of their performance measurement effort. The Philips Electronics balanced scorecard has four levels. The very highest level is the strategy review card, next is the operations review scorecard, and the third is the business unit card. The final level is the individual employee card.

The corporate quality department created very specific guidelines for how metrics should link the cascaded scorecards. These guidelines indicate that all top-level scorecard critical success factors (CSFs) for which the department is responsible must link metrically to lower-level cards. Three criteria were established to accomplish this:

1. Inclusion. Top-level CSFs must be addressed by lower-level CSFs to achieve top-level metric goals.
2. Continuity. Critical success factors must be connected through all levels. Lower-level measurements should not have longer cycle times than higher-level measurements.
3. Robustness. Meeting a lower-level CSF goal must ensure that high-level CSF goals will be met or even surpassed.

As you can see, goals in all scorecard levels align with goals in the next level above, and goals become fewer and less complex as you drill down through the organization.

The CSFs, selected by the departments that had a major controlling responsibility, were the key balanced scorecard indicators. The management team of each business unit selected CSFs that would distinguish the business unit from the competition. They used a value map to assist in determining the customer critical success factors and then derived the process CSFs by determining how process improvements could deliver customer requirements. Competence CSFs were identified by figuring out what human resource competencies were required to deliver the other three perspectives of the card. Standard financial reporting metrics were used for the financial perspective.

At this point each business unit was charged with figuring out what key indicators could best measure the critical success factors. The business units had to make some assumptions about the relationships between the processes and results to derive performance drivers and targets. These targets were set based on the gap between current performance and what was desired two and four years into the future. The criteria for these targets were that the targets had to be specific, measurable, realistic, and time-phased. The targets themselves were derived from an analysis of market size, customer base, brand equity, innovation capability, and world-class performance.

Indicators selected included:

1. Financial: Economic profit realized, income from operations, working capital, operational cash flow, inventory turns
2. Customers: Rank in customer survey, market share, repeat order rate, complaints, brand index
3. Processes: Percentage reduction in process cycle time, number of engineering changes, capacity utilization, order response time, process capability
4. Competence: Leadership competence, percentage of patent-protected turnover, training days per employee, quality improvement team participation

In cascading the scorecard throughout its different levels, six indicators were key for all business units:

1. Profitable revenue growth
2. Customer delight
3. Employee satisfaction
4. Drive to operational excellence
5. Organizational development
6. Support

In one of the business units, Philips Medical Systems North America, results are tracked in real-time. Data is automatically transferred to internal reporting systems and fed into the online balanced scorecard report with the results made immediately accessible to management. The results are then shared with employees using a Lotus Notes-based online reporting system they call Business Balanced Scorecard On-Line. To share metrics with employees they use an easy-to-understand traffic-light reporting system. Green indicates that the target was met, yellow indicates inline performance, and red warns that performance is not up to par.

Process Performance Metrics

Web analytics provide a good example of measuring business process objectives at the project level. Swamy (2002) recommends adding two new perspectives to the balanced scorecard, as shown in Figure 5.3, to properly align to e-business. We've discussed customized scorecards earlier in this book. It is entirely possible that a department with 15 projects will have 15 modified scorecards, each tailored to a specific project. In this example, note the introduction of the e-business perspective, cascading from a combination of the traditional customer and financial scorecard perspectives, and the user perspective, which links to the internal and learning

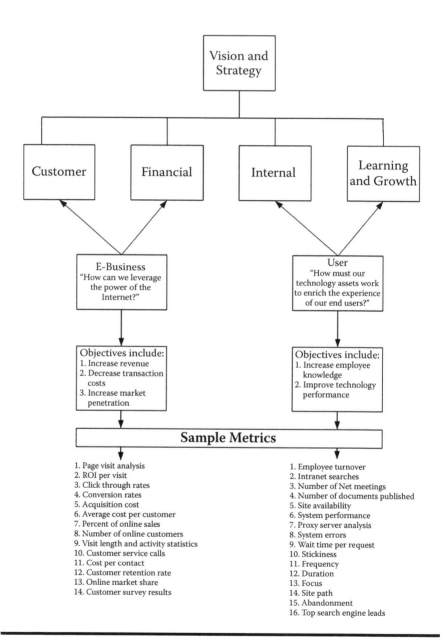

Figure 5.3   Web analytics added to the balanced scorecard.

and growth perspectives. Specific project goals are listed, with metrics originating from each goal.

Stewart (2001) makes the following metric recommendations when establishing project-specific balanced scorecards:

Financial

1. On time
2. Within budget
3. Variance from original baselined budget and final budget
4. Project costs as compared to industry standard and organizational standards for similar projects
5. Earned value

Customer

1. Project meeting intended objectives
2. Customer satisfaction (including account payment history)
3. Economic value added (strategic benefits rather than financial benefits achieved: reference-ability, increased venture capital support, etc.)

Project/Internal Business

1. Project resource requirements management
   a. Average management time of project manager related to total effort
2. Project portfolio comparatives
   a. Project cancellation rate
   b. Project backlog; awaiting startup
   c. Risk management statistics
   d. Contingency time allotted and used
3. Change management statistics (number of change records per designated period of time can show whether proper project scope has been set, percent change to customer/vendor environment, impact to scope)
4. Quality management statistics (rework, issues, etc.)
5. Project team member satisfaction

Growth and Innovation

1. Average capabilities per team member and improvement over course of project
2. Development or ongoing improvement of templates, procedures, tools, and so on
3. The rate that innovative ideas are developed (new ways of doing things)

4. Best practices identified
5. Lessons learned and applied
6. Positive achievements/impacts on the organization
7. Evaluate quantitative statistics
    a. Examine true costs of operation, evaluating impact of project slippage and inadequate support and nonsupport infrastructure costs
8. Evaluate organizational change
    a. Evaluate how the change has affected the organization's business
9. Reduce to lowest common denominator
    a. Review support costs versus costs of delay per person
    b. Review actual project costs versus plans (net present value)
10. Review strategic objectives achieved
    a. Review qualitative statistics
    b. Identify unanticipated benefits accrued
    c. Review attainment or contribution to organizational objectives versus time commitment
11. Review overall business value improvement
    a. Revenue increase/decrease
    b. Team retention and promotion
    c. Increased market share, references

We've Reached the End of Chapter 5

In this chapter you may have finally come to the realization that implementation of the balanced scorecard is much more work than you originally thought. It's much more than just dropping a bunch of metrics onto four perspectives (i.e., customer, financial, business process, and learning and growth). In reality, balanced scorecard provides a framework for re-engineering the organization for continuous improvement. Through discussion, examples, and case histories, this chapter delved into the various process improvement techniques, including the capability maturity model (CMM) and quality initiatives. These are the new processes you need to implement and then manage and measure using the balanced scorecard.

References

Gumbus, A. and B. Lyons, 2002. The balanced scorecard at Philips Electronics. *Strategic Finance.* November: 84(5): 45–49.

Kaplan, R. and D. Norton, 2004. How strategy maps frame an organization's objectives. *Financial Executive.* (Apr. 1, 2004): 20(2): 40.

Office of the Navy. Process Assets. 2004. Systems Engineering Process Office. Space and Naval Warfare Systems Center San Diego. http://sepo.spawar.navy.mil/sepo/index2.html

Solano, J., M. Perez de Ovalles, T. Rojas, A. Griman Padua, and L. Mendoza Morales. 2003. Integration of systemic quality and the balanced scorecard. *Information Systems Management*. Winter: 66–81.

Stewart, W. 2001. Balanced scorecard for projects. *Project Management Journal*. March: 32(1): 38–52.

Swamy. R. 2002. Strategic performance measurement in the new millennium: Fitting Web-based initiatives into a company's balanced scorecard is critical. Here is a guide on how to do it. *CMA Management*. 76(3, May): 44(4).

Unisys. 2003. Performance-based contracting: Measuring the performance in the information technology utility. White paper.

Zwikael, O. and S. Globerson, 2006. Benchmarking of project planning and success in selected industries. *Benchmarking: An International Journal, 13*(6): 688–700.

Chapter 6

Aligning the Project to Promote Learning and Growth

A wide variety of learning and growth metrics can be used to assess the human resource aspect of the project, department, or organization as a whole, as shown in Table 6.1. This chapter is about project staff excellence, how to accomplish it and how to measure it. The project will not be successful unless the right people are on the team and the team is effectively managed.

Liberate Rather than Empower

There is more than one way to manage. There's the way most people do it. And then there's the right way.

If you think that managing means telling your people specifically what they can do and what they can't do, keeping tabs on their phone calls, and clocking the time they spend at lunch or at the water cooler, then give back your key to the executive washroom.

If you are like most managers, you aren't quite so monstrous. But you probably are still worried that your staff may not be making the "right" decisions. What does the right decision mean, anyway? Is it the decision you would have made yourself if you were in your staff's position? Ultimately, the right decision may be different from the one you would have made. So giving your staff the impression that the

Table 6.1 Sample Learning and Growth Metrics

Learning and Growth Objectives	Measures	Targets (percent)	KPI
Create a quality workforce	Percentage of employees meeting mandatory qualification standards	>=95	L1
	Percentage of voluntary separations	>=98	L2
	Percentage of leader's time devoted to mentoring	>=45	L3
	Percentage of employees with certifications	>=54	L4
	Percentage of employees with degrees	>=75	L5
	Percentage of employees with three or more years of experience	>=75	L6
	Average appraisal rating	Baseline	L7
	Number of employee suggestions	Baseline	L8
	Percentage expert in currently used technologies	>=95	L9
	Rookie ratio[a]	<=10	L10
	Percentage expert in emerging technologies	>=75	L11
	Proportion of support staff	>=35	L12
	Availability of strategic information	>=100	L13
	Intranet searches	Baseline	L14
	Average years of experience with team	Baseline	L15
	Average years of experience with language	Baseline	L16
	Average years of experience with software	Baseline	L17
	Percentage of employees whose performance evaluation plans are aligned with organizational goals and objectives	>=98	L18

Table 6.1   Sample Learning and Growth Metrics (Continued)

Learning and Growth Objectives	Measures	Targets (percent)	KPI
	Percentage conformity with HR roadmap as a basis for resource allocation	>=95	L19
	Percentage of critical positions with current competency profiles and succession plans in place	>=98	L20
	Percentage number of net meetings	>=20	L21
	Number of new templates, procedures, tools to increase productivity	Baseline	L22
Increase employee satisfaction	Percentage of employees satisfied with the work environment	>=98	L23
	Percentage of employees satisfied with the professionalism, culture, values, and empowerment	>=98	L24
	Employee overtime	Baseline	L25
	Employee absenteeism	Baseline	L26
	Discrimination charges	Baseline	L27
	Employee grievances	Baseline	L28
	Tardiness	Baseline	L29
	Number of employee suggestions implemented	Baseline	L30
	In-house promotions	>=90	L31
Enhance employee training	Percentage of technical training goals met	>=90	L32
	Number of training sessions attended per employee	Baseline	L33
	Training budget as a percentage of overall budget	>=20	L34

(continued)

Table 6.1   Sample Learning and Growth Metrics (Continued)

Learning and Growth Objectives	Measures	Targets (percent)	KPI
	Frequency of use of new skills	>=85	L35
Enhance R&D	Research budget as a percentage of IT budget	>=35	L36
	Number of quality improvements	Baseline	L37
	Number of innovative processes deployed	Baseline	L38
	Percentage of R&D directly in line with business strategy	>=98	L39
	Number of technologies owned or possessed by company	Baseline	L40
	Number of new patents generated by R&D	Baseline	L41
	Number of patentable innovations not yet patented	Baseline	L42
	Number of patents protecting the core of a specific technology or business area	Baseline	L43
	Number of entrepreneurs in the company[b]	Baseline	L44
	Percentage of workforce currently dedicated to innovation projects	>=5	L45
	Number of new products, services, and businesses launched	Baseline	L46
	Percentage of employees who have received training in innovation	>=5	L47

[a] Rookie means new, inexperienced, or untrained personnel.
[b] Number of individuals who previously started a business.

right decision is the one you would make is a sure way to diminish motivation, creativity, accountability, and morale. As many executives like to say, "If you've got a yes person working for you, then one of you is redundant!" Ultimately, because your decision may not be the "right" one anyway, having some real thinkers on your team could only help, not hurt, your own career.

A good manager is not a robot cop overseeing clones. Instead, a good manager is one who creates an environment in which staff members take on the responsibility to work productively in self-managed, self-starting teams, then identify and solve complex problems on their own. Think of the benefits of this modus operandi. You'll be freed to think about the bigger picture. Isn't this why you wanted to become a manager in the first place?

Every field has its buzzwords. The latest one among human resources people is empowerment. Perhaps you've even taken a course on "how to empower your staff." Back to the office you go, full of new ideas. But the moment you get back, you call a meeting of everyone who reports to you. Presumably, these empowered people can't operate on their own for even a few days and need to report to mama or papa every detail of every project on which they're working. As management guru Peter Drucker always likes to say, much of what we call management is making it very difficult for people to do their jobs.

Liberating Your Staff

Oren Harari (1993), a professor at the University of San Francisco and a management consultant, relates an interesting experience with one of his clients. While he was waiting for an appointment with this particular client, he overheard two of the manager's clerical assistants calling customers and asking them how they liked the company's product. Professor Harari reflected that it was no wonder this manager had such a good reputation. When he finally met with her, he offered his congratulations on her ability to delegate the customer service task to her staff. "What are you talking about?" she asked, bewildered. "Why, your secretaries are calling up customers on their own," Harari replied. "Oh, really? Is that what they're doing?" she laughed. "You mean you didn't delegate that task to them?"

"No," she said. "I didn't even know they were doing it. Listen, Oren, my job is to get everyone on my team to think creatively in pursuit of the same goal. So what I do is talk to people regularly about why we exist as a company and as a team. That means we talk straight about our common purpose and the high standards we want to achieve. I call these our goal lines. Then we talk regularly about some broad constraints we have to work within, like budgets, ethics, policies, and legalities. Those are our sidelines.

"It's like a sport. Once we agree on the goal lines and sidelines, I leave it to my people to figure out how to best get from here to there. I'm available and attentive when they need feedback. Sometimes I praise, sometimes I criticize, but always constructively, I hope. We get together periodically and talk about who's been trying what, and we give constructive feedback to one another. I know that sounds overly simplistic, but I assure you that is my basic management philosophy.

"And that's why I don't know what my assistants are doing, because it's obviously something they decided to try for the first time this week. I happen to think it's a great idea, because it's within the playing field and helps keep high standards for being number one in our industry. I will tell you something else: I don't even know what they intend to do with the data they're collecting, but I know they'll do the right thing.

"Here's my secret: I don't know what my people are doing, but because I work face to face with them as a coach, I know that whatever it is they're doing is exactly what I'd want them to be doing if I knew what they were doing!"

The Challenge of Peopleware

The greatest productivity you can get comes from hiring within the top-10 percentile. One of technology's leading gurus, Ed Yourdon, is well-known for saying that the easiest approach to developing an efficient technology department is to bring in the better people. Because there is a 25 to 1 differential between the best people and the worst people, and a 4 to 1 differential between the best teams and the worst teams, maybe the best way to improve productivity and quality is just to improve hiring practices.

In addition to hiring, other "peopleware" techniques could go a long way toward increasing productivity. Recent studies have shown that the productivity of people with adequate office space is substantially higher than people with traditionally allocated smaller amounts of space. Training also makes a difference, particularly if workers can accrue their training days the way they accrue their vacations.

Productivity can also be improved in many other ways: by training managers to develop more skills in handling employee performance reviews, or even by focusing on the psychological makeup of the development team (see the appendices for a list of behavioral and staff competencies for employees as well as managers). Much work has been done in recent years on team dynamics. In order for a team to work together successfully, team members must complement each other. Each team needs a distribution of leaders, followers, idea people, testers, problem solvers, and so on. Even in an industry where personality profiles are skewed toward introversion, it is still possible to build an effective working team. All it needs is some good management.

Attributes of the Good Project Manager

The project manager needs to satisfy his managers, end users, and staff members while making sure that projects are delivered on time and on or under budget.

Aside from technical skills, the manager needs to be a "people person." She needs to be able to:

1. Talk the language of the end users
2. Talk the language of the tech gurus
3. Understand and deal with corporate and departmental politics

4. Cajole reluctant end users into doing something "new"
5. Resolve problems
6. Chair meetings
7. Motivate staff and end users

More specifically, the manager should be able to do the following.

Manage Expectations

Each set of stakeholders will have their own expectations about the outcome of the project.

1. End users will have expectations about what the product or service will be able to do.
2. Staff will have expectations about what role they will play in the project. Staff are usually quite excited to be involved in a new effort. Promising them a role in the new effort and then not delivering on that promise will lead to disappointment, a loss of productivity, and sometimes even the loss of the team member.
3. Senior management will have expectations about the project cost and resource utilization. It is critically important that the project manager always provide a complete picture of the status and current costs of the project.

Resolve Conflict

Any time you put two or more people together there is room for conflict. The project manager needs to be both cheerleader and referee during the lengthy project development process.

Types of conflict can include:

1. Team member to team member
2. End user to end user
3. Team member to end user
4. Department to department
5. Manager to manager
6. Customer to employee

Overcome Fears

Over time, end users develop a level of comfort with the systems and practices that they already have in place. Some might feel threatened by the aspect of change. If not handled properly, this fear of the unknown can lead to project failure.

This actually happened during the systemization of the U.S. Post Office. When more sophisticated technologies were implemented about a decade ago, the employees were not involved in any of the meetings. Hence, change was foisted upon them suddenly and dramatically. Employees, fueled by the fear of losing their jobs to this new technology, sabotaged the system.

This expensive problem could have been easily avoided had the project manager considered the effect of technological change on these employees and spent some time overcoming their fears. This can easily be done by:

1. Involving end users in the process from the beginning.
2. Keeping all employees informed about what's going on. This can be done via newsletter, e-mail, public meetings, systems demonstrations, and so on.
3. Actively listening to employees about their fears and acting on those fears.

Facilitate Meetings

What does it mean to facilitate a meeting? Meetings do not run well on their own. Instead, a meeting must be "managed." The steps for effective meeting facilitation include:

1. The project manager acts as chairperson. He schedules the meeting, invites appropriate staff, and sets the agenda.
2. The agenda is sent out to attendees in advance.
3. The chairperson moderates the meeting, moving through each item on the agenda.
4. The chairperson appoints a secretary to take meeting notes.
5. The chairperson ensures that all agenda items are covered and that the meeting adjourns on time.
6. The chairperson ensures that everyone is permitted to voice his or her opinion.
7. The chairperson resolves all disagreements.
8. After the meeting the chairperson makes sure that the meeting notes are distributed to the attendees.
9. The chairperson schedules a follow-up meeting, if necessary.

Motivate Team Members

Perhaps the most important of the project manager's responsibilities is to motivate team members. This means that the project manager must wear many hats:

1. The project manager must motivate senior management such that they retain interest in funding and supporting the project.
2. The project manager must motivate end users and end-user management so that they support the project and cooperate in its development.
3. The project manager must motivate development staff so that the effort is completed on time, on budget, and in a quality fashion.

The project manager must be all things to all people. She needs to be a constant presence in the lives of all team members, congratulating their successes as well as supporting and consoling them in the face of failure. In the end, it's people who control whether there is a productivity paradox. And people in an organization consist of everyone from senior manager to junior clerk.

The art and science of working with people is often referred to as the real technology behind the organization. And motivating them, empowering them, liberating them—and all of the buzzwords that apply—make the difference between a successful organization and one that's not so successful.

A Better Workforce

Creating a better workforce means understanding how to work with people. You'd be surprised (or maybe not) at how differently bosses look at things than do their staff, as shown in Table 6.2. The object, clearly, is to narrow the gap.

Table 6.2   What Do Employees Really Want? A Casual Survey

What Employees Want	Items	What Employers Think Employees Want
1	Interesting work	5
2	Appreciation of work	8
3	Feeling "in on things"	10
4	Job security	2
5	Good wages	1
6	Promotion/growth	3
7	Good working conditions	4
8	Personal loyalty	6
9	Tactful discipline	7
10	Sympathetic help with problems	9

One way to do so is through motivating the workforce. Now, this doesn't mean taking up the pom-poms and giving the old college cheer. It does mean taking some specific steps.

The first step is to understand your own motivations, your strengths as a manager, and your weaknesses. Probably the best approach is to ask your peers and employees to make an anonymous appraisal of your performance as a manager. Have them rate such traits as listening and communications skills, openness, and attitude. Painful as this process may be, it will actually make you seem heroic in your employees' eyes. At the same time, it will give you some food for thought on ways to improve your own performance.

The second step, one that many managers pay only lip service to, can really make the difference between having a motivated employee and one who feels that he is just another number. Take the time to learn about your employees and their families. What are their dreams? Then ask yourself how you as a manager can fulfill these dreams from a business perspective.

Perhaps the best way to learn about your employees is in a nonwork atmosphere, over lunch or on a company outing. As you learn more about your employees' motives, you can help each one develop a personalized strategic plan and vision. Ultimately, you could convert those horrible yearly performance reviews into goal-setting sessions and progress reports.

Generating a positive attitude is the third step. Studies show that 87 percent of all management feedback is negative, and that traditional management theory has done little to correct the situation. Your goal should be to reverse the trend. Make 87 percent of all feedback good.

Respect for and sensitivity toward others remains essential in developing positive attitudes. Ask employees' opinions regarding problems on the job and treat their suggestions and ideas as priceless treasures.

The partner of positive attitude in the motivational game is shared goals. A motivated workforce needs well-defined objectives that address both individual and organizational goals. This means that you should include all your employees in the strategic planning process. Getting them involved leads to increased motivation. It also acts as a quality check on whether you are doing the right thing. And you'll close the communication gap at the same time.

Just setting a goal is insufficient. You have to monitor progress. The goal-setting process should include preparing a detailed roadmap that shows the specific path each person is going to take to meet that goal. One of the things that professionals dislike the most is the feeling that they're left out of the business cycle. In essence, each project is simply part of one grand strategic plan. Many staffers frequently complain that they rarely get to see the fruits of their labor. It is still up to the manager to put project team members into the thick of things, make them feel like part of the entire organization.

Finally, recognizing employees or team achievement is the most powerful tool in the motivating manager's toolbox. Appreciation for a job well done consistently appears at the top of employee "want lists." So hire a band, have a party, send a card, or call in a clown, but thank that person or that team.

Techniques for Motivating Employees

In this section can be found a wide variety of interesting techniques useful for motivating staff as a part of continuous improvement.

Based on a study at Wichita State University, the top five motivating techniques are:

1. Manager personally congratulates employee who does a good job.
2. Manager writes personal notes about good performance.
3. Organization uses performance as basis for promotion.
4. Manager publicly recognizes employee for good performance.
5. Manager holds morale-building meetings to celebrate successes.

One doesn't actually have to give an award for recognition to happen. Giving your attention is just as effective. The Hawthorne effect says the act of measuring (paying attention) will itself change behavior.

Low-cost rewards recognition techniques that some more creative managers have used are:

1. Make a photo collage about a successful project that shows the people who worked on it, its stages of development, and its completion and presentation.
2. Create a "yearbook" to be displayed in the lobby that contains each employee's photograph, along with his or her best achievement of the year.
3. Establish a place to display memos, posters, photos, and so on, recognizing progress toward goals and thanking individual employees for their help.
4. Develop a "Behind the Scenes Award" specifically for those whose actions are not usually in the limelight.
5. Say thanks to your boss, your peers, and your employees when they have performed a task well or have done something to help you.
6. Make a thank you card by hand.
7. Cover the person's desk with balloons.
8. Bake a batch of chocolate-chip cookies for the person.
9. Make and deliver a fruit basket to the person.
10. Tape a candy bar for the typist in the middle of a long report with a note saying, "halfway there."
11. Give a person a candle with a note saying, "No one holds a candle to you."
12. Give a person a heart sticker with a note saying, "Thanks for caring."
13. Purchase a plaque, stuffed animal, anything fun or meaningful, and give it to an employee at a staff meeting with specific praise. That employee displays it

for a while, then gives it to another employee at a staff meeting in recognition of an accomplishment.

14. Call an employee into your office (or stop by his office) just to thank him; don't discuss any other issue.
15. Post a thank you note on the employee's office door.
16. Send an e-mail thank you card.
17. Praise people immediately. Encourage them to do more of the same.
18. Greet employees by name when you pass them in the hall.
19. Make sure you give credit to the employee or group that came up with an idea being used.
20. Acknowledge individual achievements by using employees' names when preparing status reports.
21. Send a handwritten note to at least one customer and one employee per week. This not only keeps your customers coming but builds loyalty internally.
22. Keep a bulletin board in your office of pictures of repeat customers and their families. This helps builds relationships and reminds everyone why they have a job.
23. When people in your organization first turn on their computers, have a message of the day such as a quotation on customer service, appear when they log in. If a day begins with inspiration, it will lift the interaction in the workplace.
24. Collect company legends and success stories on video or audiotape.
25. Create a company mascot that represents the spirit of the company. For example, one company uses a salmon because they are always "swimming upstream."
26. Designate one room as the "whine cellar," the place for anyone to go who is having a bad day. Decorate the room with treats, stuffed toys, punching bags, and the like.

McCarthy and Allen (2000) suggest that you set up your employees for success. When you give someone a new assignment, tell the employee why you are trusting him with this new challenge. "I want you to handle this because I like the way you handled _____ last week." They also suggest that you never steal the stage. When an employee tells you about an accomplishment don't steal her thunder by telling her about a similar accomplishment of yours. In addition, they suggest that you never use sarcasm, even in a teasing way. Resist the temptation to say something like, "It's about time you gave me this report on time." Deal with the "late" problem by setting a specific time the report is due. If it's done on time, make a positive comment about timeliness.

What Else Can Go Wrong

A lack of project success can be caused by managerial, organizational, economic, political, legal, behavioral, psychological, and social factors.

1. A lack of capable/competent managers
2. Project management is still very much an individual creative activity, rather than a team effort
3. Little has been done to reduce performance differences among individuals or across teams

Poor management produces:

1. Unrealistic project plans due to poor planning/scheduling/estimation skills
2. Unmotivated staff due to inability of management to manage a creative staff
3. Lack of teamwork due to inability to build and manage effective teams
4. Poor project execution due to inadequate organization, delegation, and monitoring
5. Technical problems due to lack of management understanding of departmental issues
6. Inadequately trained staff due to a short-term rather than a long-term perspective

Possible solutions to poor management problems include:

1. Training in managerial skills and techniques
2. Active mentoring and supervision by senior managers
3. Increased delegation of responsibility and matching authority

Some reasons for lack of teamwork are:

1. Desire for autonomy
2. A culture that reinforces individual efforts more than team efforts
3. Concentration of key knowledge in a few individuals
4. Desire for privacy
5. The "not invented here" syndrome translated to the "not invented by me" syndrome
6. Large productivity differences from one individual to another
7. Political considerations between powerful individuals and managers

Possible solutions to teamwork problems include:

1. Objective assessment of team contributions with appropriate rewards
2. Development of an organizational culture that condones/rewards group efforts
3. Active efforts to disperse crucial application knowledge across project staff
4. Improvements in communication and coordination across organizational layers
5. Adoption of egoless programming techniques

Large performance differences between individuals negate productivity increases. Researchers estimate that productivity ranges of 3:1 to 5:1 are typical, with some studies documenting differences as high as 26:1 among experienced staff. This variability is often due to:

1. Misguided staffing practices
2. Poor team development
3. Inattention to the critical role of motivation
4. Poor management

Techniques to increase the effective level of productivity are:

1. Enhanced training
2. Investment in productivity (tools, methods)
3. Standard practices
4. Professional development opportunities
5. Recognition
6. Effective staffing
7. Top talent
8. Job matching
9. Career progression
10. Team balance
11. Improved management

Team Dynamics

A team goes through several stages before it reaches optimal performance. When a team is first assembled it goes through the stage referred to as *forming*. At this point, team members do not yet know each other, nor what their role on the team will be. The project manager can expedite this stage by having one or more introductory meetings, where team members can meet for the first time. Off-site or social-themed meetings are also valuable team-forming techniques.

The second stage of team development is called *storming* for good reason. Although team members now accept the members in their group, individual roles have yet to be determined. The project manager will no doubt assign job- or task-oriented roles within the group (i.e., project leader, analyst, programmer), however, the social aspects of the team are still very much in play. This can cause turmoil within the team, to which the project manager needs to be attuned.

Once the team finds its inner dynamic, or balance, the team can get down to business in the *norming* phase of team development. Once a team has been together for a while, it achieves its optimal level of performance. This is referred to as the *performing* phase. As we show in the chapter on project termination, there will come a time when the project is complete and the team might be disbanded. This is the *adjourning* phase of team development.

Teams become more effective as they move through the phases discussed above. These five steps can be followed out of sequence, or simultaneously, and still be effective.

The project manager should keep in mind that there are several teaming problems of which to be aware. One problem is that a team might never move past the forming or storming stages. It is entirely possible for a team to experience such dysfunction that the project manager should consider transfers or replacements as a resolution. Another common problem is groupthink. This is defined as rationalized conformity. Groupthink is a mode of thinking that group members engage in when the desire for agreement so dominates the group that it overrides the need to realistically appraise the alternatives. How do you know if your team is suffering from groupthink? There are some common symptoms of groupthink for which you should watch out:

1. Illusions of invulnerability creating excessive optimism and encouraging risk taking
2. Rationalizing warnings that might challenge the group's assumptions
3. Unquestioned belief in the morality of the group, causing members to ignore the consequences of their actions
4. Stereotyping those who are opposed to the group as weak, evil, or stupid
5. Direct pressure to conform placed on any member who questions the group, couched in terms of "disloyalty"
6. Self-censorship of ideas that deviate from the apparent group consensus
7. Illusions of unanimity among group members, silence viewed as agreement
8. Mindguards: self-appointed members who shield the group from dissenting information

Some techniques project managers can use to prevent groupthink include:

1. Leaders should assign each member the role of "critical evaluator." This allows each member to freely air objections and doubts.
2. Higher-ups should not express an opinion when assigning a task to a group.

3. The organization should set up several independent groups working on the same problem.
4. All effective alternatives should be examined.
5. Each member should discuss the group's ideas with trusted people outside the group.
6. The group should invite outside experts into meetings. Group members should be allowed to discuss with and question the outside experts.
7. At least one group member should be assigned the role of devil's advocate. This should be a different person for each meeting.

As mentioned, there are a variety of teaming problems for which the project manager needs to be on the lookout. Aside from groupthink and improper team development, team members might harbor hidden or individual agendas, make decisions in secret, show competitive behaviors, or not take responsibility for their behavior or that of the team.

Healthy teamwork is characterized by individuals who:

1. Contribute at their highest level of experience and expertise
2. Demonstrate good faith and good will, focusing on what is best for the team
3. Willingly subordinate their personal agendas to the will of the majority
4. Honor individual diversity and contributions
5. Demonstrate open, honest, and respectful communication and confidentiality
6. Demonstrate trustworthiness in word and deed while extending trust to others
7. Consciously relinquish the need to control all decisions
8. Listen well, seeking first to understand rather than to be understood

The team unit is the fundamental component of any project. Building a successful team requires more than just randomly assigning "bodies" to a group. The psychological and sociological aspects of team dynamics must be considered and steps taken to ease team members into a new team. A variety of studies attest to the wisdom of this. Most recently, Harvards' Robert Putnam studied 30,000 Americans. He found that there is a strong positive relationship between interracial trust and ethnic homogeneity. What this translates to is that the more ethnically diverse the people around you, the less you trust them. Although his treatise was addressing neighborhoods, his study points to the fact that the ramifications of team diversity need to be addressed as well.

Team building is a process of developing and maintaining a group of people who are working toward a common goal. The process of team building usually focuses on one or more of the following objectives: (1) clarifying role expectations and obligations of team members; (2) improving superior–subordinate or peer relationships;

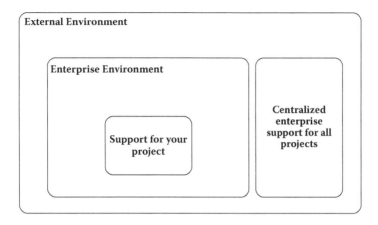

Figure 6.1   Project environmental layers.

(3) improving problem-solving, decision making, resource utilization, or planning activities; (4) reducing conflict; and (5) improving organizational climate.

Teams must be supported by the department as well as at the organizational level, as shown in Figure 6.1. Sydenham (2003) discusses several layers or support for project teams. The external environmental layer greatly influences how an organization operates. This has an impact on projects and the teams working on those projects. The enterprise environment is the layer in which all projects of the enterprise site reside. This layer constitutes the set of methodologies, tools, policies, and the like. These affect how the project, and hence, the team operates. Supporting layers include organizational (i.e., stakeholder) support for the specific project.

Social interactions may not appear to be related to successful project deployment at first glance. However, in most organizations people need to work together for a common goal to accomplish their work successfully. It is certainly easier and more enjoyable to work together in a friendly atmosphere and, most likely, more productive as well. In order to promote a friendly work environment you may wish to:

1. Encourage after-work recreational activities
2. Encourage fair treatment of all organizational members
3. Make sure work is assigned equitably
4. Ensure that work goals/standards are reasonable
5. Discourage favoritism

It is important that a spirit of cooperation and teamwork exists in all areas of the organization. When individuals are rewarded only for their own accomplishments, team efforts can suffer. Some actions include:

1. Reward team accomplishments: Utilize recognition, increased responsibilities, some time off.
2. Set aside a few hours every few months for team members to sit down together to discuss how they are working together or any problems they may be having.
3. Encourage teams to develop group identities (a logo, team name). Locate members in the same area if possible.
4. Establish cross-functional quality teams.

The U.S. Department of State *Foreign Affairs Handbook* (2006) on team building and communication suggests the following teaming techniques to encourage high team productivity:

1. Focus on "ends" (what we are here to accomplish).
2. Involve each team member in a decision that affects her.
3. Set agendas and schedules as a team.
4. Set high standards and high expectations and encourage achievement.
5. Openly support the senior service provider(s) in actions consistent with expectations.
6. Provide formative and summative assessments. Recognize and reward achievement; cite areas for improvement fairly, tactfully, and in private.
7. Maintain an effective flow of two-way communication with all team members.
8. Avoid imposing individual direction or personal standards.
9. Be sensitive to factors that cause dissatisfaction and frustration and resolve conflicts in a timely manner.
10. Avoid surprises.
11. Forgive and forget small offenses.
12. Celebrate even small successes.

Teaming Tools

Some tools involving group participation that can be utilized to define missions, goals, and objectives including the following.

Nominal Group Technique

This is a tool for idea generation, problem solving, mission and key result area definition, and goals/objectives definition. Participants should include a variety of levels (i.e., workers, supervisors, managers). A group leader addresses the subject and presents the problem or issue to be dealt with by the group. Participants spend a few minutes writing down their ideas. The leader conducts a round-robin listing of the ideas by asking each participant in turn for one idea. All ideas are written on a flipchart as stated and no judgments or evaluations are made at this time. Each item is then discussed in turn. Some ideas are combined, some discarded, and some new ideas are added. The leader then asks participants to vote for the top three, five, or seven priority items. The results are tallied, and the top five priority items (based on the voting results) are discussed. For example, as applied to key result area definition, the top five priority items would be the five key result areas chosen by the group as most important for mission accomplishment.

Roadblock Identification Analysis

This is a tool that focuses on identifying problems causing the group to be less productive than it could be. This tool utilizes the nominal group technique to identify and prioritize performance roadblocks. Action teams are formed to analyze barriers and develop proposals to remove roadblocks. The proposals are implemented, tracked, and evaluated.

Productivity by Objectives

This systematic process involves everyone in a comprehensive plan to achieve selected goals and objectives. This process involves a hierarchical system with councils, teams, and coordinators.

Management by Objectives

This approach stresses mutual goal setting by managers and subordinates, clarity and specificity in the statement of goals, and frequent feedback concerning progress toward goals. Goals should be couched in terms of specific measurable outcomes (such as units produced, product quality). Goals should be realistic and attainable.

Force Field Analysis

This is a technique involving the identification of forces "for" and "against" a certain course of action. The nominal group technique could be used in conjunction with force field analysis. The group might prioritize the forces for and against by assessing their magnitude and probability of occurrence. The group might then develop an action plan to minimize the forces against and maximize the forces for.

Table 6.3   Information Dissemination Techniques

	Same Place	*Different Place*
Same time	• Conversations • Meetings	• Teleconferences • Videoconferences • Web-based meetings • Telephone calls
Different time	• Reports • Newsletters • Videotapes • Audiotapes • Yellow sticky notes • Intranet memos	• Voicemail • E-mail • Fax • Web sites • Network-based tools • Interoffice mail • Other mail • Intranet

Team Communications

Modern project teams are often widely dispersed, often global. Table 6.3 presents some alternatives to the standard face-to-face meeting. A poll conducted by Harris Interactive on team (i.e., peers, partners, customers) collaboration (Aragon, 2006) found that:

1. More than 65 percent regularly use e-mail, fax, and audio conferencing.
2. In-person meetings are common, requiring more than 50 percent to travel for business each month.
3. Almost 33 percent say they would like to conduct more meetings via Web conferencing to reduce travel costs and time out of office, as well as better allocate already limited project budgets.
4. Only 16 percent currently use Web conferencing to facilitate meetings.

A constant theme of this 2006 Harris Interactive study was the importance of improving project collaboration and document exchange, with the chief complaints being:

1. Delays receiving input
2. Challenges of communication across time zones
3. People using incompatible software applications
4. Difficulty interpreting feedback

Team Effectiveness Leadership Model

Dr. Robert Ginnett, when a Senior Fellow at the Center for Creative Leadership (http://www.ccl.org/leadership/index.aspx), developed the Team Effectiveness Leadership Model, which can be used to identify what is required for a team to be effective and point the leader either toward the roadblocks that are hindering the team or toward ways to make the team even more effective. The U.S. Office of Personnel Management uses this technique and finds it invaluable. Their experience is the basis of the following discussion.

The model uses a systems theory approach that includes inputs (i.e., individual, team, and organizational factors), processes (i.e., what one can tell about the team by observing team members), and outputs (i.e., how well the team did in accomplishing its objectives).

Inputs are what are available to teams as they go about their work. There are multiple levels in the input stage. Input factors at both the individual and organizational levels affect the team design level, as indicated in Figure 6.2 by the direction of the arrows between these levels.

Outputs are the results of the team's work. A team is effective if (a) the team's product or service meets its stakeholders' standards for quantity, quality, and timeliness; and (b) if the group process that occurs while the group is performing its task enhances its members' ability to work together as a team in the future. An equally important result of a team working effectively is the satisfaction its members derive from that work as individuals. Those team results depend on the group process and the inputs available to the team.

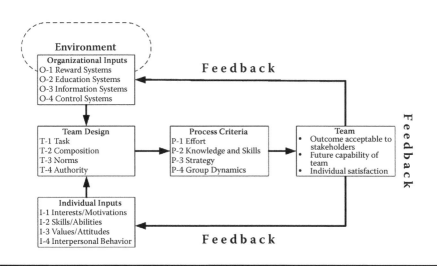

Figure 6.2   Team effectiveness leadership model.

The model identifies four process criteria yardsticks managers can use to examine the ways in which teams work, as shown in Figure 6.2. If a team is to perform effectively, it must:

1. Work hard enough (P-1 Effort)
2. Have sufficient knowledge and skills to perform the task (P-2 Knowledge & Skills)
3. Have a strategy to accomplish its work or ways to approach the task at hand (P-3 Strategy)
4. Have constructive and positive group dynamics among its members (P-4 Group Dynamics)

Research has consistently shown that effective group dynamics are the foundation upon which other teamwork proceeds. If the team is ultimately to achieve the valued outcome measures of effectiveness, a firm foundation of effective group process is critical.

Suppose a manager discovers that a team's members are not working very hard. Looking at the model's Process Criteria, an initial diagnosis would suggest a problem of effort (P-1). Instead of either encouraging or threatening the team members to get them to work harder, the manager could first consider the model's inputs to see if an underlying problem can be identified. The component in each input section with the number that corresponds to the initial problem offers a natural starting point because the items have been numbered systematically to align related concepts.

The individual inputs piece of the model asks managers to look at the interests and motivations of the individual team members (Level I-1, corresponding to a P-1 diagnosis), because team members who are interested in the group's task will be more likely to succeed at it. If the manager finds that the team members do in fact have an interest in the task, the model then leads the manager to consider another possibility.

The model emphasizes the way teams are influenced by both individual and organizational level inputs. So the next step is to look at the organizational input level. At the organization level, the model suggests the manager examine the system of rewards (or disincentives, O-1) that may be affecting the team. If the individuals have no incentives provided by the organization for putting forth effort, they might not be very inclined to work hard, or at all. Or the reward system may be structured to promote only individual performance. Such reward structures are inconsistent with team tasks where interdependence and cooperation among members is necessary.

If the manager concludes that both the individual and organizational level factors do support the team's ability to perform the task, the model offers yet another area to explore. Problems can also occur at the team design level. Here, it is likely a poorly designed task (T-1) is the culprit. If a job is meaningless, lacks sufficient autonomy, or provides no knowledge of results, team members may not put forth much effort.

Table 6.4   Problems and Solutions

Problem	Review Inputs		
	Organizational Inputs (O)	*Team Design (T)*	*Individual Inputs (I)*
Effort (P-1)	Reward Systems (O-1)	Tasks (T-1)	Interests/Motivation (I-1)
Knowledge and Skills (P-2)	Education Systems (O-2)	Design Composition (T-2)	Skills/Abilities (I-2)
Strategy	Information Systems (O-3)	Norms (T-3)	Values/Attitudes (I-3)
Critical Foundation Blocks			
Group Dynamics (P-4)	Control Systems (O-4)	Authority (T-4)	Interpersonal Behaviors (I-4)

Using this model, a manager can find key points at various levels of the input stage that would affect the way the team went about its work. In this example, a process-level problem with effort was diagnosed and the model led the manager to examine the "1" level factors at the individual, organizational, and team levels as the most likely locations for finding input problems. Ginette (2005) indicates that process criteria leverage points can be plotted against corresponding solutions, as shown in Table 6.4.

Of course, additional factors affect teams and team effectiveness, including complex interactions among the variables described in this model. Even so, this model can be useful for understanding how teams operate and can help managers analyze problems and lead more effectively.

The Virtual Team

Many modern organizations have gone virtual. Team members are dispersed across departments, campuses, states, and even countries. Virtual teams have some different requirements in terms of communication, working collaboratively, sharing information, and mutually supporting other team members. These problems are usually overcome with the use of technology: e-mail, instant messaging, faxing, Wikis, telephony, common whiteboard, application sharing, electronic meeting systems, project management software, electronic calendars, intranets and extranets, and knowledge management systems. Microsoft's Sharepoint is a leader in this particular arena.

Thompson (2005) lists the ten key issues to address to create a successful virtual team:

1. Trust building
2. Open communications
3. Accountability
4. Conflict management
5. Virtual decision-making process
6. Virtual meeting practices
7. Personal collaboration strategy
8. Collaborative document editing, techniques for planning, developing, and reviewing collaborative documents
9. Multicultural integration, tools and methods for harnessing the different cultures (business, ethnic, social) within the team as an asset rather than a weakness
10. Virtual brainstorming workflow
11. Self-managed teams; techniques for creating a "self-managed team" style

Training

Training is one of the keys to learning and growth. According to a study by Byrne (2003) the return on investment in training and development was an 8.5 percent increase in productivity compared with a 3.5 percent increase due to spending on capital improvements.

Hartford uses a balanced approach that links the employee's business opportunity plan to the organization's operating plan. Their developmental approach is centered on employee and supervisor relationships in the development and planning process.

Employees meet annually with their boss to discuss development needs. After the employee's performance review, the employee and supervisor will establish personal goals for the following years. Because the employee's plan is linked to the company's operating plan, it must then be determined which competencies the employee needs to reach corporate business goals successfully. Toward this end, all courses are mapped to a competency profile.

The Hartford corporate strategy is tied to training through what they call Prescriptive Learning Plans and Individual Learning Plans. A Prescriptive Learning Plan is a series of events, not all taking place in the classroom. These may include going to conferences, visiting Web sites, or reading white papers. It may also be reading a book or having a phone conversation with a subject matter expert within the company. Ultimately, Prescriptive Learning Plans are tied to business needs. The subset of events signed off on by a supervisor for an individual employee is called an Individual Learning Plan.

Hartford uses a balanced scorecard approach to determine its business strategy. Balanced scorecard-derived strategic plans are produced in flowchart form to ultimately create a strategy map. Ultimately, this business strategy is translated into result-focused training programs by the individual departments.

We've Reached the End of Chapter 6

In this chapter we discussed how project managers can "grow" project staff through better management techniques as well as through training and other incentives. This aspect—learning and growth—is fundamental to the success of the balanced scorecard but generally overlooked. Unless employees are rewarded in some way and unless they feel that they can grow within the organization, balanced scorecard targets will never be met.

References

Aragon, P. 2006. "Reinventing Collaboration Across Internal and External Project Teams." Retrieved September 14, from http://www.aecbytes.com/viewpoint/2006/issue_28.html

Byrne, J. 2003. How to lead now: Getting extraordinary performance when you can't pay for it. *Fast Company*, August: 62–70.

Ginette, R. 2005. "Leading a Great Team: Building Them from the Ground Up, Fixing Them on the Fly." Retrieved December 15, 2009, from http://www.executiveforum.com/PDFs/GinnettSummary.pdf

Harari, O. 1993. Stop empowering your people. *Management Review*, November: 26–29.

McCarthy, M. and J. Allen, 2000. *You Made My Day: Creating Co-Worker Recognition and Relationships*. New York: L-F Books.

Sydenham, P. 2003. *Systems Approach to Engineering Design*. Norwood, MA: Artech House.

Thompson, K. 2006. "Bioteaming: A Manifesto for Networked Business Teams." *The Bumble Bee*. Retrieved December 15, 2009, from http://www.bioteams.com/2005/04/06/bioteaming_a_manifesto.html

The U.S. Department of State Foreign Affairs. 2006. "Team Building and Communications." Retrieved from http://www.state.gov/documents/organization/89191.pdf

Chapter 7

Balanced Scorecard and Project Scope Management

Perhaps the best way to present the tie-in between project management and balanced scorecard is to discuss each of the components of a typical project plan (see the Appendices for a sample project plan). We do just this in the next several chapters. In this chapter, we examine project scope management. Definitions of goals and objectives, scope, general requirements, system context, use of external resources, and major constraints are analyzed.

Defining Business Goals

Ideas for projects can originate from virtually anyone or anyplace. Your marketing department might want a brand-new way of tracking customers. Your finance department might require some changes due to a modification of the tax code. Even your customers might be the source of a great idea. If there's one constant in business, it's change.

Change needs to be managed, however. Projects have a tendency to grow from the manageable to the not-so-manageable fairly quickly. This is usually referred to as scope creep and it's something good project management must overcome, particularly because more than a few requests for changes or new systems might not be properly aligned to business strategy.

Once an idea has been formalized, deemed feasible, and approved by the managers of the organization, a project plan should be created. The plan will detail the scope, resources, cost estimates, and schedule for the project.

From a scorecard perspective, scope must be tightly integrated with organizational goals. However, organizational goals are usually quite dynamic. Last month's goals are not necessarily this month's goals, so it's important to make sure that the goals listed are consistent with the true goals of the organization.

Most companies review their mission and goals on a yearly business. In fact, this is usually a corporatewide activity, with each department determining its own mission and goals as they relate to the corporatewide statement. Goals are usually determined after an intensive SWOT analysis (i.e., strengths, weaknesses, opportunities, and threats), where a company rigorously compares itself to its competitors.

There are actually two sets of goals: short term and long term. Short-term goals usually have a window of three to five years. However, the increasingly competitive and very global nature of business has collapsed the short-range planning cycle, in some cases, into months. Both long-term as well as short-term goals can be articulated in terms of corporate scope, products and services the company currently offers and desires to offer, market share, company size, and profitability.

Examples of business goals are:

1. Increase earnings per share by 10 percent within two years.
2. Introduce one new product per quarter within one year.
3. Introduce one new service per year within the next two years.

Notice that business goals are associated with a quantifiable metric. For example, goal number one indicates that to be successful the company is required to increase earnings per share by a certain percentage.

Defining Project Goals

Project goals are always subsets of business goals. In a project plan, one or more project goals are described and tied back to the business goals of the organization. For example, a company might decide to develop a Web-based system that matches pets with potential pet owners. The goal of this project might be defined as follows:

> The goal of DEAS (Dog e-Adoption System) is to bring together potential pet adopters and animal shelters across the country.

We can then tie this project goal to one or more of the company's stated business goals, thus:

> The goal of DEAS (Dog e-Adoption System) is to bring together potential pet adopters and animal shelters across the country. DEAS is

aligned to the corporate business goal of introducing one new service or product per year.

Defining Project Scope

The project scope is a short description of the project, which includes:

1. Justification for the project
2. What the system will do
3. How the system will generate revenue, if applicable

The project scope will flesh out the list of project goals. An example of a scope statement follows:

> The problem of pet overpopulation is severe in the United States. Animal shelters have limited capacity and every year millions of healthy animals are killed due to the shortage of potential pet adopters. The problem is economic as well as moral. Disposal of these animals is an expensive procedure and the moral implication of animal destruction is obvious.
>
> One way to address the problem is through an Internet adoption service. The potential of the Internet is not utilized in this area. There are few if any search engines with the ability to search a network of shelters for a pet or for the range of additional services and information provided by shelters.
>
> The aim of DEAS (Dog e-Adoption System) is to bring together potential pet adopters and animal shelters across the country. Shelters will have a fast and convenient option to upload a range of information about their pets to prospective pet adopters. Prospective pet adopters receive an equally fast and convenient way to look for a pet through the service. They will also gain access to a broad spectrum of information on various aspects of pet adoption and ownership—from applicable government regulations to pet care.
>
> The system will have the functionality to work with any pets present in the shelters but the design focus will be on dogs. Dog adoption holds the possibility of being the best source of pet adoptions, thus driving the economic success of the system. The system will generate revenue through shelter/adopter fees, advertising, and donations.

Like anything else, scope has to be managed. There are five components to scope management, as shown in Figure 7.1.

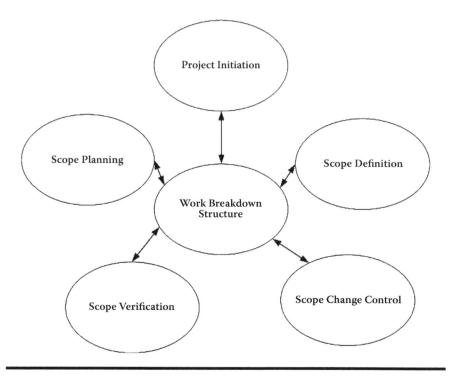

Figure 7.1   Scope management.

1. Scope Management. During the scope management phase, the project team and key stakeholders plan how they will define the scope, create the work breakdown structure (WBS), and then verify and control the scope.
2. Scope Definition. As the project evolves and goals and methods become clearer, the scope definition will change to include these requirements.
3. Creating the WBS. The WBS includes all deliverables within the project in a time-constrained projection. It basically says what will be done and when. Once laid out within the WBS, the work is tied to timeframes and costs.
4. Scope Verification. Scope verification involves formal acceptance of the completed project scope by the key stakeholders.
5. Scope Control. Scope control is the set of policies and procedures for control scope change.

Scope can be measured, as shown in Table 7.1.

Of course, there is a difference between a simple scorecard and a balanced scorecard. However, converting to a balanced scorecard is not a major hurdle if you keep in mind that not all of the four perspectives (financial, customer, internal business processes, and learning and growth) need be used for each

Table 7.1 Using a Simple Scorecard to Measure Scope

Dashboard Area	Green	Yellow	Red
Scope	• Project satisfies at least 95 percent of all business objectives • All major system components are implemented as planned	• Project satisfies at least 90 percent of all business objectives • No more than one major system component is deferred to later phase	• Project satisfies less than 90 percent of all business objectives • At least one major system component is not implemented

component of a project plan. The two measures in the Table 7.1 scorecard can be easily mapped to the internal business processes perspective. It does not make much sense to include learning and growth in this content, but both the customer and financial perspectives should be considered. If you've carefully read the first half of this book, you already understand the process for creating your own set of key performance indicators (metrics, measures, or whatever you want to call them) for one, two, or all of the perspectives.

Constraints

The project plan will usually determine the cost, resources, and time requirements for the proposed project. However, regulatory, legal, and competitive pressures might impose a specific deadline. This is referred to as "timeboxing." It is interesting to note that many governmental contracts impose a financial penalty on a contracting company that delivers the project late.

If the project is to be constrained by a set dollar amount then this too is required to be clearly articulated. Many companies create a yearly business plan that allocates financial resources to each department. Project plans, therefore, will have to live within the constraints of this preallocated budget. Savvy companies will always add a contractual stipulation that mandates all overages be absorbed by the consulting company, unless extenuating circumstances can be proven (e.g., act of war, etc.).

You might be beginning to see a pattern here, and we hope it's a balanced one. Review what I wrote. Highlight the key concepts and turn these into performance measures. For example, a specific deadline is a ready metric. Alternatively, you can measure against a baseline, for example, days late after the deadline.

General Requirements

The requirements section is the heart of the project plan. Requirements usually take the form of a list of features that the system must have. For example, the following general requirements were specified for a resource scheduling project:

- A Web-based application allowing users easy access and use
- The ability to originate or update resource reservations
- The ability to link to authorized users
- A way to search for available resources
- The ability to disallow duplicate orders from the same user
- A method to print a confirmation from the Web site
- The ability to send e-mail confirmations to the user
- The ability to print a daily list

The requirement set is closely aligned to business objectives, which we've already listed in Table 7.1: "Project satisfies at least 95 percent of all business objectives." This feature set was most likely collated during a feasibility study. Many of the desired features might have been selected as a result of competitor analysis. Web sites such as Hoovers.com or governmental regulatory agencies such as the Securities and Exchange Commission provide a wealth of detail about a company's competitors. The competitor's Web site also provides much detail, including marketing brochures and even downloadable trial software.

As you can see from Figure 7.2, the feasibility study is the very first phase of a typical product development effort. This is the phase where ideas are discussed, evaluated, and then deemed feasible or infeasible. If the ideas are deemed feasible the next phase, the project plan, can then be initiated.

In some organizations feasibility studies are not performed. In these organizations the project plan is created as the requirements are being determined during analysis. In all cases, the functionality of the project must be ascertained, as scheduling and cost estimation are dependent upon knowing what the project is going to do. The feasibility study can also serve as a useful checkpoint to ensure that the project is proceeding in alignment with organizational goals. In the excitement of discovering a new cutting edge technology, project teams often lose sight of the business goals and focus instead on the technology. A continual reassessment of the project is recommended.

Figure 7.2   Product development life cycle.

Technical Requirements

Most projects are built under a series of constraints. For example, a particular product must be built using a particular machine part. These constraints must be addressed in the project plan. This includes, but is not limited to: standards, existing systems, security, disaster recovery, availability, scalability, and reliability.

Standards

The goal of each standard is to provide a set of benchmarks, enabling the project team to complete the task and be assured that it meets at least a minimum level of quality.

An organization might adhere to one or more standards. In particular, ISO 9000 is frequently cited as a requirement for many companies. ISO 9000 is the most recognizable of ISO standards. It defines the criteria for quality in the manufacturing and service industries. It was first popularized in Europe but its popularity has spread worldwide as more and more companies deem "ISO certification" to be a competitive advantage.

ISO 9000 is actually a "family" of standards:

1. ISO 9000 is the actual standard. ISO 9001, ISO 9002, and ISO 9003 are the three quality assurance models against which organizations can be certified.
2. ISO 9001 is the standard of interest for companies that perform the entire range of activities from design and development to testing. ISO 9001 is of most interest to the software developer. It is this standard that provides the all-important checklist of quality initiatives such as:
   a. Develop your quality management system
   b. Implement your quality management system
   c. Improve your quality management system
3. ISO 9002 is the standard for companies that do not engage in design and development. This standard focuses on production, installation, and service.
4. ISO 9003 is the appropriate standard for companies whose business processes do not include design control, process control, purchasing, or servicing. This standard is focused on testing and inspection.

Project managers should make sure they fully understand the requirements of each standard that is to be adopted. These requirements can be adapted to scorecard metrics. For example, the ISO 9000 standard has a multidimensional set of foci, including management commitment, quality policy, and customer focus. A internal business processes measure for management commitment might be *number of times (once per year minimum) conducting management reviews of the quality policies* and a customer perspective measure for customer focus might be *number of programs used to increase customer satisfaction.*

Table 7.2 Measuring Change

Dashboard Area	Green	Yellow	Red
Scope	• Total cost of all change requests is 50 percent or less of change request budget • All major components will be implemented as planned	• Total cost of all change requests is 75 percent or less of change request budget • Major component will be deferred to later phase in order to meet current phase's schedule or budget	• Total cost of all change requests is at least 75 percent of the change request budget • Major component will not be implemented

Existing System(s)

Not all projects involve the development of something new. In many cases, existing products will need to be modified. This is referred to as maintenance. Table 7.2 demonstrates a basic scorecard approach for maintenance vis-à-vis scope.

Hardware/Software

This section of the project plan describes:

1. Existing and proposed hardware (e.g., computers, copiers, telephones, milling machines, tractors, etc.) that is required to be used
2. Existing and proposed software that is to be used

So how does one turn a list of hardware and software into viable metrics? If you think in terms of a cost–benefits analysis, then you should be able to visualize the approach. We discuss project estimation in Chapter 9. Table 7.3 provides a quick

Table 7.3 Simple Cost–Benefit Analysis

Costs/One Time	Benefits/Year
$1,000	1. Rental computer savings: $75 × 12 = $900
	2. Typing income: $300 ×12 = $3,600
Totals: $1,000/one time	Totals: $4,500/year
Potential savings/earnings	$3,500/first year; $4,500 subsequent years

Table 7.4   Cost Benefits Translated to a Balanced Scorecard

Perspective	Measures
Customer	Percentage increase in customer satisfaction
Internal business processes	Percentage increase in customer productivity
Financial	Percentage increase in yearly income
Learning and growth	Number of new skills acquired

overview of what a simple cost–benefits analysis looks like for the purchase of a personal computer, which you've already seen in Chapter 3.

Obviously, a cost–benefits analysis compares costs to benefits. This may encompass one, two, three, or even four of the balanced scorecard perspectives, as shown in Table 7.4.

Security

Most organizations have security requirements that must be adhered to by all products or services. This should be included in the project plan. A security statement might contain the following information:

> The system will provide a number of different security features. Firstly, all members must log into the system at member PCs and must provide a username and password before gaining access to the system. Similarly, the librarian and administrator access the system via their respective PCs and are authenticated by username and password. Secondly, remote users access the system via a gateway that provides a firewall. The firewall allows access to services designated as remote access services, but blocks access to all other services, such as administrator services. Cookies will also be used to aid in identifying remote users.
>
> The DBMS provides a high level of security. Security profiles for the different user types will be created so that specific users have permissions (create, update, delete) only on selected data objects. For example, only the administrator will have create and delete permissions in the asset database. Stored procedures will be used to maintain referential integrity in the databases.

Again, highlighting the key concepts will assist in determining appropriate key measures. I picked out the following concepts in a quick reading of this: login with an id/password, gateway/firewall, cookies, security profiles, and stored procedures. It is up to the project manager to determine which of the four balanced scorecard perspectives to apply. Obviously, internal business processes predominate here. However, one could make an argument to include the financial perspective to assist in tracking the costs of security; the customer perspective to track how all of this will affect the customer; and, finally, the learning and growth perspective as developers will have to learn how to do all of this.

Scalability, Availability, and Reliability

Scalability, availability, and reliability provide a set of measures as they are always referred to in a quantitative fashion. Scalability indicates expandability. A scalability statement might specify the following:

> The system will be able to expand to 200 users without breaking down or requiring major changes in procedure.

Availability refers to the percentage of time that a system is available for use. It is also referred to as *uptime*, that is, the amount of time the system is up. Availability is an important component of information systems. An availability statement might specify the following:

> System uptime will not be lower than 99 percent. Providing a reliable and continuous service to users is one of the key requirements of the system. When a failure occurs, system downtime will be kept to a minimum. The target is to have the system operational within two hours following a serious failure.

Reliability refers to the accuracy, correctness, and quality of the product. Some common measures are:

1. Fault density. This measure can be used to predict remaining faults by comparison with expected fault density, determine if sufficient testing has been completed, and establish standard fault densities for comparison and prediction.
2. Defect density. This metric measures the concentration of errors in a product. If the defect density is outside the norm after several inspections, it is an indication of a problem.
3. Cumulative failure profile. A plot is drawn of cumulative failures versus a suitable time base.
4. Fault-days number. This measure represents the number of days that faults spend in the product from their creation to their removal. For each fault detected and removed, during any phase, the number of days from its creation to its removal is determined (fault-days). The fault-days are then summed for all faults detected and removed, to get the fault-days number

at system level, including all faults detected and removed up to the delivery date. In those cases where the creation date of the fault is not known, the fault is assumed to have been created at the middle of the phase in which it was introduced.

Disaster Recovery

Disaster recovery is associated with risk analysis and mitigation planning. Before a disaster recovery (contingency) plan can be created, risks associated with the project should be identified. A sample risk plan can be seen in Table 7.5. Each "risk" should have an associated contingency plan.

Table 7.5 was sorted first by probability and then by impact value. Risks are discussed in more detail in Chapter 10. For the purposes of the Goals and Objectives statement, all that is required is a brief statement such as:

Table 7.5   Risk Table

Risks	Category[a]	Probability (%)	Impact[b]
Customer will change or modify requirements	PS	70	2
Lack of sophistication of end users	CU	60	3
Users will not attend training	CU	50	2
Delivery deadline will be tightened	BU	50	2
End users resist system	BU	40	3
Server may not be able to handle larger number of users simultaneously	PS	30	1
Technology will not meet expectations	TE	30	1
Larger number of users than planned	PS	30	3
Lack of training of end users	CU	30	3
Inexperienced project team	ST	20	2
System (security and firewall) will be hacked	BU	15	2

[a] Category abbreviations: BU, business impact risk; CU, customer characteristics risk; PS, process definition risk; ST, staff size and experience risk; TE, technology risk.
[b] Impact values: 1, catastrophic; 2, critical; 3, marginal; 4, negligible.

The DBMS software will provide a backup capability to ensure protection of the data in the database. In addition, the DBMS software provides a transaction recording feature that can be used to keep track of all transactions during normal day time operation. If a failure occurs, the transaction record can be used to rollback to the last successful transaction so that a minimum amount of information is lost.

It is the risk table itself, however, that will provide the input into the balanced scorecard. This table supplies both a probability of occurrence as well as an impact assessment, both of which can be used to determine acceptable measures.

Training and Documentation

All documents created should be assigned a tracking number and stored in a repository for future use. This includes all internal design documentation, operation policies and procedures, and testing plans, as well as user manuals and any online help, if applicable.

Appropriate measures would include number of manuals, number of revisions of manuals, percentage of completeness of manuals, percentage of frequency of use (if accessed online), cost to prepare, user satisfaction, and so on.

Organizations have a wide variety of training options. Most do not settle for just one mode of training, particularly because training is an ongoing process. The project plan should specify which training options should be utilized.

Training options include:

1. Tutorials
2. Courses and seminars
3. Computer-aided instruction

Similarly to documentation, training efforts and materials can and should be tracked via one or more scorecard perspectives.

Installation Issues

The project plan should specify what, if any, requirements are to be imposed on the installation of the developed product. These may include:

1. Timing constraints. There might be certain periods of time when installation processes are prohibited, for example, end of month reconciliation or start of day, among others.
2. Resource constraints. Installation might require the participation of a wide variety of people such as the database administrator, various end users, and so on. One or more of these people might have limited availability.

3. Redundancy requirements. The request for proposal (RFP) should specify whether redundant systems are to be maintained after installation of the proposed system.

In addition to the constraints imposed on the installation process, the RFP should specify that a detailed log of all installation issues be maintained. Issues might be categorized as follows:

- 0—Only severe errors logged
- 1—Errors
- 2—Warnings
- 3—Information
- 4—Detailed information useful for debugging

We've Reached the End of Chapter 7

The Project Plan must be carefully constructed as it is the controlling document. Project managers must work with the various project stakeholders (i.e., managers, end users, clients, customers, etc.) to determine all internal and external constraints and restraints on the effort as well as the scope and general requirements. Project managers also need to translate each step of the scope to one or more balanced scorecard perspective measures, targets, and initiatives.

Chapter 8

Balanced Scorecard and Project Scheduling

Scheduling is one of the two major project planning tasks, the other being cost estimation. There are a variety of tools and methodologies that can be used to assist in creating an accurate schedule. In this chapter we review some of these, for example, the work breakdown structure (WBS), network diagrams, and PERT and Gantt charts, as well as critical path. We discuss all of this within the context of performance management and measurement using the balanced scorecard approach.

The Task Network

The critical key performance indicators in the scheduling process are whether the deadline has been met, and how many days late (or early if we're very optimistic) the project was delivered, if applicable. However, the scheduling process itself, and the attendant tasks being scheduled, can also be measured.

A project is composed of one or more tasks. Each of these tasks has interdependencies, usually based on their sequence. Most projects have more than one person involved in the engineering process, so it is likely that some tasks will be done in parallel; for example, Task A and Task B are developed concurrently. It is very important that tasks be carefully coordinated so that, for example, if Task C depends on Task D, then Task D has available to it on a timely basis the work product output by Task C. How the tasks are ordered depends not only on the requirements and dependencies, but also on a host of other, but very measurable, variables such as the risk level of the task, cost of development of each task, number

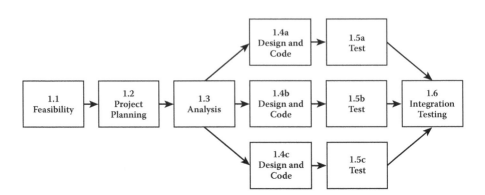

Figure 8.1 A WBS for an incremental software development project

of days task development is past deadline, number of new skills learned as a result of developing the code for the task, and so on. More importantly, each task represents a facet of a requirement that should trace back to a particular stakeholder as well as connect to a business goal.

Figure 8.1 shows a simple work breakdown structure. A WBS is sometimes referred to as a task network for a software engineering project that is developed using an incremental methodology. Criteria for completeness of the WBS include (Wysocki, 2009):

1. Status and completion are measurable.
2. The activity is bounded.
3. The activity has a deliverable.
4. Time and cost are easily estimated.
5. Activity duration is within acceptable limits.
6. Work assignments are independent.

Notice that there are three 1.4 (a, b, and c) and three 1.5 (a, b, and c) tasks. This reflects the fact that this system has split design, coding, and testing into three increments. Each increment may be done in parallel, as shown in this diagram, or completed on a staggered schedule.

To create a work breakdown structure will require that much information be elicited about the project that is required to be tasked. A statement of work (SOW) is typically created after a feasibility study or upon request of one or more stakeholders. A careful reading of the SOW will help to determine exactly what needs to be done to satisfy the SOW (i.e., figure out what tasks are needed to accomplish this goal). For each task, the inputs, outputs, resources, and milestones need to be determined. Some of the tasks might be too complex to remain as stand-alone tasks. In this case, the task is broken down into one or more additional subtasks. Similarly to a major task, all subtasks must have inputs, outputs, resources, and milestones defined. It would be advisable to also record task ownership (i.e., for requirements traceability) and business goal traceability, generally on the highest level tasks. Although the business goal is included at the very highest level task, the lower-level tasks could, and should, include appropriate performance measures, as shown in Table 8.1.

You'll note that the business goal in this example is measureable. Those responsible for setting business goals usually use the SMART methodology (i.e., specific, measurable, attainable, relevant, timely). Our listed business goal easily fits these criteria.

Readers may wonder just how the scheduler arrived at the dates, seemingly out of thin air, in Table 8.1. As discussed in the chapter on cost estimation, there is both art as well as science involved in the process of project management. Just as one might use "guesstimation" techniques to arrive at a cost estimate, a scheduler might use a best estimate to arrive at the *first cut* of a schedule. The key here is that this is a first cut. Project management is a discipline within the field of software engineering. As with all components of software engineering (i.e., requirements document, design specification, test plan), a project plan is continually revised as more is understood and known about the project. In other words, the development of a project plan is an iterative process.

Once a preliminary schedule is articulated it can be fine-tuned as the project manager gains a better understanding of tasks, dependencies, and specific milestone and due date requirements.

Many project managers use a top-down approach to task identification. Using this methodology a complex project is decomposed (i.e., divided up) into less complex subprojects, or tasks. Top-down design is a tenet of good software engineering, so it follows that the top-down approach to task identification would offer similar quality attributes. Top-down methodologies promote usability, efficiency, reliability, maintainability, and reusability.

When using a top-down approach we proceed from top to bottom. We conceptualize the highest-order tasks and then break these down into subtasks. For example, two high-order tasks might be:

Develop modifications to system
Produce faculty training

Next, we proceed to identify the subtasks for each of the higher-order tasks that we have already identified:

Develop modifications to system
    Clean up and finalize for delivery
    Develop additional perks

Produce faculty training
    Create in-house training
    Create campus training

Table 8.1   A Typical WBS

Number	Tasks	Deliverable	Dates/ Days	Precedence	Milestone	Task Owner	Business Goal or Metric
A0000	Start of Project	Agreement/Contact	02/04/10			Paul Smith	Increase profitability 100 percent within one year by selling our periodicals via the Internet
A9999	Project Ends	Delivery			10/05/10		
A0010	Hold Meetings	Weekly meetings	02/04/10		07/05/10		
A0101		Assess functional requirements	4				
A0102			8				
A0103	Develop	Demonstrate system via a prototype	2	A0102, A0103, A0104	01/03/10		Stakeholders will approve 90 percent of the prototype's functionality
A0104	Requirements	Evaluation of testing needs	9				
A0105		Assess nonfunctional requirements	4				
		Final requirements specification					

A0201	Develop Documentation	Quality assurance plan	2		03/05/10
A0202		Project plan	8		
A0203		Requirements document	13		
A0204		Design document	11		
A0205		User guide	5		
A0206		Final project notebook	4		
A0207		Maintenance plan	4		
A0301	Produce Programmer Training	Web design training	6	A0202, A0204	03/12/10
A0302		Database design training	4		
A0401	Create Preliminary Design	Brainstorming	1	A0203, A0204	03/20/10
A0402		Architectural layout	5	A0204, A0401	
A0501	Create Detailed Design	Design user interface	10		04/01/10
A0502		Database design	10		

(continued)

Table 8.1   A Typical WBS (Continued)

Number	Tasks	Deliverable	Dates/ Days	Precedence	Milestone	Task Owner	Business Goal or Metric
A0602	Perform Coding	Build database	0		04/19/10		
A0603		User interface of campus version	14				
A0604		User interface of in-house version	14				
A0701	Perform	In-house testing	4 3	A0104	04/26/10		
A0702	Integration Testing	Necessary modifications					
A0801	Perform Post-Test	On campus testing	4	A0701,	05/03/10	Paul	95 percent
A0802		Necessary modifications	4	A0702		Smith	stakeholder acceptance
A0901	Develop	"Clean up" and finalized for delivery	1		05/07/10		
A0902	Modification	Additional "perks"					
A1001	Produce Faculty	In-house training	0	A0901,	05/10/10		
A1002	Training	Campus training	1	A0205			

An alternative to the top-down methodology is the bottom-up ("grass roots") methodology. In a bottom-up approach you start by defining the low-level tasks, such as "develop additional perks," and then figure out how these will be put together to create successively higher-level tasks (i.e., develop modifications to the system), and ultimately the entire system.

There are many advantages to using a bottom-up methodology. The most important advantage is that we are assured that we will conform to requirements as each requirement is tasked at a low level, thus satisfying our end users. Therefore, it can be said that bottom-up estimating is the most precise of all methodologies.

The system developer creating the table shown in Table 8.1 could have created this task list using a bottom-up approach. She would have done this by listing the deliverables (column 3), grouping these deliverables (i.e., subtasks), and, finally, creating the major tasks (column 2). To create a bottom-up task list requires the developer to have detailed information and can be quite time-consuming as a result.

Accurate task identification is critical to the successful development and implementation of a project. Guidelines should be developed and published such that the methodology deployed to create the WBS is a repeatable process within the organization. Configuration management is the recommended repeatable process by which task identification is managed.

Project Scheduling

People who perform project scheduling are often referred to as estimators. These employees are usually senior members of the staff who have years of experience working on a wide variety of projects as well as in-depth knowledge of the organization and its systems. These folks usually have a good handle on both technology and business, and can grasp the significance of trying to balance the technological goals against the strategic goals of the organization. Their estimate should articulate this in terms of risk and variance metrics. Just how long will it take to perform a particular task? There are several estimation approaches from which to choose:

1. Stochastic approach: It is unlikely that one can ever calculate the duration of a task with certainty. The stochastic approach takes this uncertainty into consideration by estimating a task duration along with a variance. This variance should be measured against the baseline.
2. Deterministic approach: Most project schedulers do not want to deal with uncertainty, so the deterministic approach is the preferred method. A deterministic estimate is based on past experiences where the number used is the average time it took to perform the task in the past. There is risk in adopting this approach as well: Just because it took x days to complete task y, doesn't means it will take x days to complete a task similar to y. Thus, the variance against the baseline should be measured here as well.

3. Modular approach: This technique, the most popular of those listed here, is similar to the top-down method of task identification. A task is first decomposed into its subtasks. Each subtask is then estimated. The sum of the estimates is "rolled up" to provide an estimate for the major task. For example,

   A2000 Develop Modifications to System
   A2010 Clean up and finalize for delivery
   A2020 Develop additional perks

   A2000 has two subtasks. If we estimate A2010 to take 20 days and A2020 to take 30 days, then the duration for task A2000 is calculated to be 50 days.

   This method is very popular because the estimator can involve the actual developers in the process of cost estimation. Who better to estimate how long it would take to program a task than the person doing the actual programming? Because multiple people are involved in this process (the estimator and those he asks to provide a task cost estimate), the estimate can be deemed a bit more reliable than those generated through use of other methodologies. Thus risk and, presumably, variance are reduced. Still, these two variables should be measured.

4. Benchmark job technique: This technique is best used for repetitive tasks where a task duration has proven to be consistent over time (i.e., benchmark). For example, let's say it takes 20 minutes to install virus software on a PC. The company has 100 PCs. Given that each PC is similar and the process of installing the virus software is the same for each PC, we can estimate the duration for the complete install task to be (20 minutes × 100 PCs) 33.33 hours.

5. Experience is best: The very best estimators are those with years of experience in the organization and with in-depth knowledge of the systems and policies and procedures used by the organization. This is a sort of "Father Knows Best" approach. It works best when the estimator is also the project manager and also has the political clout to "push" the team and stakeholders to adhere to the stated schedule.

The most prevalent unit of measure for a schedule is days. In a time-critical system (i.e., person-rated where life and death is often at stake), it is quite possible that hours and even minutes might need to be used. When summarizing the project schedule it is customary to roll up the schedule to provide an overview. In this case, time spans longer than days are permissible.

The project stakeholders (i.e., the end users) will most likely review the overview of the project schedule, and will either approve or disapprove it. Keep in mind that projects are not created in a vacuum. They are the result of business planning. Thus, the final schedule needs to be synchronized to the schedule as identified in that business, strategic, or tactical plan. The key question is how do you keep a single project on track when the goals, and dates, in the business plan itself might change.

Project Management Charts

There are a variety of project management charting techniques that can be used to assist the resource allocation activity:

1. Gantt charts assist the project manager in scheduling tasks.
2. PERT (Program Evaluation and Review Techniques) charts utilize a systemic network of nodes and arrows to allocate the various project tasks or activities. These nodes are then analyzed to determine the critical path (i.e., the longest path) through the tasks.

PERT charts show task interdependencies (i.e., which tasks are dependent upon which other tasks for their successful completion) but do not clearly show how these tasks might overlap. Gantt charts, on the other hand, do show task overlap as well as interdependencies.

Most project managers prefer Gantt over PERT as Gantt is far easier to use and easier to understand. However, both Gantt and PERT can be used simultaneously.

Gantt

The Gantt chart is the most commonly used of all business charting tools. It is widely used outside of the information technology department, as all business processes are task-based. Figure 8.2 is an example of a typical Gantt chart as created by Microsoft Project. Notice that it is a chart with two dimensions: tasks and time.

Gantt charts are easily understandable:

1. Tasks are listed on the vertical dimension.
2. Time is shown on the horizontal dimension using a bar whose length signifies the length of time it will take to complete the task. In our example, the name of the person assigned to the task is located at the end of the bar.

Project "task notes" can be used to store information about applicable metrics and correlation of business goals.

Program Evaluation and Review Technique (PERT)

PERT charts—also known as network diagrams or precedence diagrams—show tasks and the dependencies between tasks. Figure 8.3 shows a network of six tasks (i.e., Task A through Task F). Each task contains a task description as well

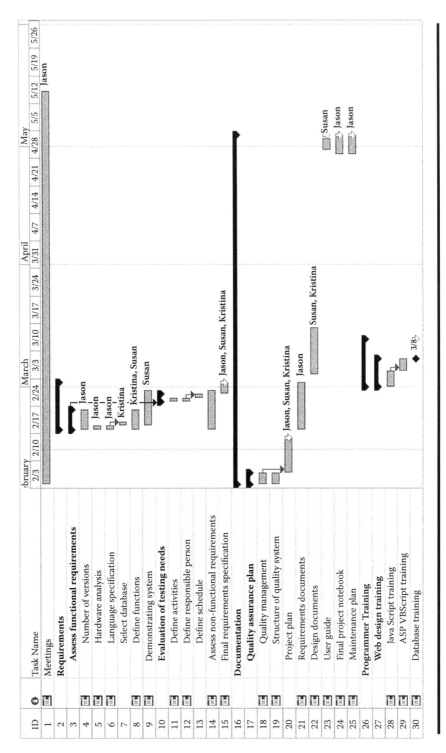

Figure 8.2 Gantt chart as created by Microsoft Project.

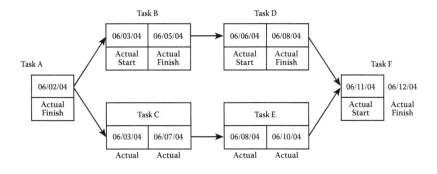

	Task B			Task D	
	06/03/04	06/05/04		06/06/04	06/08/04
	Actual Start	Actual Finish		Actual Start	Actual Finish

Task A	
06/02/04	
Actual Finish	

Task F	
06/11/04	06/12/04
Actual Start	Actual Finish

Task C	
06/03/04	06/07/04
Actual	Actual

Task E	
06/08/04	06/10/04
Actual	Actual

Figure 8.3 A sample PERT chart with six tasks.

as a scheduled start and finish date (the two dates we see in each task box) and an actual start and finish date. We can clearly see, for example, that Task A must be completed before Tasks B and C are initiated. We can also see that Tasks A through E must be completed before Task F is begun. In other words, the PERT chart enables us to visualize the order of the tasks as well as the dependencies between the tasks.

The project manager can also use the Microsoft Visio software tool to create a PERT chart. There are variations on this format. One might also choose to include slack (i.e., free) time and duration in the diagram.

Critical Path

The critical path is the sequence, or chain, of tasks that determines the duration of the project. It is calculated by figuring out the longest path through the tasks, giving us the "outside date" the project will be completed.

A variation on the PERT chart is the task activity network or network diagram, as shown in Figure 8.4. Circles are called events and are arbitrarily identified in this figure as event 10 (the initiating task) through event 50 (the final task). The arrows represent the activities and duration of that activity. "A, 5," for example, refers to an activity named "A" that takes five days to complete.

As you can see the duration (critical path) for the project can be readily calculated. To determine the length of the project, all we need do is add up the total number of days along each path and select the one with the longest duration.

Path 10-20-40-50 has a length of (5 + 20 + 3) 28 days.
Path 10-30-40-50 has a length of (10 + 20 + 3) 33 days

The critical path is 33 days as it is the longest of the two paths calculated.

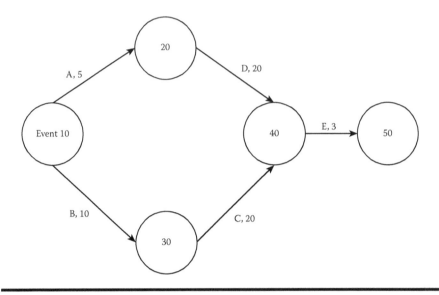

Figure 8.4 Using a task activity network to calculate critical path.

Leveling and Resource Allocation

In a typical work environment there will always be staff members who are over-utilized and others who are underutilized. This is especially true for key human resources assigned to a project. Leveling refers to the optimization technique of efficiently allocating human resources to a project by essentially evening out the workload by the reallocation of tasks. The manager first looks at how each human resource is utilized. Next, "slack" time (i.e., free time) for each resource is examined. Finally, tasks are reallocated based on an analysis of resource utilization and available slack time, although, on occasion, reallocation will be done regardless of the amount of slack time available.

There are several methods that can be used to level human resource utilization, including:

1. Split a task into subtasks so that work can be suspended and then restarted when a resource is available.
2. Allocate additional human resources to a particular task.
3. Replace the human resource assigned to the task.
4. Delay lower-priority tasks until higher-priority tasks are completed.

Leveling can be a complicated statistical process, particularly when precedence of tasks must be considered. This is why tools such as Microsoft Project are so useful. When you use leveling, Microsoft Project checks each of the selected resources. If a resource is overallocated, Microsoft Project searches for the tasks that are causing the overallocation and identifies which of those tasks can be delayed. Microsoft Project does not delay tasks that:

- Have a constraint of Must Start On, Must Finish On, or As Late As Possible
- Have a Do Not Level priority
- Have an actual start date

After determining which tasks can be delayed, Microsoft Project picks the task to delay based on its task relationships, start date, priority, and constraints. Note that Microsoft Project cannot resolve overallocations in projects that are scheduled from the finish date.

Questions to ask prior to resource optimization include:

1. Which human resources can be allocated to which tasks (e.g., skillsets required for each task)?
2. Can the project finish date be delayed?
3. Can a task be subdivided?
4. What are the task's dependencies?
5. Can a task be shared?

Slack

In terms of project management, slack is the timing difference between an activity's earliest start date and its latest possible (critical) start date. If the slack of an activity is zero then that activity can be considered to be on the critical path. The critical path is the succession of tasks such that if any one of them is completed x days late, the project itself will be x days late.

Slack management is the process by which a project manager fine-tunes a schedule to correspond to the project's budget dollar availability. At times the cash flow of a budget (i.e., the budget dollars available during a certain period) precludes one or more tasks from being completed as per the schedule. Slack management is the art and science of redistributing the tasks so that the project stays within budget and on schedule while, at the same time, allowing a buffer for emergencies. For example, if critical Task A is redistributed to the tail end of the schedule due to budgeting problems, and an unforeseen emergency precludes Task A from being completed on schedule, the entire project might be delivered late.

Slack time management is also heavily used in manufacturing. Jobs are prioritized in accordance with their slack time, with the slack time being divided by the number of operations remaining. Each operation is an opportunity for delay. The lower the slack time per operation, the higher the job's priority is.

Crashing

What do you do if the project is behind and is in danger of being late? *Crashing* is the practice of doing one or more activities in a shorter than normal period of time. This can be done by:

1. Using different technologies to speed up the process
2. Adding or deleting resources

Questions that should be answered prior to crashing are:

1. How much does it cost to crash activities?
2. Do the benefits of completing the project in a shorter than normal time outweigh the extra cost of crashing activities?

When the Resources Are Human

Project managers should be reminded that each task on a Gantt chart, PERT chart, or critical path represents something done by a human being (i.e., resource). When creating a schedule estimators need to take into account (see Appendix I on staff competency):

1. The experience of the resource
2. The educational level of the resource
3. The amount of work the resource has already been allocated
4. How long it typically takes a particular resource to complete a particular task
5. How well the resource works with team members

To ensure smooth sailing the project manager should:

1. Make continuous training of human resources a priority.
2. Keep the staff motivated.
3. Utilize effective project control techniques.
4. Institute reward and recognition systems.
5. Develop an organizational culture that condones or rewards group efforts.
6. Make active efforts to disperse crucial application knowledge across project staff.
7. Improve communication and coordination across organizational layers.
8. Adopt egoless programming techniques.

Large performance differences between individuals negate productivity increases. Boehm (1991) estimates that productivity ranges of 3:1 to 5:1 are typical with some studies documenting differences as high as 26:1 among experienced programmers.

Techniques to increase the effective level of productivity include:

1. Enhanced training
2. Investment in productivity (tools, methods)
3. Use of standard practices
4. Professional development opportunities
5. Recognition
6. Effective staffing
7. Using top talent
8. Matching the job to the employee's skillsets
9. Providing a career progression
10. Providing team balance

It should be remembered that all of this has balanced scorecard ramifications. From an internal business process perspective, a project is composed or tasks and subtasks, the development and implementation of which satisfy one or more business goals. From a customer perspective, each scheduled task satisfies one or more stakeholder requirements. From a financial perspective, each task is related to a cost, which is discussed more in depth in the next chapter. Finally, from a learning and growth perspective, end users, customers, managers, and the organization as an entity benefit in some way from the project's artifacts (e.g., the product itself) as well as the project's competitive, psychological, and sociological impact. Each of these perspectives can be viewed, and ultimately managed, through the prism of appropriate performance measures.

We've Reached the End of Chapter 8

Creating the project schedule is one of the most difficult project management tasks. Many, if not most, projects wind up exceeding time estimates. Successful time estimation requires a great deal of experience, the use of tools (i.e., PERT, Gantt, etc.) with which to model the project's tasks, and an intimate understanding of the human resources being scheduled. Measuring the creation of, and adherence to, the project schedule, is necessary and quite possible through a balanced scorecard.

References

Boehm, Barry W. 1991. *Software Engineering Economics*. New York: Prentice-Hall.

Wysocki, R.K. 2009. *Effective Project Management: Traditional, Agile, Extreme*. 5th ed. Indianapolis, IN: Wiley.

Chapter 9

Balanced Scorecard and Project Estimation

The topic of project estimation lends itself nicely to balanced scorecard. Cost estimation and budgeting utilize quantitative methods, which can be easily tied to measures in one or more of the four scorecard perspectives. In this chapter we examine a variety of estimation techniques such as process-based and bottom-up estimation. Use of historical data and estimation of external resources is addressed. Various budgeting methodologies such as top-down, bottom-up, iterative, and overburden are examined. Budget analysis techniques such as cost–benefit analysis, breakeven analysis, ROI, and NPV are analyzed.

The Importance of Project Estimation

Menlo Worldwide had been reworking its transportation and supply-chain management system, known as Emco, since 1996. Over time, the project size grew and the scope began to drift. Then September 11th happened and in its wake the United States Transportation Security Administration created the "known shipper" program to electronically match cargo to legitimate shipping companies.

This new requirement (i.e., business goal) threw a wrench into Emcon's fragile works. Not only did the entire product need to be retrenched, but all the internal business processes associated with it needed to be retrenched as well.

The project manager had a real problem on his hands. He was faced with a project that had been creeping along for years and a product architecture that was over 30 years old. His decision was to overhaul this most critical application but to do so in a carefully controlled, planned way.

The project manager put the project back into a business context and narrowed its scope, including a total redesign of some of the base architecture to remove some of the complexity that was impeding progress. He also made a decision to delay some components, such as handheld devices for delivery drivers, until later in the project.

Doing all of this was no easy feat. According to the project manager, the most difficult part of the project was understanding what had to be changed and then developing a viable project plan and accompanying estimate.

WBS: The Basis for Project Estimates

One of the first things Emcon's project manager did was create a work breakdown structure (WBS). This enabled him to understand and then effectively allocate and organize project tasks. To execute these tasks, Emcon's project manager also had to allocate sufficient resources, time, and budget dollars (i.e., the triple constraint).

Figure 9.1 shows a partial WBS for a Web-based veterinarian service called "Dog E-Doctor System (DEDs)." Once a project is broken down into manageable tasks it becomes possible to begin the estimation process. As we discussed in the chapter on scheduling, each of these tasks is related in some way to a business goal.

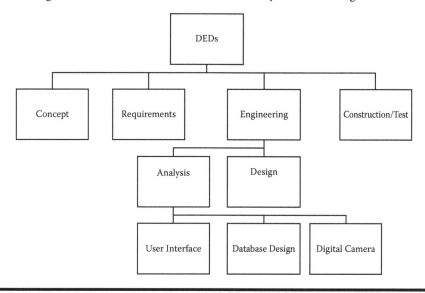

Figure 9.1 The WBS assists the project planner in identifying discrete project tasks. The WBS in this figure is a small subset of the complete WBS for this project.

The Process of Human Resource Estimation

Project managers use a wide variety of techniques to perform the project cost estimation effort. It is customary, in fact, for the estimator to use at least two techniques and then triangulate the two (i.e., discuss the reasons why the two estimates have differences). Often, the best estimate is the average of the results of the various estimation methods used.

An example of this methodology follows. Notice that we account for all three dimensions of the "triple constraint."

1.0 PROJECT ESTIMATES

This portion of the document provides cost, effort, and time estimates for the project using various estimation techniques.

1.1 HISTORICAL DATA USED FOR ESTIMATES

Local data was collected to determine the average salaries for professionals in Roanoke, Virginia. Table 9.1 summarizes this data and shows the average salary for seven different types of professionals (e.g., marketing, systems, sales, etc.) required by our sample project. The average salary values do not include the administrative costs associated with the employee. These administrative costs are typically 40 percent of the employee's salary. Therefore, the real cost of the employee is 1.4 times the average salary. This adjusted salary value is shown in the second to last column of the table. The last column adjusts the salary to a per month basis.

Table 9.1   Average Salaries

Profession	Average Salary	Average Adjustment (40%)	Per Month
Resource 1	$50,328	$70,459	$5,871
Resource 2	$44,949	$62,928	$5,244
Resource 3	$53,923	$75,492	$6,291
Resource 4	$48,406	$67,768	$5,647
Resource 5	$77,619	$108,666	$9,055
Resource 6	$58,325	$81,655	$6,804
Resource 7	$58,395	$81,753	$6,812

It is important that current "real world" data always be used. All too often estimates are based on "gut" feelings about what the true cost of development is. Many job Web sites provide comparative cost data. In addition, the human resources department presumably has accurate cost information as well. Because we intend to use these cost estimates as the basis for performance measurement, it is important that the numbers are accurate and reflect what's going on in the industry.

1.2 ESTIMATION TECHNIQUES APPLIED AND RESULTS

Two estimation techniques were used for planning purposes. Two were used so that the results could be compared and contrasted to ensure that the plan was as accurate as possible. The two estimation techniques used were:

Process-based
Bottom-up estimation

1.2.1 PROCESS-BASED ESTIMATION

Process-based estimation bases the estimate on the project to be used. This is accomplished by breaking down (decomposing) the project into a relatively small set of tasks. The time required to accomplish each task is then estimated. The major functions for this system are:

Control Engineering	UICE
Algorithm Engineering	SIAE
Data Management	DDM
Automated Notification	ANA
Digital Camera System	DCS
Credit Card Transaction	CCT
Automated Backup Recovery System	ABRS

This is where the WBS comes in handy. Work breakdown structures enable the estimator to successively decompose a system into multiple levels of subtasks. This makes it easier to provide an accurate cost estimate. The process-based estimation results show that the project will require 9.15 person-months of time to complete.

Estimation is one part science and one part "guesstimation." Table 9.2 represents a series of time estimates based on months for each task. For example, the project manager who created this estimate decided that it would take about a quarter of a month (.25) to complete the analysis of the user interface (UICE). From where did she get that quarter of a month? In our example, one person is being

Table 9.2 Process-Based Human Resources Estimation Table

Activity Task Function	Cust. Comm.	Planning	Risk Analysis	Engineering		Construction Release			Totals
				Analysis	Design	Code	Test	Cust. Eval.	
UICE	0.38	0.08	0.03	0.25	0.38	0.38	0.38	0.15	2.03
SIAE	0.23	0.03	0.02	0.13	0.25	0.15	0.25	0.08	1.14
DDM	0.08	0.03	0.05	0.38	0.5	0.13	0.25	0.03	1.45
ANA	0.15	0.03	0.03	0.13	0.15	0.13	0.13	0.03	0.78
DCS	0.08	0.03	0.02	0.13	0.38	0.5	0.38	0.03	1.55
CCT	0.08	0.02	0.02	0.13	0.25	0.25	0.25	0.03	1.03
ABRS	0.08	0.03	0.02	0.13	0.25	0.25	0.38	0.03	1.17
Total	1.08	0.25	0.19	1.28	2.16	1.79	2.02	0.38	9.15
Effort (%)	12	3	2	14	24	20	22	4	100%

shared among this and four other projects. Therefore, one-fifth of the cost of this person will be applied to this project.

Table 9.2 shows that the project requires 9.15 person-months of work. However, this does not mean that four workers can complete the project in one-fourth of the time. There are two reasons for this. The more workers on a project, the more lines of communication there are that must be maintained.

Communications can dominate productivity. Most project problems arise as the result of poor communications among workers. If there are n workers on the team, then there are $n(n - 1)/2$ interfaces across which there may be communications problems. This is also a learning and growth issue, so it should be encapsulated within this scorecard perspective as well.

Maintaining these lines of communication takes project resources away from the actual work. Also, the critical path may not be able to be completed in one-fourth of the time. Therefore, the actual amount of time required to complete the project will be estimated at 35 percent higher than the time shown in Table 9.2. The amount of time required to complete the project will be $(9.15 \times 1.35)/4 = 3.08$ months.

The project manager might need to reduce or increase this figure depending on political, administrative, or other constraints. Inasmuch as each task, and group of tasks, is somehow related to a business goal, and should list the task owner (responsible end user), making these changes will be easily traceable and auditable.

The cost of the project team will be $84,795.

Resource 7: $20,708 (From Table 9.1, Resource 7 is costed at $6,812. Multiply this by 3.04 months, a reduction from the 3.08 months listed, and you get $20,708)

Resource 7: $20,708

Resource 7: $20,708

Resource 4: $17,166

Resource 5: $5,505

Note: Three people who perform the role of resource 7 are required for this project example.

Other Estimation Techniques

The most important thing for you to understand about project estimation is that uncertainty is inherent in most estimation endeavors, so you need to plan on it as well as measure it! Using a variety of estimation techniques will ensure that your estimate is as accurate as possible. A typical project plan will include the results of at least two estimation methodologies.

Estimating by analogy relates the cost of a system to the cost of a known similar system through comparisons of key technical and management characteristics.

This technique is useful when little data is available and is based on actual costs. The major problem with this technique is that its accuracy is highly dependent on a similarity between items.

Bottom-up, or grass roots, estimating builds up an estimate of a system using detailed information (i.e., you start from the lowest-level tasks and build your system upwards. It's analogous to bottom-up design versus top-down design when designing software systems). This is considered the most precise of all estimation techniques, and is the one most commonly used. The problem with this technique is that it requires detailed design information and, ultimately, depends on the stability of the design and skills of the team.

The parametric estimation method relates the cost of a system to one or more parameters of the system such as physical or performance characteristics utilizing a mathematical model. Parametric cost modeling techniques were first developed in the 1950s by the Rand Corporation. The big advantage of this technique is that it is very sensitive to significant design changes, so a changing scope can be easily reflected in the estimation. This method also provides quick reproducible results, based on the "real world" experience of many systems. Parametric estimation might be the best approach to estimation for the purposes of aligning to a business strategy and being measured by balanced scorecard. NASA provides a good downloadable manual, which explains this technique in detail. It can be found at: http://cost.jsc.nasa.gov/pcehg.html

Estimating Resources

Earlier we discussed how the scope of the project plan should detail the nonhuman resources required by the project. This includes all hardware, software, office supplies, training, and even travel-related expenses necessitated by the project. The cost of these resources must be estimated as well. These costs may be ascertained by researching the Internet or directly from the various vendors. The total estimated project cost, therefore, is the sum of the human resource estimate and nonhuman resource estimate.

A variety of human resources may be assigned to a project. These resources have a variety of titles and pay scales. The project plan's section on estimation will contain historical data for these various pay scales, which is then used to calculate the project's cost. The project plan will also contain much information that describes the people involved in the project as well as the equipment (i.e., nonhuman resources) that are needed for the project.

Human Resources

An excerpt of a typical project plan that deals with this requirement follows.

> This project will require four developers. Three of them are Software Engineers and one is a Database Analyst. A Software Design Manager

will manage the project. The team is well rounded and each team member has several years of experience in the IT field. Since the team members have a wide range of expertise, this project should require very little additional training.

The one part of the project that may require some minimal training is the digital camera system. One of the Software Engineers will be sent to a two-day training course on the system that will be purchased. This will insure that the risks involved with the most technically challenging aspect of the project will be limited. The cost of the training class and travel will be $2,000.

The project team will also be made up of one of the SPCA's employees that will be the main point of contact for gathering end user feedback from the SPCA's perspective. This end user will not be paid for their participation since they will have a vested interest in insuring the project's success.

There will also be a group of five end users that will be paid for their testing of the system. They will provide feedback from the user's perspective (individuals looking to adopt a dog). Their feedback will be solicited during regular dinner sessions. They will be served dinner while the latest changes to the system are discussed. After dinner they will be allowed to test out the system for ~1 hour. They will each be paid $20 for each of the testing sessions (5 sessions).

Nonhuman Resources

This includes costs for resources such as hardware (e.g., personal computers, servers, digital cameras, etc.), software (e.g., operating system, database management system, etc.), office supplies (e.g., desks), training, travel, and the like. The project manager determines the nonhuman resources for each low-level task by asking, "What does the human resource require to perform this task?"

Budgeting

All projects have budgets. A budget is the total sum of all costs of a project. This includes:

1. Salaries
2. Hardware
3. Software
4. Training, as applicable
5. Other equipment such as telephones, stamps, paper, and so on

One talks about costs from two perspectives:

1. Fixed costs are those costs that never vary. For example, let's say that a proposed system requires the company to purchase Microsoft Office. The price of Office is fixed, therefore this can be identified as a fixed cost.
2. Overhead costs are costs not directly related to the project. For example, the project team's office space is considered overhead. Most project estimations will include overhead as a factor of salaries. This is referred to as administrative overhead and is generally estimated to be 30 to 40 percent of the salary. For example, if $50 is the dollar amount we are using for a typical programmer's hourly cost, then the project manager will craft a budget using a hourly rate of $65 (i.e., $50 + (30% of $50)).

There are several different methods of preparing a budget: top-down, bottom-up, and iterative. In all cases, the main goal of the budgetary process is to craft an accurate assessment of the costs of completing the project without overburdening the budget with extraneous costs.

Top-Down

Budgeting within organizations is multitiered. The organization itself prepares a budget (strategic) as do the departments within the organization (tactical). The organization's master budget is the result of long-range planning, whereas each department prepares a budget based on short-range planning.

Top-down budgeting requires the project planner to be constrained by whatever dollar allocations are made available via the long-range plan. Problems with this methodology include the inevitable competition for scarce budget dollars and a lack of understanding on the part of senior management of the specifics of the project.

Bottom-Up

Bottom-up is the preferred budgeting approach from the project manager's perspective. In this scenario, each project manager prepares a budget proposal for each project under his direction. The advantage to this approach is a granular level of detail for each project's budget, making the budgeting process far more accurate.

A disadvantage of this methodology is a loss of control by senior management. Once the many project budgets are aggregated, it is very likely that the gap between the resultant tactically created budget and the organization plan and budget will be quite wide.

Iterative

An iterative approach to budgeting tries to combine the advantages of both bottom-up and top-down budgeting while avoiding their respective disadvantages.

The iterative approach starts with management's crafting of a strategic budgetary framework, which is then passed down to the lower levels of the organization. Project managers use the guidance from the framework to develop their respective project budgets. These project budgets are then aggregated at the departmental (i.e., functional) level, and then finally into an organizational budget. Senior management then reviews this budget based on organizational goals, schedule, available resources and cost; makes its comments; and returns the budget to the functional areas for revision. Once revised, the project budgets are then reaggregated at the functional level and resubmitted to senior management. This iterative process is at times quite time-consuming.

Budget Monitoring

We discussed cost–benefit analysis, breakeven analysis, ROI, earned value management (EVM), and rapid economic justification in Chapter 3, so they won't be reiterated here. Suffice it to say that you will note that tangibles (e.g., reduced turnaround time) as well as intangibles (e.g., enhanced customer satisfaction) can be easily included in one or more of the balanced scorecard perspectives.

The budget approved by management (i.e., the estimated budget for the time cycle) is referred to as the baseline budget. The key word here is "baseline", meaning that to which actual budget costs are compared. Project budgets are usually monitored on a continuous basis with a status report submitted to management on a monthly basis. The status report will report on any variations (i.e., actual budget) from this baseline budget as well as projections (i.e., projected budget) for future status reporting periods.

The goal of budget monitoring is to keep project costs within an acceptable deviation (e.g., 10 percent) from the baseline. There are many reasons why a budget would deviate. The estimate could have been flawed from the outset, or a key resource may decide to quit and need to be replaced with a more expensive resource. These two problems are internal to the department and project. However, there are some business goal-related reasons a budget might deviate from the baseline. The end users might well decide to change the priority of a project component, or decide the scope must change for a variety of reasons (i.e., competitive, regulatory, etc.). In all cases, the deviation would be noted in the status report.

We've Reached the End of Chapter 9

The main reasons for inaccurate cost estimates are:

1. Many estimates for complex projects are rushed; a rough order of magnitude (ROM) estimate is provided before the requirements are really understood and defined. These estimates tend to be lower than later, more accurate, ones.
2. A lack of expertise by the estimator and lack of data on which to base the estimate.
3. The human bias toward underestimation. This may result from an overestimation of staff productivity capabilities, or an oversight of necessary supplemental activities.
4. The push from management for competitive estimates; it must be low to win the bid!

Accurate project estimation relies on a thorough understanding of the discrete tasks that require automation. The work breakdown structure is a visual tool enabling the project manager to decompose a system into a series of tasks and subtasks. From this base, the project manager can use a variety of estimation techniques to arrive at a dollar cost for the project. To this must be added nonhuman resources such as travel and office equipment. The total cost of a project will ordinarily be evaluated to determine whether the project is cost justified. Budget monitoring, using techniques we discussed here and in Chapter 3, can be used to assess performance using at least the four scorecard perspectives.

Chapter 10

Balanced Scorecard and Project Risk

In this chapter we examine the concept of project risk, with careful attention to the mitigation of risks. We examine the different varieties of risks, such as business, environment, product, employee, and so on; learn how to apply probability to each risk; understand the impact of each risk; devise a contingency plan for each risk; and ultimately learn how to measure risk.

The Proactive Risk Strategy

Project risk management addresses the following questions, all measureable in some way:

1. Are we losing sight of goals and objectives as the project moves forward?
2. Are we ensuring that the results of the project will improve the organization's ability to complete its mission? The result should be an improvement over previous process.
3. Are we ensuring sufficient funds are available, including funds to address risks?
4. Are we tracking implementation to ensure "quicker/better/cheaper" objectives are being met?
5. Are we applying appropriate risk management principles throughout the project?

6. Are we taking corrective action to prevent or fix problems, rather than simply allocating more money and time to them?
7. Have changes in the environment, such as new systems or leadership, created new risks that need to be managed?

A proactive risk strategy should always be adopted, as shown in Figure 10.1. It is better to plan for possible risk then have to react to it in a crisis.

Sound risk assessment and risk management planning throughout project implementation can have a big payoff. The earlier a risk is identified and dealt with, the less likely it is to negatively affect project outcomes. Risks are both more probable and more easily addressed early in a project. By contrast, risks can be more difficult to deal with and more likely to have significant negative impact if they occur later in a project. As explained below, risk probability is simply the likelihood that a risk event will occur. Conversely, risk impact is the result of the probability of the risk event occurring plus the consequences of the risk event. Impact, in laymen's terms, is telling you how much the realized risk is likely to hurt.

The propensity (or probability) of project risk depends on the project's life cycle, which includes five phases: initiating, planning, executing, controlling, and closing. Although problems can occur at any time during a project's life cycle, problems have a greater chance of occurring earlier due to unknown factors.

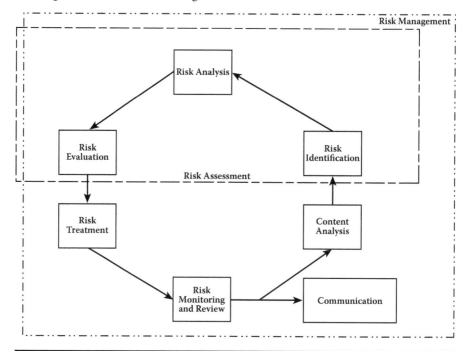

Figure 10.1   Risk management feedback loop.

The opposite can be said for risk impact. At the beginning of the project the impact of a problem, assuming it is identified as a risk, is likely to be less severe than it is later in the project life cycle. This is in part because at this early stage there is much more flexibility in making changes and dealing with the risk, again, assuming it is recognized as a risk. In addition, if the risk cannot be prevented or mitigated, the resources invested—and potentially lost—at the earlier stages are significantly lower than later in the project. Conversely, as the project moves into the later phases, the consequences become much more serious. This is attributed to the fact that as time passes, there is less flexibility in dealing with problems, significant resources have likely already been spent, and more resources may be needed to resolve the problem.

Risk Management

The first thing that needs to be done is to identify risks. One method is to create a risk item checklist. A typical project plan might list the following risks:

1. Customer will change or modify requirements
2. Lack of sophistication of end users
3. Delivery deadline will be tightened
4. End users resist system
5. Server may not be able to handle larger number of users simultaneously
6. Technology will not meet expectations
7. Larger number of users than planned
8. Lack of training of end users
9. Inexperienced project team
10. System (security and firewall) will be hacked

Keil (1998) developed a framework for identifying software project risks by interviewing experienced software project managers in different parts of the world. The following questions are ordered by their relative importance to the ultimate success of a project:

1. Have top software and customer managers formally committed to support the project?
2. Are end users enthusiastically committed to the project and the system or product to be built?
3. Are requirements fully understood by the software engineering team and their customers?
4. Have customers been involved fully in the definition of requirements?
5. Do end users have realistic expectations?
6. Is the project scope stable?

7. Does the software engineering team have the right mix of skills?
8. Are project requirements stable?
9. Does the project team have experience with the technology to be implemented?
10. Is the number of people on the project team adequate to do the job?
11. Do all customer or user constituencies agree on the importance of the project and on the requirements for the system or product to be built?

Based on the information uncovered by this questionnaire we can begin to categorize risks. Software risks generally include project risks, technical risks, and business risks.

Project risks can include budgetary, staffing, scheduling, customer, requirement, and resource problems. Risks are different for each project, and risks change as a project progresses. Project-specific risks could include, for example, the following:

1. Lack of staff buy-in
2. Loss of key employees
3. Questionable vendor availability and skills
4. Insufficient time
5. Inadequate project budgets
6. Funding cuts
7. Cost overruns

Technical risks can include design, implementation, interface, ambiguity, technical obsolescence, and leading-edge problems. An example of this is the development of a project around a leading-edge technology that has not yet been proven.

Business risks include building a product or system no one wants (market risk), losing support of senior management (management risk), building a product that no longer fits into the strategic plan (strategic risk), losing budgetary support (budget risks), and building a product that the sales staff does not know how to sell.

Tan (2002) proposes a method of risk analysis that requires modularizing the project into measurable parts. Risk can then be calculated as follows:

1. Exposure Factor (EF) = Percentage of asset loss caused by identified threat.
2. Single Loss Expectancy (SLE) = Asset Value × Exposure factor.
3. Annualized Rate of Occurrence (ARO) = Estimated frequency of a threat occurring within a year and characterized on an annual basis. A threat occurring ten times a year has an ARO of ten.
4. Annualized Loss Expectancy (ALE) = Single Loss Expectancy × Annualized Rate of Occurrence.

5. Safeguard Cost–Benefit Analysis = (ALE before implementing safeguard) – (ALE after implementing safeguard) – (annual cost of safeguard) = value of safeguard to the company.

Charette (1989) proposes that risks also be categorized as known, predictable, or unpredictable risks. Known risks are those that can be uncovered upon careful review of the project plan and the environment in which the project is being developed (e.g., lack of development tools, unrealistic delivery date, or lack of knowledge in the problem domain). Predictable risks can be extrapolated from past experience. For example, your past experience with the end users has not been good so it is reasonable to assume that the current project will suffer from the same problem. Unpredictable risks are hard, if not impossible, to identify in advance. For example, no one could have predicted the events of September 11th but this one event affected computers worldwide.

Once risks have been identified most managers project these risks in two dimensions: likelihood and consequences. As shown in Table 10.1, a risk table is a simple tool for risk projection. First, based on the risk item checklist, list all risks in the first column of the table. Then in the following columns fill in each risk's category, probability of occurrence, and assessed impact. Afterward, sort the table by probability and then by impact, study it, and define a cut-off line (i.e., the line demarking the threshold of acceptable risk). Table 10.2 describes the generic criteria used for assessing the likelihood that a risk will occur.

All risks above the designated cut-off line, as designated by a metric created and incorporated into the balanced scorecard, must be managed and discussed. Factors influencing their probability and impact should be specified.

A risk mitigation, monitoring, and management plan (RMMM) is the tool to help avoid risks. Causes of the risks must be identified and mitigated. Risk monitoring activities take place as the project proceeds and should be planned early. Table 10.3 describes typical criteria that can be used for determining consequences of each risk.

Table 10.1   A Typical Risk Table

Risks	Category[a]	Probability (%)	Impact[b]
Risk 1	PS	70	2
Risk 2	CU	60	3

[a] Category abbreviations: CU, customer characteristics risk; PS, process definition risk.

[b] Impact values: 1, catastrophic; 2, critical; 3, marginal; 4, negligible.

Table 10.2   Criteria for Determining Likelihood of Occurrence

Likelihood: What Is the Probability That the Situation or Circumstance Will Happen?	
5 (Very High)	Very likely to occur. Project's process cannot prevent this event, no alternate approaches or processes are available. Requires immediate management attention.
4 (High)	Highly likely to occur. Project's process cannot prevent this event, but a different approach or process might. Requires management's attention.
3 (Moderate)	Likely to occur. Project's process may prevent this event, but additional actions will be required.
2 (Low)	Not likely to occur. Project's process is usually sufficient to prevent this type of event.
1 (Very Low)	Very unlikely. Project's process is sufficient to prevent this event.

Risk can be mapped to a balanced scorecard, most often in the internal business process perspective, as shown in Table 10.4. An excerpt of a typical risk mitigation, monitoring and management plan is presented below.

3.1   SCOPE AND INTENT OF RMMM ACTIVITIES

This project will be uploaded to a server and this server will be exposed to the outside world, so we need to develop security protection. We will need to configure a firewall and restrict access to only "authorized users" through the linked Faculty database. We will have to know how to deal with load balance if the amount of visits to the site is very large at one time.

We will need to know how to maintain the database in order to make it more efficient, what type of database we should use, who should have the responsibility to maintain it, and who should be the administrator. Proper training of the aforementioned personnel is very important so that the database and the system contain accurate information.

3.2   RISK MANAGEMENT ORGANIZATIONAL ROLE

The software project manager must maintain track of the efforts and schedules of the team. They must anticipate any "unwelcome" events that may occur during the development

Table 10.3 Criteria for Determining Consequences

	1 (Very Low)	2 (Low)	3 (Moderate)	4 (High)	5 (Very High)
Technical	Minimal or no impact on mission or technical success/exit criteria or margins. Same approach retained.	Minor impact on mission or technical success/exit criteria, but can handle within established margins. Same approach retained.	Moderate impact on mission or technical success/exit criteria, but can handle within established margins. Workarounds available.	Major impact on mission or technical success criteria, but still meets minimum mission success/exit criteria, threatens established margins. Workarounds available.	Major impact on mission or technical success criteria, cannot meet minimum mission or technical success/exit criteria. No alternatives exist.
Schedule	Minimal or no schedule impact, and can be handled within schedule reserve; no impact on critical path.	Minor schedule impact, but can handle within schedule reserve; no impact on critical path.	Impact on critical path, but can handle within schedule reserve, no impact on milestones.	Significant impact on critical path, and cannot meet established lower-level milestone.	Major impact on critical path and cannot meet major milestone.
Cost	Minimal or no cost impact or increase over that allocated, and can be handled within available reserves.	Minor cost impact, but can be handled within available reserves.	Causes cost impact and use of allocated reserves.	Causes cost impact, may exceed allocated reserves, and may require resources from another source.	Causes major cost impact and requires additional budget resources from another source.

Table 10.4   Balanced Scorecard Metrics for Reducing Risk Objective

Measure	Target (%)
Percentage definitional uncertainty risk: Low degree of project specification. Rate risk probability from 0 to 100 percent.	<=10
Percentage technological risk: Use of bleeding-edge technology. Rate risk probability from 0 to 100 percent.	<=45
Percentage developmental risk	<10
Percentage nonalignment risk: Resistance of employees or end users to change. Rate probability of risk from 0 to 100 percent.	<=4
Percentage service delivery risk: Problems with delivering system (e.g., interface difficulties). Rate risk probability from 0 to 100 percent.	<=5
Number of fraudulent transactions	<=1
Percentage of systems that have risk contingency plans	>=95
Percentage of systems that have been assessed for security breaches	>=95

or maintenance stages and establish plans to avoid these events or minimize their consequences.

It is the responsibility of everyone on the project team with the regular input of the customer to assess potential risks throughout the project. Communication among everyone involved is very important to the success of the project. In this way, it is possible to mitigate and eliminate possible risks before they occur. [This is known as a proactive approach or strategy for risk management.]

3.3   RISK DESCRIPTION

This section describes the risks that may occur during this project.

3.3.1   DESCRIPTION OF POSSIBLE RISKS

Business Impact Risk: (BU)

This risk would entail that the software produced does not meet the needs of the client who requested the product. It would also have a business impact if the product no longer fits into the overall business strategy for the company.

Customer Characteristics Risks: (CU)

This risk is the customer's lack of involvement in the project and their nonavailability to meet with the developers in a timely manner. Also the customer's sophistication as to the product being developed and ability to use it is part of this risk.

Development Risks: (DE)

Risks associated with the availability and quality of the tools to be used to build the product. The equipment and software provided by the client on which to run the product must be compatible to the software project being developed.

Process Definition Risks: (PS)

Does the software being developed meet the requirements as originally defined by the developer and client? Did the development team follow the correct design throughout the project? The above are examples of process risks.

Product Size: (PR)

The product size risk involves the overall size of the software being built or modified. Risks involved would include the customer not providing the proper size of the product to be developed, and if the software development team misjudges the size or scope of the project. The latter problem could create a product that is too small (rarely) or too large for the client and could result in a loss of money to the development team because the cost of developing a larger product cannot be recouped from the client.

Staff Size and Experience Risk: (ST)

This would include appropriate and knowledgeable programmers to code the product as well as the cooperation of the entire software project team. It would also mean that the team has enough team members who are competent and able to complete the project.

Technology Risk: (TE)

Technology risk could occur if the product being developed is obsolete by the time it is ready to be sold. The opposite affect [sic] could also be a factor: if the product is so "new" that the end-users would have problems using the system and resisting the changes made. A "new" technological product could also be so new that there may be problems using it. It would also include the complexity of the design of the system being developed.

3.4 RISK TABLE

The risk table provides a simple technique to view and analyze the risks associated with the project. The risks were listed and then categorized using the description of risks listed in Section 3.3.1. The probability of each risk was then estimated and its impact on the development process was then assessed. A key to the impact values and categories appear at the end of the table.

PROBABILITY AND IMPACT FOR RISK

Risks	Category	Probability	Impact
Customer will change or modify requirements	PS	70 percent	2
Lack of sophistication of end users	CU	60 percent	3
Users will not attend training	CU	50 percent	2
Delivery deadline will be tightened	BU	50 percent	2
End users resist system	BU	40 percent	3
Server may not be able to handle larger number of users simultaneously	PS	30 percent	1
Technology will not meet expectations	TE	30 percent	1
Larger number of users than planned	PS	30 percent	3
Lack of training of end users	CU	30 percent	3
Inexperienced project team	ST	20 percent	2
System (security and firewall) will be hacked	BU	15 percent	2

Impact values:
    1 – Catastrophic
    2 – Critical
    3 – Marginal
    4 – Negligible

Category abbreviations:
   BU – Business impact risk
   CU – Customer characteristics risk
   PS – Process definition risk
   ST – Staff size and experience risk
   TE – Technology risk

RMMM Strategy

Each risk or group of risks should have a corresponding strategy associated with it. The RMMM strategy discusses how risks will be monitored and dealt with. Risk plans (i.e., contingency plans) are usually created in tandem with end users and managers. An excerpt of a RMMM strategy follows:

Project Risk RMMM Strategy

The area of design and development that contributes the largest percentage to the overall project cost is the database subsystem. Our estimate for this portion does provide a small degree of buffer for unexpected difficulties (as do all estimates). This effort will be closely monitored, and coordinated with the customer to ensure that any impact, either positive or negative, is quickly identified. Schedules and personnel resources will be adjusted accordingly to minimize the effect, or maximize the advantage as appropriate.

Schedule and milestone progress will be monitored as part of the routine project management with appropriate emphasis on meeting target dates. Adjustments to parallel efforts will be made as appropriate should the need arise. Personnel turnover will be managed through use of internal personnel matrix capacity. Our organization has a large software engineering base with sufficient numbers to support our potential demand.

Technical Risk RMMM Strategy

We are planning for two senior software engineers to be assigned to this project, both of whom have significant experience in designing and developing web-based applications. The project progress will be monitored as part of the routine project management, with appropriate emphasis on meeting target dates, and adjusted as appropriate.

Prior to implementing any core operating software upgrades, full parallel testing will be conducted to ensure compatibility with the system as developed. The application will be developed using only public Application Programming Interfaces (APIs), and no "hidden" hooks. While this doesn't guarantee compatibility, it should minimize any potential conflicts. Any problems identified will be quantified using cost–benefit and trade-off analysis; then coordinated with the customer prior to implementation.

The database subsystem is expected to be the most complex portion of the application, however it is still a relatively routine implementation. Efforts to minimize potential problems include the abstraction of the interface from the implementation of the database code to allow changing the underlying database with minimal impact. Additionally, only industry standard SQL calls will be used, avoiding all proprietary extensions available.

Business Risk RMMM Strategy

The first business risk, lower than expected success, is beyond the control of the development team. Our only potential impact is to use the current state of the art tools to ensure performance, in particular database access, meets user expectations; to this end, graphics are designed using industry standard look-and-feel styles.

Likewise, the second business risk, loss of senior management support, is really beyond the direct control of the development team. However, to help manage this risk, we will strive to impart a positive attitude during meetings with the customer, as well as present very professional work products throughout the development period.

Williams, Walker, and Dorofee (1997) advocate use of a risk information sheet, an example of which appears in Table 10.5.

Risk Avoidance

Risk avoidance can be accomplished by evaluating the critical success factors (CSF) of a business or business line. Managers are intimately aware of their missions and goals, but they don't necessarily define the processes required to achieve

Table 10.5   A Sample Risk Information Sheet

Risk id: PO2-4-32   Date: March 4, 2007   Probability: 80 percent   Impact: High
Description: Over 70 percent of the software components scheduled for reuse will be integrated into the application. The remaining functionality will have to be custom developed.
Refinement/context: 1. Certain reusable components were developed by a third party with no knowledge of internal design standards.   2. Certain reusable components have been implemented in a language that is not supported on the target environment.
Mitigation/monitoring: 1. Contact third party to determine conformance to design standards.   2. Check to see if language support can be acquired.
Management/contingency plan/trigger: Develop a revised schedule assuming that 18 additional components will have to be built.   Trigger: Mitigation steps unproductive as of March 30, 2007
Current status: In process
Originator: Jane Manager

these goals, in other words, "How are you going to get there?" In these instances, technologists must depart from their traditional venue of top-down methodologies and employ a bottom-up approach. They must work with the business units to discover the goal and work their way up through the policies, procedures, and technologies that will be necessary to arrive at that particular goal. For example, the goal of a fictitious business line is to be able to cut down the production/distribution cycle by a factor of ten, providing a customized product at no greater cost than that of the generic product in the past. To achieve this goal, the technology group needs to get the business managers to walk through the critical processes that need to be invented or changed. It is only at this point that any technology solutions are introduced.

One technique, called process quality management or PQM, uses the CSF concept. IBM originated this approach, which combines an array of methodologies to solve a persistent problem: how do you get a group to agree on goals and ultimately deliver a complex project efficiently, productively, and with a minimum of risk (Hardaker and Ward, 1987)?

PQM is initiated by gathering, preferably off site, a team of essential staff. The team's components should represent all facets of the project. Obviously, all teams have leaders and PQM teams are no different. The team leader chosen must have a skill mix closely attuned to the projected outcome of the project. For example, in a PQM team where the assigned goal is to improve plan productivity, the best team leader just might be an expert in process control, albeit the eventual solution might be in the form of enhanced automation.

Assembled at an off-site location, the first task of the team is to develop, in written form, specifically what the team's mission is. With such open-ended goals as, "Determine the best method of employing technology for competitive advantage," the determination of the actual mission statement is an arduous task, best tackled by segmenting this rather vague goal into more concrete subgoals.

In a quick brainstorming session the team lists the factors that might inhibit the mission from being accomplished. This serves to develop a series of one-word descriptions. Given the ten-minute timeframe, the goal is to get as many of these inhibitors as possible without discussion and without criticism.

It's at this point that the team turns to identifying the critical success factors that are the specific tasks that the team must perform to accomplish its mission. It is vitally important that the entire team reach a consensus on the CSFs.

The next step in the IBM PQM process is to make a list of all tasks necessary for accomplishing the CSF. The description of each of these tasks, called business processes, should be declarative. Start each with an action word such as: study, measure, reduce, negotiate, or eliminate.

Table 10.6 and Figure 10.2 show the resulting project chart and priority graph, respectively, that diagram this PQM technique. The team's mission, in this example, is to introduce just-in-time (JIT) inventory control, a manufacturing technique that fosters greater efficiency by promoting stocking inventory only to the level of need. The team, in this example, identified six CSFs and eleven business processes labeled P1 through P11.

The project chart is filled out by first ranking the business process by importance to the project's success. This is done by comparing each business process to the set of critical success factors. A check is made under each CSF that relates significantly to the business process. This procedure is followed until each of the business processes has been analyzed in the same way. The final column of the project chart permits the team to rank each business process relative to current performance, using a scale of A = excellent to D = bad, and E = not currently performed.

Table 10.6 CSF Project Chart

Number	Business Process	Critical Success Factors						Count	Quality
		1	2	3	4	5	6		
P1	Measure delivery performance by suppliers	x	x					2	B
P2	Recognize/reward workers				x	x		2	D
P3	Negotiate with suppliers	x	x	x				3	B
P4	Reduce number of parts	x	x	x	x			4	D
P5	Train supervisors					x	x	2	C
P6	Redesign production line	x		x	x			3	A
P7	Move parts inventory	x						1	E
P8	Eliminate excessive inventory buildups	x	x					2	C
P9	Select suppliers	x	x					2	B
P10	Measure				x	x	x	3	E
P11	Eliminate defective parts		x	x	x			3	D

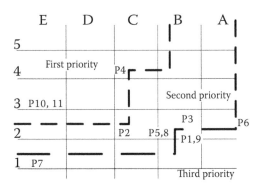

Figure 10.2 CSF priority graph.

The priority graph, when completed, will steer the mission to a successful, and prioritized, conclusion. The two axes to this graph are Quality, using the A through E grading scale, and Priority, represented by the number of checks noting each business process received. These can be lifted easily from the project chart from the Quality and Count columns, respectively

The final task as a team is to decide how to divide the priority graph into different zones representing first priority, second priority, and so on. In this example, the team has chosen as a first priority all business processes, such as "negotiate with suppliers" and "reduce number of parts," that are ranked from a quality of fair, degrading to a quality of not currently performed, and having a ranking of three or greater. Most groups employing this technique will assign priorities in a similar manner.

Determining the right project to pursue is one factor in the push for competitive technology. It is equally as important to be able to "do the project right," which can greatly reduce risk.

Quantitative Risk Analysis

Many methods and tools are available for quantitatively combining and assessing risks. The selected method will involve a tradeoff between sophistication of the analysis and its ease of use. There are at least five criteria to help select a suitable quantitative risk technique:

1. The methodology should be able to include the explicit knowledge of the project team members about the site, design, political conditions, and project approach.
2. The methodology should allow quick response to changing market factors, price levels, and contractual risk allocation.
3. The methodology should help determine project cost and schedule contingency.
4. The methodology should help foster clear communication among the project team members and between the team and higher management about project uncertainties and their impacts.
5. The methodology should be easy to use and understand.

Three basic risk analyses can be conducted during a project risk analysis: technical performance analysis (will the project work?), schedule risk analysis (when will the project be completed?), and cost risk analysis (what will the project cost?). Technical performance risk analysis can provide important insights into technology-driven cost and schedule growth for projects that incorporate new and unproven technology. Reliability analysis, failure modes and effects analysis (FMEA), and fault tree analysis are just a few of the technical performance analysis methods commonly used. However, this discussion of quantitative risk analysis concentrates on cost and schedule risk analysis only (U.S. Department of Transportation (n.d.)).

At a computational level there are two considerations about quantitative risk analysis methods. First, for a given method, what input data are required to perform the risk analysis? Second, what kinds of data, outputs, and insights does the method provide to the user?

The most stringent methods are those that require as inputs probability distributions for the various performance, schedule, and cost risks. Risk variables are differentiated based on whether they can take on any value in a range (continuous variables) or whether they can assume only certain distinct values (discrete variables). Whether a risk variable is discrete or continuous, two other considerations are important in defining an input probability: its central tendency and its range or dispersion. An input variable's mean and mode are alternative measures of central tendency; the mode is the most likely value across the variable's range. The mean is the value when the variable has a 50 percent chance of taking on a value that is greater and a 50 percent chance of taking on a value that is lower.

The other key consideration when defining an input variable is its range or dispersion. The common measure of dispersion is the standard deviation, which is a measure of the breadth of values possible for the variable. Normally, the larger the standard deviation is, the greater the relative risk. Finally, its shape or the type of distribution may distinguish a probability variable. Continuous distribution shapes that are commonly used in project risk analysis are the normal distribution, the lognormal distribution, and the triangular distribution.

All three distributions have a single high point (the mode) and a mean value that may or may not equal the mode. Some of the distributions are symmetrical about the mean, whereas others are not. Selecting an appropriate probability distribution is a matter of which distribution is most like the distribution of actual data. In cases where insufficient data are available to completely define a probability distribution, one must rely on a subjective assessment of the needed input variables.

The type of outputs a technique produces is an important consideration when selecting a risk analysis method. Generally speaking, techniques that require greater rigor, demand stricter assumptions, or need more input data generally produce results that contain more information and are more helpful. Results from risk analyses may be divided into three groups according to their primary output:

1. Single parameter output measures
2. Multiple parameter output measures
3. Complete distribution output measures

The type of output required for an analysis is a function of the objectives of the analysis. If, for example, a project manager needs approximate measures of risk to help in project selection studies, simple mean values (a single parameter) or a mean and a variance (multiple parameters) may be sufficient. On the other hand, if a project manager wishes to use the output of the analysis to aid in assigning contingency to a project, knowledge about the precise shape of the tails of the output distribution or the cumulative distribution is needed (complete distribution measures). Finally, when identification and subsequent management of the key risk drivers are the goals of the analysis, a technique that helps with such sensitivity analyses is an important selection criterion.

Sensitivity analysis is a primary modeling tool that can be used to assist in evaluating individual risks, which is extremely valuable in risk management and risk allocation support. A "tornado diagram" is a useful graphical tool for depicting risk sensitivity or influence on the overall variability of the risk model. Tornado diagrams graphically show the correlation between variations in model inputs and the distribution of the outcomes; in other words, they highlight the greatest contributors to the overall risk. Figure 10.3 is a tornado diagram for a sample project. The length of the bars on the tornado diagram corresponds to the influence of the items on the overall risk.

The selection of a risk analysis method requires an analysis of what input risk measures are available and what types of risk output measures are desired. These methods range from simple empirical methods to computationally complex, statistically based methods.

Traditional methods for risk analysis are empirically developed procedures that concentrate primarily on developing cost contingencies for projects. The method assigns a risk factor to various project elements based on historical knowledge of the relative risk of those elements. For example, documentation costs may exhibit a low degree of cost risk, whereas labor costs may display a high degree of cost risk. Project contingency is determined by multiplying the estimated cost of each element by its respective risk factors. This method profits from its simplicity and produces an estimate of cost contingency. However, the project team's knowledge of risk is only implicitly incorporated in the various risk factors. Because of the historical

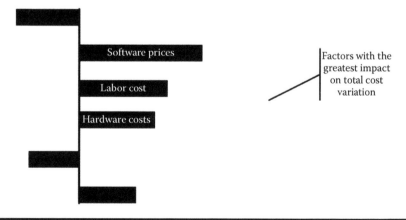

Figure 10.3　A tornado diagram.

or empirical nature of the risk assessments, traditional methods do not promote communication of the risk consequences of the specific project risks. Likewise, this technique does not support the identification of specific project risk drivers. These methods are not well adapted to evaluating project schedule risk.

Analytical methods, sometimes called second-moment methods, rely on the calculus of probability to determine the mean and standard deviation of the output (i.e., project cost). These methods use formulas that relate the mean value of individual input variables to the mean value of the variables' output. Likewise, there are formulas that relate the variance (standard deviation squared) to the variance of the variables' output. These methods are most appropriate when the output is a simple sum or product of the various input values. The formulas below show how to calculate the mean and variance of a simple sum.

> For sums of risky variables, $Y = x1 + x2$; The mean value is $E(Y) = [E(x1) + E(x2)]$ and the variance is $\sigma_{[Y]}^2 = \sigma_{[x1]}^2 + \sigma_{[x2]}^2$.
> For products of risky variables, $Y = x1 \times x2$; The mean value is $E(Y) = [E(x1) \times E(x2)]$ and the variance is $\sigma_{[Y]}^2 = ([E[x1]]^2 \times \sigma_{[x2]}^2) + ([E(x2)]^2 \times \sigma_{[x1]}^2) + (\sigma_{[x1]}^2 \times \sigma_{[x2]}^2)$.

Analytical methods are relatively simple to understand. They require only an estimate of the individual variable's mean and standard deviation. They do not require precise knowledge of the shape of a variable's distribution. They allow specific knowledge of risk to be incorporated into the standard deviation values. They provide for a practical estimate of cost contingency. Analytical methods are not particularly useful for communicating risks; they are difficult to apply and are rarely appropriate for scheduled risk analysis.

Simulation models, also called Monte Carlo methods, are computerized probabilistic calculations that use random number generators to draw samples from probability distributions. The objective of the simulation is to find the effect of multiple uncertainties on a value quantity of interest (such as the total project cost or project duration). Monte Carlo methods have many advantages. They can determine risk effects for cost and schedule models that are too complex for common analytical methods. They can explicitly incorporate the risk knowledge of the project team for both cost and schedule risk events. They have the ability to reveal, through sensitivity analysis, the impact of specific risk events on the project cost and schedule.

However, Monte Carlo methods require knowledge and training for their successful implementation. Input to Monte Carlo methods also requires the user to know and specify exact probability distribution information, mean, standard deviation, and distribution shape. Nonetheless, Monte Carlo methods are the most common for project risk analysis because they provide detailed illustrative information about risk impacts on the project cost and schedule.

Monte Carlo analysis histogram information is useful for understanding the mean and standard deviation of analysis results. The cumulative chart is useful for determining project budgets and contingency values at specific levels of certainty or confidence. In addition to graphically conveying information, Monte Carlo methods produce numerical values for common statistical parameters, such as the mean, standard deviation, distribution range, and skewness.

Probability trees are simple diagrams showing the effect of a sequence of multiple events. Probability trees can also be used to evaluate specific courses of action (i.e., decisions), in which case they are known as decision trees. Probability trees are especially useful for modeling the interrelationships between related variables by explicitly modeling conditional probability conditions among project variables. Historically, probability trees have been used in reliability studies and technical performance risk assessments. However, they can be adapted to cost and schedule risk analysis quite easily. Probability trees have rigorous requirements for input data. They are powerful methods that allow the examination of both data and model risks. Their implementation requires a significant amount of expertise, therefore, they are used only on the most difficult and complex projects.

Risk Checklists

The checklists in this section can assist in coming up with the risks for a project as well as developing the balanced scorecard metrics that can help assess and then manage the risks.

Checklist 10.1, Framework for Project Plan, sets forth the key aspects of project implementation that need to be addressed and the important issues that need to be considered for each aspect. To help managers consider the wide variety of risks any project could face, Checklist 10.2, Examples of Common Project-Level Risks, sets forth examples of major areas in which risks can occur and examples of key risks that could arise in each area.

Monitoring will be most effective when managers consult with a wide range of team members and, to the maximum extent possible, use systematic quantitative data on both implementation progress and project objectives. Checklist 10.3, Ongoing Risk Management Monitoring for Projects, provides a useful framework for monitoring of individual projects. Checklist 10.4, To Ensure Risks Are Adequately Addressed in Project Plan, is useful for ensuring that risks are discussed in detail.

Checklist 10.1   Framework for Project Plan

Project	
Responsible Manager	
Mission	Articulate clearly the mission, goal, or vision for the project.
Objectives	Ensure that the project is feasible and will achieve the project mission. Clearly define what you hope to achieve by executing the project and make sure project objectives are clear and measurable.
Scope	Ensure that an adequate scope statement is prepared that documents all the work of the project.
Deliverables	Ensure that all deliverables are clearly defined and measurable.
Milestones/costs	Ensure that realistic milestones are established and costs are properly supported.
Compliance	Ensure that the project meets legislative requirements and that all relevant laws and regulations have been reviewed and considered.
Stakeholders	Identify team members, project sponsor, and other stakeholders. Encourage senior management support and buy-in from all stakeholders.
Roles and responsibilities	Clarify and document roles and responsibilities of the project manager and other team members.
Work breakdown structure (WBS)	Make sure that a WBS has been developed and that key project steps and responsibilities are specified for management and staff.
Assumptions	Articulate clearly any important assumptions about the project.
Communications	Establish main channels of communications and plan for ways of dealing with problems.
	(continued)

Checklist 10.1   Framework for Project Plan (Continued)

Risks	Identify high-level risks and project constraints and prepare a risk management strategy to deal with them.
Documentation	Ensure that project documentation will be kept and is up to date.
Boundaries	Document specific items that are not within the scope of the project and any outside constraints to achieving goals and objectives.
Decision-making process	Ensure that the decision-making process or processes for the project are documented.
Signatures	Key staff signature sign off.

Checklist 10.2   Examples of Common Project-Level Risks

Category	*Risk*
Scope	Unrealistic or incomplete scope definition
	Scope statement not agreed to by all stakeholders
Schedule	Unrealistic or incomplete schedule development
	Unrealistic or incomplete activity estimates
Project management	Inadequate skills and ability of the project manager
	Inadequate skills and ability of business users or subject matter experts
	Inadequate skills and ability of vendors
	Poor project management processes
	Lack of or poorly designed change management processes
	Lack of or poorly designed risk management processes
	Inadequate tracking of goals/objectives throughout the implementation process.

Checklist 10.2   Examples of Common Project-Level Risks (Continued)

Category	Risk
Legal	Lack of legal authority to implement project
	Failure to comply with all applicable laws and regulations
Personnel	Loss of key employees
	Low availability of qualified personnel
	Inadequate skills and training
Financial	Inadequate project budgets
	Cost overruns
	Funding cuts
	Unrealistic or inaccurate cost estimates
Organizational/business	Lack of stakeholder consensus
	Changes in key stakeholders
	Lack of involvement by project sponsor
	Loss of project sponsor during project
	Changes in office leadership
	Organizational structure
Business	Poor timing of product releases
	Unavailability of resources and materials
	Poor public image
External	Input or interest
	Changes in related systems, programs, etc.
	Labor strikes or work stoppages
	Seasonal or cyclical events
	Lack of vendor and supply availability
	Financial instability of vendors and suppliers
	Contractor or grantee mismanagement

(continued)

Checklist 10.2   Examples of Common Project-Level Risks (Continued)

Category	Risk
Internal	Unavailability of business or technical experts
Technical	Complex technology
	New or unproven technology
	Unavailability of technology
Performance	Unrealistic performance goals
	Immeasurable performance standards
Cultural	Resistance to change
	Cultural barriers or diversity issues
Quality	Unrealistic quality objectives
	Quality standards unmet

Checklist 10.3 Ongoing Risk Management Monitoring for Projects

Review period[a]: _____

Section 1: Progress and Performance Indicators

Project Implementation or Outcome Objective	*Progress/ Performance Indicator*	*Status of Indicator*	*Are Additional Actions Needed?*	*Notes*
A				
B				
C				
D				

Section 2: Reassessment of Risks

Identified Risk	*Actions to Be Taken*	*Status and Effectiveness of Actions*	*Are Additional Actions Needed?*	*Notes*
1				
2				
3				
4				

[a] Managers should establish timeframes for periodic reviews in addition to ongoing monitoring of program data.

Checklist 10.4   To Ensure Risks Are Adequately Addressed in Project Plan

	Project Design		Project Implementation		
Risk Management Action	*Yes*	*No*	*Yes*	*No*	*Comments*
In developing the project plan, were stakeholders and experts outside the responsible project office consulted about their needs?					
Does the project plan address both internal and external hazards that could impede implementation or performance (see Checklist 10.2)?					
• Have all relevant laws and regulations been considered?					
• Have all safety/security concerns been considered (patient safety, animal safety, data and property security, etc.)?					
Has a strategy been implemented to prevent or mitigate all identified risks?					
Is reliable, up-to-date data available to allow tracking of project implementation and performance so that problems can be identified early?					
• If not, has an expectation been set that this will be done?					
Are expectations clear and reasonable for the project and for each team member (what, when, and how) and consistent with available resources?					

Checklist 10.4   To Ensure Risks Are Adequately Addressed in Project Plan (Continued)

	Project Design		Project Implementation		
Risk Management Action	*Yes*	*No*	*Yes*	*No*	*Comments*
Are mechanisms in place to ensure effective communication with responsible officials, both within the team and with other stakeholders as necessary?					
If problems occur, can decisions be made quickly?					
Does project have clear goals and objectives that are being continually tracked to ensure they are being achieved?					
Is there a clear statement of how the new process or system will be an improvement over the current process or system?					
Is there clear and accurate baseline data for comparing the new process to the old process?					
Is there a lessons-learned component so we will be able to use and share the good and bad lessons from the project?					

We've Reached the End of Chapter 10

Risk is inherent in all projects. The key to project success is to identify risk and then deal with it. Doing this requires the project manager to identify as many risks as possible, categorize those risks, develop a contingency plan to deal with each risk, and then measure and manage those risks.

References

Charette, R.N. 1989. *Software Engineering Risk Analysis and Management*. New York: McGraw-Hill/Intertext.

Hardaker, M. and B. Ward,1987. How to make a team work. *Harvard Business Review* 65 (6, November/December): 112, 6 p.

Keil M. 1998. A framework for identifying software project risks. *CACM* 41(11, November): 76–83.

Tan, D. 2002. "Quantitative Risk Analysis Step-By-Step." Retrieved from :http://www.sans. org/reading_room/whitepapers/auditing/849.php

U.S. Department of Transportation n.d. "Risk Assessment and Allocation." Retrieved from http://international.fhwa.dot.gov/riskassess/risk_hcm06_04.htm

Williams, R.C., J.A. Walker, and A.J. Dorofee.1997. Putting risk management into practice. *IEEE Software* (May) 14(3): 75–81.

Chapter 11

Balanced Scorecard and Procurement Management

In this chapter we examine the concept of procurement management, the need for a procurement plan, and the issue of outsourcing. External resources need to be carefully controlled, monitored, and measured.

Procurement has a direct relationship to the financial perspective of the balanced scorecard, although human resources issues would touch the remaining three perspectives of learning and growth, customer, and internal business process. Still, it is the financial aspects of procurement that have the most impact on the organization. Table 11.1 details a few related balanced scorecard measures and associated targets for this perspective.

Outsourcing

Outsourcing has been part of the IT landscape for some time. Quite a few companies have outsourced globally (i.e., offshored) to reduce project costs. Whether you outsource globally or closer to home, an analysis still must be done to determine feasibility of outsourcing and appropriateness of vendor selection. Both of these can be assisted by use of metrics.

Outsourcing is actually a three-phase process:

Phase 1. Analysis and evaluation
Phase 2. Needs assessment and vendor selection
Phase 3. Implementation and management

Table 11.1 Sample Procurement Measures for the Financial Perspective of a Balanced Scorecard

Measures	Targets (%)
Cost to spend ratio: Operational costs/purchasing obligations (goods and services purchased).	<1
Negotiated cost savings: Cost savings compared to total costs.	>=20
Costs avoided/total costs: Costs avoided compared to total costs. You can avoid costs by reusing hardware/software, utilizing a partner, etc.	>=10
Percentage of goods and services obtained through competitive procurement practices: Difference between average qualified bid and the cost of the successful bid. The sum of each calculation is aggregated into a new savings ratio for all transactions.	>=19

Phase 1. Analysis and Evaluation

In order to understand the services that need to be outsourced, organizational goals need to be identified, particularly the core competencies. Once the goals and core competencies are identified, information related to these activities is gathered to compare the cost of performing the functions in-house with the cost of outsourcing them. This enables the company to answer nonfinancial questions such as, "How critical are these functions/activities?" or "What are the dependencies on these activities?" or "Will this activity become a mission-critical activity?" This will help organizations reach decisions about whether to outsource. Long-term cost and investment implications, work morale, and support should also be considered.

Phase 2. Needs Assessment and Vendor Selection

The objective of this phase is to develop a detailed understanding of the needs of the organization and the capabilities of possible solution providers. In this phase a request for a proposal (RFP) is developed and delivered to applicable vendors. The RFPs need to be structured in a manner to facilitate assessment and comparison of the various vendors. The RFP should contain the complete requirements, problem that needs to be resolved, desires, and so on. A clearly structured and documented RFP also helps vendors understand and evaluate what a company is looking for and assists them in assessing whether they can provide the required service.

When evaluating the vendor proposals, the organization should look not only at the technological capability of the vendor but also at factors such as the vendor's financial stability, track record, and customer support reputation. Contacting the vendors' existing and previous clients would give the organization a good idea

Table 11.2 Pugh Matrix

Alternatives	Baseline	1	2	3	4	5
Criteria (mark with "+" or "–" or "S")						
Quality						
Cost						
Responsiveness						
Credentials						

about the vendor's abilities. A matrix, such as the one shown in Table 11.2, can be used to aid in the decision-making process.

1. Choose or develop the criteria for comparison and the weight (importance) of each.
2. Select the alternatives to be compared.
3. Generate scores. For each comparison the product should be evaluated as being better (+), the same (S), or worse (–).
4. Compute the total score.

We could give each of these criteria a weight and get the composite score of the alternate criterion to determine the better alternative. For each column, determine the total number of pluses, minuses, and sames. Alternately, take the sum of the alternate score multiplied by the weight of the criterion.

Once a vendor is selected, the organization needs to make sure that a fair and reasonable contract, beneficial to the organization, is negotiated. It is imperative that the organization clearly defines service levels and the consequences of not meeting them. Both parties should make sure that they understand the performance measurement criteria.

Phase 3. Implementation

The final phase in the outsourcing decision process is the implementation. During this phase a clear definition of the task needs to be identified and establishing a timeframe would be very helpful. Mechanisms need to be established to monitor and evaluate performance during the vendor's developmental process. This is important even after implementation to make sure that the outsourced tasks are being delivered by the vendor as they are supposed to be delivered. Ability to identify, communicate, and resolve issues promptly and fairly will help the company achieve mutual benefits and make a relationship successful.

Depending on the size of the outsourcing contract, the manager responsible for the program's delivery and integration may be responsible for all of the process, or only a part of it. These are the horizontal and vertical factors of outsourcing management. A manager of the horizontal process is often involved in the decision to outsource, and is then responsible for defining the work, selecting and engaging the vendor, and managing the delivery and completion of the program. This manager normally handles all day-to-day negotiations. With larger programs, particularly those on a global scale, there is often a decision taken at senior levels to outsource. A negotiation team is appointed to work through the complex agreements, usually under strict confidentiality, until the agreement is finalized and announced. It is then the role of the manager of the vertical component to implement and manage the ongoing program. Part of this role is the interpretation of the agreement, and identification of areas not covered by the agreement.

Procurement Planning

Procurement planning, which encompasses the outsourcing decision, should be every bit as rigorous as project planning. Once you've made a decision to go outside the organization, a procurement plan should be created. Although all companies do things differently, there are still some very common elements in a procurement plan. A sample plan is described in this section.

Description of the Project

The description provides an overview of the proposed procurement request. The project itself should be described. At a minimum, the project plan should be referenced. Those practicing configuration management will have the benefit of a standardized policy for configuration identification. Configuration identification incrementally establishes and maintains the definitive current basis for control and status accounting of a system and its configuration items (CIs) throughout their life cycle. The configuration identification process ensures that all processes have common sets of documentation as the basis for developing a new system, or modifying an old one. Hence, a project plan in this environment would have a unique identifying number and would be easily referenced.

The description should also indicate whether the project requires commercial-off-the-shelf (COTS), modified-off-the-shelf (MOTS), or custom software development. The percentage of each should be calculated. Other questions that should be answered by this section are:

1. Does the project require integration or is the project a stand-alone system with minimal integration?
2. What is the system maintenance strategy?

3. Which databases or legacy systems are required to be used or created?

Market Research

Market research, which is a marketing term, is related to the research one typically does when performing a feasibility study. Research needs to be done to determine what is available on the market: who the vendors are and what their products or services are. It is advisable to request meetings with customers of each product, preferably in a related industry. At a minimum, you will want to conduct a reference check detailing your findings as shown in Table 11.3.

Most importantly, you will want to assess the stability of the vendor company itself. How long has the company been in business? Is it in danger of being acquired or merged with another company? You then need to request a price estimate from interested bidders or sources.

The procurement plan should describe this effort in terms of approach to the market survey, functional requirements of the product or services to be acquired, prospective sources, and competitive environment.

Acquisition Methodology Steps

In this section of the procurement plan, the proposed acquisition methodology should be described. Describe why this will be a competitive or noncompetitive bid. If consultants are being used, explain why in-house staff can't be used.

Describe how sources for competition will be sought, promoted, and sustained throughout the acquisition. If competition is not contemplated or achievable, discuss the basis of that decision. Justify why the requirement(s) cannot be modified to take advantage of competition.

Describe the proposed procurement steps. For example, a request for proposal can be structured using all or a combination of a request for information (RFI), conceptual, technical, draft, and final proposal methodologies. Discuss key deliverables, including management plans and reports that will be used to monitor the contractor's performance. For best value solicitations, describe the evaluation factors and values (percentage or points) assigned for the functional/technical requirements. As shown in Table 11.4, the evaluation factors must be based on functional requirements.

Discuss the evaluation factors and scoring methodology. If appropriate, include additional scoring or evaluation worksheets as appendices, as shown in Tables 11.5 and 11.6. Discuss mandatory and desirable requirements and indicate if reference checks will be performed. If weighted scores are used, indicate how the weighted score is computed, and how the weighting is applied. Indicate why the weights were chosen, as shown in Table 11.7.

Table 11.3　Reference Check Statements

#	Bidder Name: _____	Did the response meet expectations?					
		RC1		RC2		RC3	
	Statement	Yes	No	Yes	No	Yes	No
1	Effectiveness of contractor collaboration with the on-site project manager						
2	Ability of contractor to facilitate discussions with other stakeholders						
3	Ability of the contractor to integrate easily with other project staff						
4	Overall satisfaction with contractor method of introducing issues/problems encountered on project						
5	Speed with which contractor brought forward identified issues						
6	Did contractor bring forward feasible solutions at the same time they presented issues or problems?						
7	Was the assignment of staff personnel stable?						
8	Were deliverables timely and in conformance with contract specifications?						
9	What was your overall satisfaction with contractor?						

Table11.4   Sample Evaluation Factors and Values

Evaluation Factor	Value Assigned (e.g., % or points)
Development and conversion	45
Training tasks and deliverables	25
Costs	30

Table 11.5   Mandatory Requirements

Requirement Number	Description of Requirement	Score

Table 11.6   Weighted Desirable Requirements

Requirement Number	Description of Requirement	Weight	Score	Weighted Score

Procurement Risk Management

In this section, methods to protect the company's investment and ensure adequate contractor performance are described. Protections might include:

1. Payment holdbacks
2. Performance bond requirements
3. Warranty provisions
4. Liquidated damage provisions

Like anything else in project management, procurement risks must be managed. This can be done similarly to the project risk management discussed in the last chapter. One of the most popular techniques is to include language in the statement of work (SOW) that requires the acceptance of deliverables for the company to pay the vendor's invoice. The vendor should be required to take timely and appropriate measures to correct or remediate the reason(s) for nonacceptance, and demonstrate that they have successfully completed the scheduled work for each deliverable before payment is made.

Table 11.7 Scoring Values

Score	Description
0	No Value: Fails to address the component or the bidder does not describe any experience related to the component.
1	Poor: Minimally addresses the component, but one or more major considerations of the component are not addressed. Low degree of confidence in the bidder's response or proposed solution.
2	Fair: The response addresses the component adequately, but minor considerations may not be addressed. Acceptable degree of confidence in the bidder's response or proposed solution.
3	Good: The response fully addresses the component and provides a good quality solution. Good degree of confidence in the bidder's response or proposed solution.
4	Very Good: All considerations of the component are addressed with a high degree of confidence in the bidder's response or proposed solution.
5	Excellent: All considerations of the component are addressed with the highest degree of confidence in the bidder's response or proposed solution. The response exceeds the requirements in providing a superior solution.

Contract Management Approach

In this section of the procurement plan, the project's specific approach, tools, and processes should be described, including:

1. Contract management plan
2. Issue and action item process
3. Problem tracking process
4. Status reporting process
5. System acceptance process
6. Invoice process
7. Deficiency management process
8. Dispute resolution process
9. Deliverable management process

Describe the tools used to manage the contract, contractual requirements, and deliverables (e.g., Microsoft Project and IBM's Rational RequisitePro). The status reporting approach, including written reports and meetings, should also be documented. Discuss how meeting minutes, issues, and action items are recorded, tracked, and resolved. Detail specific approaches to monitoring and managing contractor performance and how performance problems and issues will be resolved, including the dispute process and payment withholds/liquidated damages.

Perhaps the best way to manage risk is to prevent problems from happening in the first place. Keeping a tight rein over outsider contracts is critically important. Status meetings, walkthroughs, quality and performance management, and measurement techniques such as balanced scorecard should be used.

We've Reached the End of Chapter 11

Procurement in many organizations is a hit or miss affair. Project managers need to recognize that this is an important aspect of the project, as selecting the correct vendor (and solution) can make or break a project. The process of procurement management needs to be standardized, monitored, and measured.

Chapter 12

Balanced Scorecard and Project Termination

It's amazing how little attention project termination actually gets. Yet this is the project management phase that can ultimately determine success or failure. Most certainly, it's the step that can contribute to institutional knowledge through a careful gleaning of lessons learned. In this chapter, particular attention is given to the steps for project completion, the concept of change control, and project auditing using a balanced scorecard approach.

All Good Things Must Come to an End

All good things must come to an end. Projects do as well. For the most part, project termination is a carefully controlled process where the artifacts of the effort are evaluated and the resulting system turned over to *production*. However, not all projects actually make it that far.

The best possible ending for a system is that it is successfully completed and placed into production. From a systems development life cycle (SDLC) methdodology perspective this means the following:

1. The system is thoroughly tested (e.g., unit, system, integration, parallel and acceptance testing) and ultimately *accepted* by the end users. Many companies have quality assurance (QA) departments that are responsible for testing.

2. Procedure manuals are written, published, and disseminated to appropriate stakeholders. These include manuals for end users (i.e., how to use the system) and operators (i.e., how to run the system).
3. End users are trained.
4. The system is *turned over* to the systems operations group to be placed on the production computers. Computer systems are typically developed on a "development computer." The reason for this is to make sure that the programming *bugs* that often plague *systems-in-progress* do not negatively affect systems already being used by end users. As a one-time programmer I was personally responsible for *bringing down* computers on a weekly basis. Indeed, among programmers, it is a badge of honor to have one's bug bring down a computer. The process of turning over a system to be placed in production requires paperwork to be filled out specifying the program modules, databases, and other files to be moved from the development computer to the production computer.
5. Project completion reports are written and submitted to management. Depending upon the project, management might engage the marketing or public relations department to announce the introduction of the system to the organization's clients, suppliers, and public.
6. Project documentation is stored, usually in an online repository.
7. Project staff is reassigned. If contractors are used, these resources are reassigned or terminated as per the organization's contractual obligations.
8. Other project resources are reassigned (e.g., equipment).
9. System monitoring is put into place. These are metrics that measure the quality and reliability of the system, as shown in Table 12.1.
10. Once a system *goes into production* it is not forgotten. Because it is quite common that a project placed in production already has a list of requested changes waiting for it, a *maintenance* team is assigned to the system (i.e., change control). Often, members of the original development team are assigned this job.

Not all systems end successfully, however. A systems developer once worked on a project to bring voice recognition to the floor of a major stock exchange. They were not able to get the technology to distinguish voices from background noise on the floor of the exchange. This project, then, was a failure. Project termination in the event of failure still requires the project manager to:

1. Prepare a preliminary report and meet with management and end users.
2. Reassign resources after performing a performance evaluation on each human resource.
3. Terminate contracts, after meeting with attorneys.
4. Dispose of equipment.
5. Close out financial documents and audit final charges and costs.

Table 12.1 Internal Business Processes Metrics that Can Be Used to Increase System Reliability and Quality

Measures	Targets
Percentage reduction in demand for customer or tech support	>=25 percent
Number of end-user queries handled	Baseline
Average time to address an end-user problem	<=4 hours
Equipment downtime	<=1 percent
Mean time to failure	<=1000 hours
Percentage remaining known product faults	<=5 percent
Percentage of projects with lessons learned in database	>=95 percent
Fault density: Faults of a specific severity/thousand	<=3 percent
Defect density: Total number of unique defects detected during code inspection/thousand lines of code	<=3 percent
Cumulative failure: Failures per period	Baseline
Fault days number: Number of days that faults spend in the system from their creation to their removal	<=1
Functional test coverage: Number of requirements for which test cases have been completed/total number of software functional requirements	>=95 percent
Requirements traceability: Number of requirements met by the architecture/number of original requirements.	>=98 percent
Software maturity index: Number of functions in current delivery (adds + changes + deletes)/number of functions in current delivery	>=1
Percentage of conflicting requirements	<=5 percent
Test coverage (implemented capabilites/required capabilites)*(program primitives tested)/total program primitives)*100%. Note: Primitives are datatypes provided by a programming language as basic building blocks. This includes functions.	>=92 percent

(continued)

Table 12.1 Internal Business Processes Metrics That Can Be Used to Increase System Reliability and Quality (Continued)

Measures	Targets
Cyclomatic complexity: Equals the number of decisions plus one. Decisions are caused by conditional statements. In Visual Basic they are If, Then. Else, Select Case, For, Next, Do, Loop, and While, Wend/End While. The cyclomatic complexity of a procedure with no decisions equals 1. There is no maximum value because a procedure can have any number of decisions.	
Cyclomatic complexity, also known as V(G) or the graph-theoretic number, is calculated by simply counting the number of decision statements. A multiway decision, the select case statement, is counted as several decisions. This version of the metric does not count Boolean operators such as And and Or, even if they add internal complexity to the decision statements	
A high cyclomatic complexity denotes a complex procedure that's hard to understand, test, and maintain. There's a relationship between cyclomatic complexity and the "risk" in a procedure.	<=20
CC Type of procedure: Risk	
1–4 A simple procedure: Low	
5–10 A well-structured and stable procedure: Low	
11–20 A more complex procedure: Moderate	
21–50 A complex procedure, alarming: High	
>50 An error-prone, extremely troublesome, untestable procedure: Very high	
Percentage of project time allocated to quality testing	>=15 percent

6. Prepare final report, including information from steps 1 through 5.
7. Work with public relations, if necessary, to put the best possible face on a bad situation.
8. Update appropriate lessons-learned databases.

Figure 12.1 provides an overview of the close-out processes. Snedaker (2005) stresses that inputs to the final project close are the final project deliverables as well as the most current project plan. The course of action in this close-out phase is

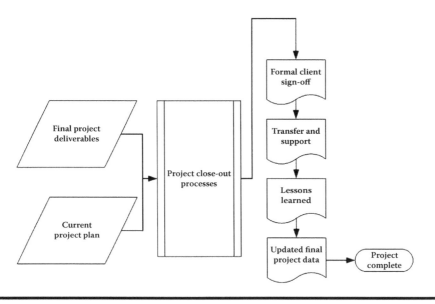

Figure 12.1   Close-out steps.

to update project data and documentation ensuring that deliverables are formally accepted and ongoing operations and support processes are in place.

It should also be noted that not all systems are terminated as a resolute *success* or *failure*. Sometimes a project is terminated midstream. There are a wide variety of possible reasons:

1. Requirements change
2. Regulations change
3. New technologies are introduced
4. Technologies in use are deemed obsolete
5. Functionality is outsourced or merged into another department or company
6. Employee illness, vacations, departure, and unanticipated developer-related difficulties in developing the system

Any one or more of these problems might serve to terminate a project prematurely. In all cases, information about the causes of the termination should be recorded quantitatively as well as qualitatively, where possible.

The Project Audit

Deciding whether to terminate a project midstream is not always easy. In fact, there are often mitigating factors that complicate the decision-making process. Lockheed, a major avionics company, continued on with the development of the

L1011 Tri-Star aircraft although the project accumulated enormous losses. Lockheed never really expected to earn a profit from it. Instead, they saw the L1011 as their re-entry into commercial aviation. The same can be said for Digital Equipment Corporation's AltaVista search engine. AltaVista was one of the first search engines on the Internet. Development and maintenance was costly, but Digital saw it as a vehicle for modernizing their company and improving their image. (Note: DEC was bought by Compaq, which itself was bought out by Hewlett Packard. AltaVista is now owned by Overture.)

As we've discussed, most projects are not clear successes or failures. What this means is that a particular project might reach a point where it is not really obvious to its stakeholders whether the project will ultimately be a success or a failure or whether it should be continued or terminated. Therefore, management should continually monitor all projects. Throughout the book, we've talked about project tracking and control. However, this is usually done from within the project team. A project audit is a form of project tracking and control that is done by people external to the project team.

The project audit reviews a large number of variables, including:

1. Schedule
2. Costs, including ongoing or annual costs
3. Technology
4. Risk
5. Probability of success
6. Investment return
7. Degree of innovation
8. Degree of linkage with other projects
9. Degree of management support
10. Degree of staff support
11. Resource use
12. Personnel
13. Information assets
14. Future trends

Shtub (1994) discusses a series of questions designed to provide management with a methodology for reaching the termination decision:

1. Did the organization's goals change sufficiently so that the original project definition is inconsistent with the current goals?
2. Does management still support the project?
3. Is the project's budget consistent with the organizational budget?
4. Are technological, cost, and scheduling risks acceptable?
5. Is the project still innovative? Is it possible to achieve the same results with current technology faster at lower cost without completing the project?
6. How is the project team's morale?

7. Can the team complete the project successfully?
8. Is the project still profitable and cost effective?
9. Can the project be easily integrated into the organization's functional units?
10. Is the project still current? Do sufficient environmental or technological changes make the project obsolete?
11. Are there opportunities to use the project's resources elsewhere that would be more cost effective or beneficial?

These questions need to be asked repeatedly throughout the project's life cycle. The responses to these questions, in conjunction with analysis of the project and budgetary issues we've already discussed earlier in this book, should give management the ammunition it needs to decide whether to red or green flag the project before a mistake might be made.

The project audit encompasses all four perspectives of the balanced scorecard. Representative objectives, measures, and targets can be seen in Table 12.2.

Change Control

Change happens. Once a system has been completed, it will inevitably need to be modified, for the general reasons listed below.

1. Requirements change. It is not uncommon for end users to start crafting their "wish lists" before a system ever gets placed in production. For the most part, project managers freeze changes to a system while the system is being constructed, hence the wish list. Most of the time changed requirements can be accommodated by the wish list process. However, there are occasions when the requirements have changed so dramatically there is no choice but to terminate the system and, perhaps, start again.
2. Regulations change. Many organizations are governed by a variety of state, local, and federal regulatory guidelines. These have a habit of changing. For example, the cellular phone number portability mandate will require extensive change to many systems. There might well be one or two in development mode that might be terminated altogether as a result of this regulatory modification.
3. New technologies are introduced.
4. Technologies in use are deemed obsolete.
5. Functionality is outsourced or merged into another department or company. Mergers and acquisitions have a way of terminating projects midstream for obvious reasons. Today's organizational propensity for outsourcing jobs to lower-cost countries affects a project.
6. Employee illness, vacations, departure, and unanticipated developer-related difficulties in developing the system.

Table 12.2 Project Audit Balanced Scorecard with All Four Perspective-Representative Measures

	Measures	*Targets*
Financial Objectives		
Optimize cost efficiency of purchasing	Cost to spend ratio	<1 percent
	Negotiated cost savings	>=20 percent
	Costs avoided/total costs	>=10 percent
	Percentage of goods and services obtained through competitive procurement practices	>=19 percent
Control costs	Dollar amount under IT budget	Baseline
	Dollar amount over budget	Baseline
	IT budget as a percentage of revenue	<=30 percent
	IT expenses per employee	<=35,000
Customer Objectives		
Increase customer satisfaction	Percentage of customers satisfied with system timeliness (speed)	>=92 percent
	Percentage of customers satisfied with responsiveness to questions	>=92 percent
	Percentage of customers satisfied with quality	>=92 percent
	Percentage of customers satisfied with sales/customer service representatives	>=92 percent
	Length of time to resolve disputes	<=4 hours
Conformance with customer requests	Percentage of baselined projects with a plan	>=90 percent
	Percentage customer requests satisfied	>=90 percent

Table 12.2   Project Audit Balanced Scorecard with All Four Perspective-Representative Measures (Continued)

	Measures	*Targets*
Internal Business Processes Objectives		
Improve development processes	Percentage resources devoted to planning and review of IT activities	>=25 percent
	Percentage resources devoted to applications development	Baseline
	Average time required to develop a standard-sized new application	Baseline
	Percentage of applications programming with reused code	>=80 percent
	Percentage of time spent to repair bugs and fine-tune new applications	<=10 percent
	Response time to answer design queries	<=4 hours
	Person-months of effort/project	Baseline
	Percentage requirements fulfilled	>=90 percent
	Number of code modules	Baseline
	Pages of documentation	Baseline
Learning and Growth Objectives		
Create a quality workforce	Percentage of employees meeting mandatory qualification standards	>=95 percent
	Percentage of voluntary separations	>=98 percent
	Percentage of leaders' time devoted to mentoring	>=45 percent
	Percentage of employees with certifications	>=54 percent
	Percentage of employees with degrees	>=75 percent
	Percentage of employees with three or more years of experience	>=75 percent

Change control combines human procedures and automated tools to provide a mechanism for the control of changes that, if uncontrolled, can rapidly lead a project to chaos. The change control process begins with a change request, leads to a decision to make or reject the request, and culminates with a controlled update of the software that is to be changed.

An organization is made up of many departments such as marketing, sales, and finance among others. All of these departments are called end-user departments and may make requests of the IT department. These requests for service may be for new systems or maintenance of an existing system, that is, change requests.

Most IT organizations have policies and procedures to control the flow of requests made to the IT department. End users are often required to fill out one or more forms that specify the type of change and the reason for the work request.

It is critically important to provide detailed instructions for:

1. Identifying changes
2. Requesting changes
3. Classifying
4. Documenting requests for changes
5. Change impact assessment
6. Change approval

As the new system is implemented and users begin to work with it, errors occur or changes are needed. Just as in the development of a new system, maintenance requires that steps be taken carefully in making changes or fixing errors. In the event of an error this can be even more critical. Each step of the maintenance process is similar to steps in the systems development life cycle, as shown in Figure 12.2. This is a logical extension of the development process, as changes are being made to the system that can affect the whole system and need to be controlled and measured.

SDLC					
Project identification and selection	Project initiation and planning	Analysis	Logical design	Physical design	Implementation
Obtain maintenance requests	Requests into changes		Design changes		Implementing changes
Maintenance					

Figure 12.2 The maintenance life cycle compared to the development life cycle.

Table 12.3 Represented Balanced Scorecard Metrics for Maintenance

Objectives	Measures	Target
Monitor change management	Number of change requests per month	Baseline
	Percentage of change to customer environment	Baseline
	Changes released per month	Baseline
Enhance applications portfolio	Age distribution of applications	Baseline
	Technical performance of applications portfolio	Baseline
	Rate of product acceptance	>=95 percent

An important part of managing maintenance is to understand and measure the effectiveness of the maintenance process. As a system is implemented, service requests may be quite high as bugs are still being worked out and needs for change are discovered. If the maintenance process is operating properly, an immediate decrease in failures should be seen. Good management of maintenance should include the recording of failures over time and analyzing these for effectiveness. If a decrease is not noticed the problem should be identified and resolved.

Another measure of success of the maintenance process is the time between failures. The longer the time between failures is, the more time can be spent on improving the system and not just fixing the existing system. Failures will happen, but more costly is the time spent fixing even the simplest failure.

Recording the type of failure is important to understanding how the failure happened and it can assist in avoiding failures in the future. As this information is recorded and maintained as a permanent record of the system, solutions can be developed that fix the root cause for a variety of failures.

Typical balanced scorecard objectives, measures, and targets for the internal business processes perspective are shown in Table 12.3. Note that we've included an objective for the Enhance Applications Portfolio. These metrics can be used as predictors of future maintenance requests. Some targets have the word "Baseline" encoded. Baseline indicates that the metric is informational; for example, only the raw value will be displayed (i.e., aggregated by the specified period: weekly, monthly, etc.). The targets should be set to default (or zero in the case of baselined targets).

We've Reached the End of Chapter 12

A project can be terminated for many reasons. Determining whether a project should be terminated can be decided through use of a project audit, which is generally done externally from the project team. Whatever the reason for termination, it is important that project close-out be planned and methodologically executed. Close-out steps include staff reassignment, project reporting, meetings, and project roll-downs via a lessons-learned brainstorming session.

If a project has been terminated via successful completion, the system will then move into maintenance mode where changes to the system must be managed, controlled, and measured.

References

Shtub, A., J. Bard, and S. Globerson. 1994. *Project Management: Engineering, Technology and Implementation*. Englewood Cliffs, NJ: Prentice-Hall.

Snedaker, S. 2005. *How to Cheat at IT Project Management*. Rockland, MA: Syngress.

Appendix A: Business Strategy Primer

You just heard through the company grapevine that your biggest competitor is about to launch the Web site to end all Web sites. From what you hear, this Web site is not only going to enable the competitor's customers to order online, but they'll also be able to check order status and even communicate real-time with sales staff. If this isn't bad enough, simultaneously your competitor will be turning on an internal Web site that will enable them to buy all of their supplies and parts online and even control and monitor their supply chain. Just how will you approach this challenge? At what issues will you look? Whom will you interview? What will you study?

Don't think this doesn't happen.

The success of Amazon.com came as a big surprise to Barnes & Noble. Who would have thought that a no-name virtual start-up would soon outpace and outsell the biggest bookseller in the world? Barnes & Noble (B&N) started life as a sleepy bookseller chain. In the late 1980s, it morphed itself into the largest chain of superstore bookstores in the United States. When the Internet crept onto the scene in the early 1990s, Barnes & Noble joined a host of other companies that took a wait and see approach to the newfangled concept of e-business. It waited and watched as tiny Amazon.com, a company no one had ever heard of, opened its e-doors in 1995. Unfortunately, it continued to wait and watch, as Amazon.com became the world's largest bookstore, leaving B&N in the dust.

B&N found out the hard way that it was impossible to compete without jumping on the e-business bandwagon. And jump it did, by launching barnesandnoble.com with German-based megamedia firm Bertlesmann in 1997. B&N's stated strategy is to be an e-commerce leader in the sale of books, music, and DVDs/videos. Although Amazon had the luxury of building its e-business from the ground up, Barnes & Noble was a well-established company. E-business, therefore, had to be retrofitted to existing business processes and functions. They geared up quickly, however, they still find themselves a very distant second to uber-bookstore Amazon.com.

Trying to replicate the profitable moves of the market leader, however, is fraught with danger in the online world. B&N found this out the hard way. In December of 1999, the U.S. District Court for the Western District of Washington issued a preliminary injunction to bar B&N from infringing on Amazon's patented "1-Click" shopping feature.

Competing with a first mover, particularly one as creative and dynamic as Amazon.com, is no mean feat. Over the years, Amazon has morphed from, as the media so succinctly put it, the Earth's biggest bookstore to the Earth's biggest anything store. B&N is in the process of morphing as well. It has begun to go beyond books and CDs and is now selling calendars, providing free courses, and selling the Nook, an e-book. Can other electronics and clothing be far behind?

The goal, then, is to create a viable strategic plan that will, if not make you a first mover, at least let you effectively compete with first movers. In the world of high-tech, this is often a make or break scenario.

Strategic Planning

It is said that, "Failing to plan is planning to fail." Strategic management can be defined as the art and science of formulating, implementing, and evaluating cross-functional decisions that enable an organization to achieve its objectives. Put simply, strategic management is planning for an organization's future. The plan becomes a roadmap to achieve the goals of the organization, with marketing as a centerpiece of this plan. Much as for a person taking a trip to another city, the roadmap serves as a guide for management to reach the desired destination. Without such a map, an organization can easily flounder.

The value of strategic planning for any business is to be proactive in taking advantage of opportunities while minimizing threats posed in the external environment. The planning process itself can be useful to rally the troops toward common goals and create "buy-in" to the final action plan. The important thing to consider in thinking about planning is that it is a process, not a one-shot deal. The strategy formulation process, which is shown in Figure A-1, includes the following steps:

1. Strategic planning to plan (assigning tasks, time, etc.)
2. Environmental scanning (identifying strengths and weaknesses in the internal environment and opportunities and threats in the external environment)
3. Strategy formulation (identifying alternatives and selecting appropriate alternatives)
4. Strategy implementation (determining roles and responsibilities, and timeframe)
5. Strategy evaluation (establishing specific benchmarks and control procedures, revisiting plan at regular intervals to update plan, etc.)

Figure A.1 Strategy formulation

Business tactics must be consistent with a company's competitive strategy. A company's ability to successfully pursue a competitive strategy depends upon its capabilities (internal analysis) and how these capabilities are translated into sources of competitive advantage (matched with external environment analysis). The basic generic strategies a company can pursue are shown in Figure A.2:

1. Cost leadership
    a. Lower prices
    b. Lower costs
    c. Experience curve
    d. "One size fits all"
    e. Large volume
    f. Conformance quality
    g. Example: Cheapest car wash in town (self-serve).
2. Differentiation
    a. Higher prices
    b. Product innovation
    c. Higher value added
    d. A product for each market
    e. High relative perceived quality
    f. Example: "Touch-Free" car wash (drive-through)

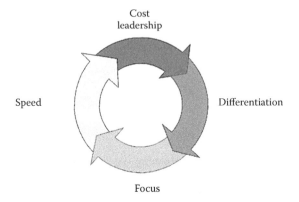

Figure A.2   Basic competitive strategies

3. Focus
    a. Specific customers
    b. Specific market segment
    c. Either focused cost leadership or focused differentiation
    d. Target cost leadership or differentiation strategy to specific segments of the market.
    e. Example: Car wash catering to high-end vehicles, hand detail, polish, wax specifically designed for Mercedes, Lexus, and so on.
4. Speed
    a. Speed of new product innovation and product introduction
    b. Example: Applies mainly to software and biotech products

In all strategy formulation, it is vital for the company to align the strategy tactics with its overall source of competitive advantage. For example, many small companies make the mistake of thinking that product giveaways are the best way to promote their business or add sales. In fact, the opposite effect may happen if there is a misalignment between price (lowest cost) and value (focus).

Michael Porter's (Harvard Business School) Five Forces model gives another perspective on an industry's profitability. This model helps strategists develop an understanding of the external market opportunities and threats facing an industry generally, which gives context to specific strategy options.

Specific strategies that a company can pursue should align with the overall generic strategy selected. Alternative strategies include forward integration, backward integration, horizontal integration, market penetration, market development, product development, concentric diversification, conglomerate diversification, horizontal diversification, joint venture, retrenchment, divestiture, liquidation, and a combined strategy. Each alternative strategy has many variations. For example, product development could include research and development pursuits, product improvement, and so on. Strategy selection will depend on management's assessment of the company's strengths, weaknesses, opportunities, and threats (SWOT) with consideration of strategic "fit." This refers to how well the selected strategy helps the company achieve its vision and mission.

Strategy Implementation

A 1999 study found that nearly 70 percent of strategic plans and strategies are never successfully implemented (Corboy and O'Corrbui, 1999). Strategies frequently fail because the market conditions they were intended to exploit change before the strategy takes effect. An example of this is the failure of many telecoms that were born based on projected pent-up demand for fiber-optic capacity fueled by the growth of the Internet. Before much of the fiber could even be laid, new technologies were introduced that permitted a dramatic increase of capacity on the existing infrastructure. Virtually overnight, the market for fiber collapsed (Sterling, 2003).

Over a three-year period Downes (2001) studied strategy execution mistakes and concluded that the execution obstacles are of two varieties: problems generated by forces external to the company, as our telecom example demonstrates, and problems internal to the company. According to Downes, internal issues test the flexibility of companies to launch initiatives that represent significant departures from longstanding assumptions about who they are and what they do. Can they develop new marketing techniques appropriate to new channels without destroying existing brand equity? Can they integrate new software into their infrastructure? Can they align their human resources?

What could these companies have done to ensure that their programs and initiatives were implemented successfully? Did they follow best practices? Were they aware of the initiative's critical success factors? Was there sufficient senior-level involvement? Was planning thorough and all-encompassing? Were their strategic goals aligned throughout the organization? And most important, were their implementation plans able to react to continual change?

Although planning is an essential ingredient for success, implementing a strategy requires more than just careful initiative planning. Allocating resources, scheduling, and monitoring are indeed important, but it's often the intangible or unknown that gets in the way of ultimate success. The ability of the organization to adapt to the dynamics of fast-paced change as well as the desire of executive management to support this challenge is what really separates the successes from the failures.

TiVo was presented with a challenge when it opted to, as its CEO puts it, "forever change the way the world watches TV." The company pioneered the digital video recorder (DVR), which enables viewers to pause live TV and watch it on their own schedules. There are millions of self-described "rabid" users of the TiVo service. In a company survey, over 40 percent said they'd sooner disconnect their cell service than unplug their TiVo.

TiVo is considered disruptive technology because it forever changes the way the public does something. According to Forbes.com's Sam Whitmore (2004), no other $141 million company has come even close to transforming government policy, audience measurement, direct response and TV advertising, content distribution, and society itself.

But TiVo started off on shaky footing and continues to face challenges that it must address to survive. Therefore, TiVo is an excellent example of continual adaptive strategic implementation and is worth study.

Back in the late 1990s Michael Ramsey and James Barton, two forward thinkers, came up with the idea that would ultimately turn into TiVo. They quickly assembled a team of marketers and engineers to bring their product to market and unveiled their product at the National Consumer Electronics show in 1999. TiVo hit the shelves a short four months later. Ramsey and Barton, founders and C-level executives, were actively involved every step of the way, a key for successful strategic implementations.

Hailed as the "latest, greatest, must have product" TiVo was still facing considerable problems. The first was consumer adoption rates. It takes years before any new technology is widely adopted by the public at large. To stay in business, TiVo needed a way to jumpstart its customer base. On top of that the firm was bleeding money so it had to find a way to staunch the flow of funds out of the company.

Their original implementation plan did not include solutions to these problems. But the firm reacted quickly to their situation by jumping into a series of joint ventures and partnerships that would help them penetrate the market and increase their profitability. An early partnership with Philips Electronics provided them with funding to complete their product development. Deals with DirectTV, Comcast Interactive, and other satellite and cable companies gave TiVo the market penetration it needed to be successful. The force behind this adaptive implementation strategy was Ramsey and Barton, TiVo's executive management team. Because implementations often engender a high degree of risk, the executive team must be at the ready should there be a need to go to "Plan B". Ramsey and Barton's willingness to jump into the fray to find suitable partnerships enabled TiVo to stay the course and stay in business.

But success is often fleeting, which is why performance monitoring and a continual modification of both the strategic plan and resulting implementation plan is so very important. Here again the presence of executive oversight must loom large. Executive management must review progress on an almost daily basis for important strategic implementations. Although many executives might be content just to speak to their direct reports, an actively engaged leader will always involve others lower on the chain of command. This approach has many benefits, including reinforcing the importance of the initiative throughout the ranks and making subordinate staff feel as if they are an important part of the process. The importance of employee buy-in to strategic initiatives cannot be underestimated in terms of ramifications for the success of the ultimate implementation. Involved, excited, and engaged employees lead to success. Unhappy, fearful, disengaged employees do not.

TiVo competes in the immense and highly competitive consumer electronics industry where being a first mover (Porter, 1980) isn't always a competitive advantage. Competition comes in fast and hard. ReplayTV and EchoStar, the owner of the DISH network, with over seven million subscribers, are direct competitors. It's the indirect competitors, however, for which TiVo needs to watch out. Although Microsoft phased out its UltimateTV product, the company still looms large by integrating some extensions into its Windows operating system that provide similar DVR functionality. TiVo's main indirect competitor (Pearce and Robinson, 2005), however, is digital cable's pay-per-view and video-on-demand services. The question becomes: will DVRs be relegated to the technological trash heap of history where they can keep company with the likes of Betamax and eight-track tapes? Again, this is where executive leadership is a must if implementation is to be successful. Leaders must continually assess the environment and make adjustments to the organization's strategic plan and resulting implementation plans. They must provide their staff with the flexibility and resources to quickly adapt to changes that might result from this reassessment.

In spite of all its partnerships, the massive market for TiVo has yet to materialize. In the United Kingdom, TiVo stopped selling its DVRs in 2003 giving credence to the "flop theory." Part of the reason is that despite its rabid customer base and multiple partnerships, widespread adoption of the technology continues to be slow. There are several reasons for this. One is the perceived lack of privacy. Because the device is truly personal it is quite possible to track exact viewing habits. There have been at least two humorous TV movies on attempts by some men to outfox their machines by recording lots of macho war movies, therefore causing their TiVos to gather incorrect preference data ("UK company: Heave ho, TiVo!," 2003). TiVo's reaction to this problem was renewed vigor in informing its customers of its privacy and opt-out policies. TiVo is combating consumer lethargy through a combination of consumer education, benefits-focused advertising, and clever product placement on popular TV.

An even bigger challenge is the changing face of its partnerships. In 2005, DirecTV sold off all but the company's core satellite TV operations. Among the assets sold were its TiVo equity partnership. Given this particular challenge, it's not too surprising that TiVo has begun to search for new paths for its technology, essentially continually updating its implementation plan as conditions change. They continue to seek partnerships with content providers, consumer electronics manufacturers, and technology providers to focus on the development of interactive video services. One of its more controversial ideas was the promotion of "advertainment". These are special-format commercials that TiVo downloads onto its customers' devices to help advertisers establish what TiVo calls "far deeper communications" with consumers.

TiVo continues to try to dominate the technology side of the DVR market by constant R&D. They currently have 70 granted patents and 106 patents pending ("TiVo granted eight new domestic and foreign patents," 2005). Even if TiVo—the product—goes under, TiVo's intellectual property will provide a continuing strategic asset.

Heraclitus, a Greek philosopher living in the sixth century, BC said, "Nothing endures but change." That TiVo has survived up to this point is a testament to their willingness to adapt to continual change. That they managed to do this when so many others have failed demonstrates a wide variety of strategic planning and implementation skillsets. They have an organizational structure that is able to adapt quickly to whatever change is necessary. Although a small company, their goals are carefully aligned throughout the organization, at the organizational, divisional, as well as employee level. Everyone at TiVo has bought into the plan and is willing to do what it takes to be successful. They have active support from the management team, a critical success factor for all strategic initiatives. Most important, they are skillful at performance management. They are acutely aware of all environmental variables (i.e., competition, global economies, consumer trends, employee desires, industry trends, etc.) that might affect their outcomes and show incredible resourcefulness and resiliency in their ability to reinvent themselves.

Pearce and Robinson (2005) assert that "The strategy and the firm must become one." In doing so the firm's managers must direct and control actions and outcomes and, most critically, adjust to change. Executive leadership can do this by not only being actively engaged themselves but in making sure all employees involved in the implementation are on the same page. How is this done? There are several techniques, including the ones already mentioned. Executive leadership should frequently review the progress of the implementation and jump into the fray when required. This might translate to finding partnerships, as was the case with TiVo, or simply quickly signing off on additional resources or funding. More importantly, executive leadership must be an advocate—cheerleader—for the implementation with an eye toward rallying the troops behind the program. Savvy leaders can accomplish this through frequent communications with subordinate employees. Inviting lower-level managers to meetings, such that they become advocates within their own departments, is a wonderful method for cascading strategic goals throughout the organization. E-mail communications, speeches, and newsletters also provide a pulpit for getting the message across.

Executive leadership should also be mindful that the structure of the organization can have a dramatic impact on the success of the implementation, as Pearce and Robinson discuss. The authors dissect the twenty-first century organizational structure that includes the following characteristics: bottom-up, inspirational, employees and free agents, flexible, change, and "no compromise" to name a few. Merge all of this with a fair rewards system and compensation plan and you have all the ingredients for a successful implementation. As you can see, organizational structure, leadership, and culture are the key drivers for success.

Implementation Problems

Microsoft was successful at gaining control of people's living rooms through the Trojan horse strategy of deploying the now ubiquitous Xbox. Hewlett Packard was not so successful in raising its profile and cash flow by acquiring rival computer maker Compaq, to the detriment of its CEO, who was ultimately ousted. Segway, the gyroscope-powered human transport brainchild of the brilliant Dean Kamen, received a lukewarm reception from the public. Touted as "the next great thing" by the technology press, the company had to re-engineer its implementation plan to reorient its target customer base from the general consumer to specific categories of consumers, such as golfers and cross-country bikers, as well as businesses.

Successful implementation is essentially a framework that relies on the relationship among the following variables: strategy development, environmental uncertainty, organizational structure, organizational culture, leadership, operational planning, resource allocation, communication, people, control, and outcome (Okumus, 2003). One major reason why so many implementations fail is that there are no practical, yet theoretically sound, models to guide the implementation process. Without an adequate model, organizations try to implement strategies without a good understanding of the multiple variables that must be simultaneously addressed to make implementation work (Alexander, 1991).

In HP's case one could say that the company failed in its efforts at integrating Compaq because it did not clearly identify the various problems that surfaced as a result of the merger, and then use a rigorous problem-solving methodology to find solutions to the problems. Segway, on the other hand, framed the right problem (i.e., "the general consumer is disinterested in our novel transport system") and ultimately identified alternatives such that they could realize their goals.

The key is first to recognize that there is a problem. This isn't always easy as there will be differences of opinions among the various managerial groups as to whether one exists and as to what the problem actually is. In HP's case the problems started early on when the strategy to acquire Compaq was first announced. According to one fund manager who didn't like the company before the merger, the acquisition just doubled the size of its worst business (De Aenlle, 2005). We should also ask about the role of executive leadership in either assisting in the problem determination process or verifying that the right problem has indeed been selected. Although HP's Carly Fiorina did a magnificent job of implementing her strategy using what Pearce and Robinson (2005) describe as the three key levers (i.e., organizational structure, leadership, and culture), she most certainly dropped the ball by disengaging from the process and either not recognizing that there was a problem within HP or just ignoring the problem for other priorities. Elizabeth Bailey (2003), a director on diverse boards including CSX and Honeywell, says that the management team needs to pull together to solve problems. The goal is to help position the company for the future. You are not just dealing with the issues of the day, but you are always looking for the set of issues that are over the next hill. A management team that is working well sees the next hill, and the next hill. It's problem solving at its highest degree.

There are many questions that should be asked when an implementation plan appears to go off track. Is it a people problem? Was the strategy flawed in the first place? Is it an infrastructural problem? An environmental problem? Is it a combination of problems? Asking these questions will enable you to gather data that will assist in defining the right problem to be solved. Of course, responding yes to any one or more of these questions is only the start of the problem-definition phase of problem solving. You must also drill down into each of these areas to find the root causes of the problem. For example, if you determine there is a people problem, you then have to identify the specifics of this particular problem. For example, in a company that has just initiated an offshoring program, employees may feel many emotions: betrayed, bereft, angry, scared, and overwhelmed. Unless management deals with these emotions at the outset of the offshoring program, employee productivity and efficiency will undoubtedly be negatively affected.

Radical change to the work environment may also provoke more negatively aggressive behavior. When the U.S. Post Office first automated its postal clerk functions management shared little about what was being automated. The rumor mill took over and somehow employees got the idea that massive layoffs were in the works. Feeling that they needed to fight back, some postal employees actually sabotaged the new automated equipment. Had management just taken a proactive approach by providing adequate and continuing communications to the employees prior to the automation effort none of this would have happened. Dr. Lyle Sussman, chairman and professor of management, University of Louisville, (Lynch, 2003) neatly sums up management's role in avoiding people problems through use of what he calls "the new metrics": return on intellect (ROI), return on attitude (ROA), and return on excitement (ROE). As the title of the Lynch article suggests, it is important that leaders challenge the process, inspire a shared vision, enable others to act, model the way, and encourage the heart.

It is also quite possible to confuse symptoms of a problem with the problem itself. For example, when working with overseas vendors it is sometimes hard to reach these people due to the difference in time zones. This is particularly true when working with Asian firms, as they are halfway across the globe. Employees working with these external companies might complain of lack of responsiveness when the actual problem is that real-time communications with these companies are difficult due to time zone problems. The problem, then, is not "lack of responsiveness" by these foreign vendors, but lack of an adequate set of technologies that enable employees and vendors to more easily communicate across different time zones, vast distances, and in different languages (i.e., Webcast tools and instant messaging tools are all being used for these purposes).

Once the problem has been clearly framed, the desired end state and goals need to be identified and some measures created so that it can be determined whether the end state has actually been achieved. Throughout the problem-solving process relevant data must be collected and the right people involved. Nowhere are these two seemingly simple caveats more important than in identifying the end state and the metrics that will be used to determine whether your goals have been achieved.

Strategy implementation usually involves a wide variety of people in many departments. Therefore, there will be many stakeholders that will have an interest in seeing the implementation succeed (or fail). To assure success, the implementation manager needs to make sure that these stakeholders are aligned and have bought into the strategy and will do whatever it takes to identify and fix the problems that have been identified. The definition of the end state and associated metrics are best determined in cooperation with these stakeholders, but must be overseen and approved by management. Once drafted, these must become part of the operational control system.

In recent years the balanced scorecard approach has been linked to strategy implementation. The scorecard technique aims to provide managers with the key success factors of a business and to facilitate the alignment of business operations with the overall strategy (Kaplan and Norton, 1996). Kaplan and Norton addressed strategy implementation specifically in their approach by identifying four main implementation factors: (1) clarifying and translating the vision and strategy, (2) communication and linking, (3) planning and target setting, and (4) strategic feedback and learning. Each of the four balanced scorecard perspectives, as shown in Figure A.3, has associated metrics and other indicators that can be used to assess the success of an implementation. If the implementation was properly planned, and performance planning and measurement well integrated into the implementation

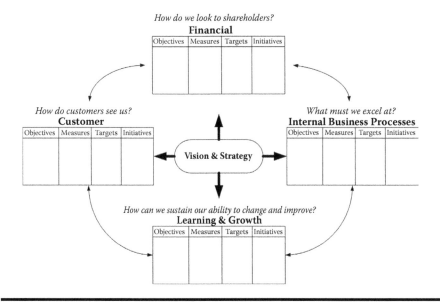

Figure A.3   The four balanced scorecard perspectives

plan, a variety of metrics and triggers will already be available for review and possible adaptation to the current problem-solving task.

A variety of alternatives will probably be identified by the manager. Again, the quality and quantity of these alternatives will be dependent upon the stakeholders involved in the process. Each alternative will need to be assessed to determine: (1) viability, (2) completeness of the solution (i.e., does it solve 100 percent of the problem, 90 percent, 50 percent, etc.), (3) costs of the solution, (4) resources required by the solution, and (5) any risk factors involved in implementing the alternative. In a failed implementation situation that resulted from a variety of problems, there might be an overwhelming number of possible alternatives. None of these might be a perfect fit. For example, replacing an overseas vendor gone out of business only solves a piece of the problem and, by itself, is not a complete solution. In certain situations it is quite possible that a complete solution might not be available. It might also be possible that no solution is workable. In this case, a host of negative alternatives such as shutting down the effort or selling the product/service/division might need to be evaluated.

Once a decision is made on the appropriate direction to take, based on the alternative or combination of alternatives selected, a plan must be developed to implement the solution. We can either develop an entirely new implementation plan or fix the one we already have. There are risks and rewards with either approach and the choice you make will depend upon the extent of the problems you identified in the original plan.

Strategic planning is not a one-time event. It is rather a process involving a continuum of ideas, assessment, planning, implementation, evaluation, readjustment, revision, and, most of all, good management.

References

Alexander, L.D. 1991. Strategy implementation: Nature of the problem, in D. Hussey (Ed.), *International Review of Strategic Management* (Vol. 18, pp. 91–97). New York: John Wiley & Sons.

Bailey, E. 2003. Interview with Elizabeth Bailey. Retrieved December 15, 2009 from http://execed.wharton.upenn.edu/ebuzz/0306/thoughtleadersi.html

Corboy. M. and D. O'Corrbui. 1999. The seven deadly sins of strategy. *Management Accounting* 77(10, November).

De Aenlle, C. 2005. See you, Carly. Goodbye, Harry. Hello Investors. *The New York Times* March 13.

Downes, L. 2001. Strategy can be deadly – Industry trend or event. *The Industry Standard* May 14. Retrieved December 15, 2009, from http://findarticles.com/p/articles/mi_m0HWW/is_19_4/ai_75213359/

Kaplan, R.S. and D.P. Norton. 1996. *The Balanced Scorecard – Translating Strategy into Action*. Boston: Harvard Business School Press.

Lynch, K. 2003. Leaders challenge the process, inspire a shared vision, enable others to act, model the way, encourage the heart. *The Kansas Banker* 93(4, April).

Okumus, F. 2003. A framework to implement strategies in organizations. *Management Decision* 41(9).

Pearce, H.A. and R.B. Robinson. 2005. *Strategic Management: Formulation, Implementation and Control.* 9th ed. New York: McGraw-Hill-Irwin.

Porter, M.E. 1980. *Competitive Strategy.* New York: Free Press.

Sterling, J. 2003. Translating strategy into effective implementation: Dispelling the myths and highlighting what works. *Strategy and Leadership* 31(3): 27–34.

TiVo granted eight new domestic and foreign patents. 2005. *PR Newswire* March 1.

UK company: Heave ho, TiVo! 2003. *EIU ViewsWire* February 7.

Whitmore, S. 2004. What TiVo teaches us. *Forbes*, July 7:174(1).

Appendix B: Value Measuring Methodology

The purpose of the value measuring methodology (VMM) is to define, capture, and measure value associated with electronic services unaccounted for in traditional return-on-investment (ROI) calculations, to fully account for costs, and to identify and consider risk. Developed in response to the changing definition of value brought on by the advent of the Internet and advanced software technology, VMM incorporates aspects of numerous traditional business analysis theories and methodologies, as well as newer hybrid approaches.

VMM was designed to be used by organizations across the federal government to steer the development of an e-government initiative, assist decision makers in choosing among investment alternatives, provide the information required to manage effectively, and maximize the benefit of an investment to the government.

VMM is based on public and private sector business and economic analysis theories and best practices. It provides the structure, tools, and techniques for comprehensive quantitative analysis and comparison of value (benefits), cost, and risk at the appropriate level of detail.

This appendix provides a high-level overview of the four steps that form the VMM framework. The terminology used to describe the steps should be familiar to those involved in developing, selecting, justifying, and managing an IT investment:

Step 1: Develop a decision framework
Step 2: Alternatives analysis
Step 3: Pull the information together
Step 4: Communicate and document

Step 1. Develop a Decision Framework

A decision framework provides a structure for defining the objectives of an initiative, analyzing alternatives, and managing and evaluating ongoing performance. Just as an outline defines a paper's organization before it is written, a decision framework creates an outline for designing, analyzing, and selecting an initiative for investment, and then managing the investment. The framework can be a tool that management uses to communicate its agency, governmentwide, or focus-area priorities.

The framework facilitates establishing consistent measures for evaluating current or proposed initiatives. Program managers may use the decision framework as a tool to understand and prioritize the needs of customers and the organization's business goals. In addition, it encourages early consideration of risk and thorough planning practices directly related to effective e-government initiative implementation.

The decision framework should be started as early as possible in the development of a technology initiative. Employing the framework at the earliest phase of development makes it an effective tool for defining the benefits that an initiative will deliver, the risks that are likely to jeopardize its success, and the anticipated costs that must be secured and managed. The decision framework is also helpful later in the development process as a tool to validate the direction of an initiative, or to evaluate an initiative that has already been implemented.

The decision framework consists of value (benefits), cost, and risk structures, as shown in Figure B.1. Each of these three elements must be understood to plan, justify, implement, evaluate, and manage an investment.

The tasks and outputs involved with creating a sound decision framework include:

Tasks
1. Identify and define value structure.
2. Identify and define risk structure.

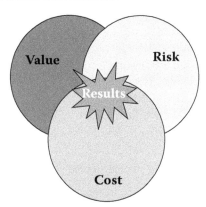

Figure B.1   The decision framework.

3. Identify and define cost structure.
4. Begin documentation.

Outputs
1. Prioritized value factors
2. Defined and prioritized measures within each value factor
3. Risk factor inventory (initial)
4. Risk tolerance boundary
5. Tailored cost structure
6. Initial documentation of basis of estimate of cost, value, and risk

Task 1: Identify and Define the Value Structure

The value structure describes and prioritizes benefits in two layers. The first considers an initiative's ability to deliver value within each of the five value factors (user value, social value, financial value, operational and foundational value, and strategic value). The second layer delineates the measures to define those values.

By defining the value structure, managers gain a prioritized understanding of the needs of stakeholders. This task also requires the definition of metrics and targets critical to the comparison of alternatives and performance evaluation.

The value factors consist of five separate, but related, perspectives on value. As defined in Figure B.2, each factor contributes to the full breadth and depth of the value offered by the initiative. Because the value factors are usually not equal in importance, they must be weighted in accordance to their importance to executive management.

Identification, definition, and prioritization of measures of success must be performed within each value factor, as shown in Figure B.3. Valid results depend on project staff working directly with representatives of user communities to define

Value Factor	Definitions and Examples
Direct Customer (User)	Benefits to users or groups associated with providing a service through an electronic channel
	Example: Convenient Access
Social (Nonuser/Public)	Benefits to society as a whole
	Example: Trust in government
Govt/Operational Foundational	Improvements in government operations and enablement of future initiatives
	Example: Cycle Time; Improved Infrastructure
Strategic/Political	Contributions to achieving strategic goals, priorities, and mandates
	Example: Fulfilling the organizational mission
Government Financial	Financial benefits to both sponsoring and other agencies
	Example: Reduced cost of correcting errors

Figure B.2   Value factors.

Direct User Value Factor		
Concise, Illustrative Name		
24/7 Access to Real-Time Information & Services, Anytime & Anywhere		
Brief Description		
Are customers able access real-time electronic travel services and policy information from any location 24 hours a day?		
Metrics and Scales		
	% of remote access attempts that are successful (10 points for every 10%)	
	% of travel services available electronically 10 points = 25% 90 points = 75% (threshold requirement) 100 points = 100%	
	Is data updated in the system in real time? No = 0 Yes = 100	

Figure B.3   A value factor with associated metrics.

and array the measures in order of importance. These measures are used to define alternatives, and also serve as a basis for alternatives analysis, comparison, and selection, as well as ongoing performance evaluation.

In some instances, measures may be defined at a higher level to be applied across a related group of initiatives, such as organizationwide or across a focus-area portfolio. These standardized measures then facilitate "apples-to-apples" comparisons across multiple initiatives. This provides a standard management yardstick against which to judge investments.

Whether a measure has been defined by project staff or at a higher level of management, it must include the identification of a metric, a target, and a normalized scale. The normalized scale provides a method for integrating objective and subjective measures of value into a single decision metric. The scale used is not important; what is important is that the scale remain consistent.

The measures within the value factors are prioritized by representatives from the user and stakeholder communities during facilitated group sessions.

Task 2: Identify and Define Risk Structure

The risk associated with an investment in a technology initiative may degrade performance, impede implementation, or increase costs. Risk that is not identified cannot be mitigated or managed causing a project to fail either in the pursuit of funding or, more dramatically, during implementation. The greater the attention paid to mitigating and managing risk, the greater the probability of success.

The risk structure serves a dual purpose. First, the structure provides the starting point for identifying and inventorying potential risk factors that may jeopardize an initiative's success and ensures that plans for mitigating their impact are developed and incorporated into each viable alternative solution.

Second, the structure provides management with the information it needs to communicate their organization's tolerance for risk. Risk tolerance is expressed in terms of cost (what is the maximum acceptable cost "creep" beyond projected cost) and value (what is the maximum tolerable performance slippage).

Risks are identified and documented during working sessions with stakeholders. Issues raised during preliminary planning sessions are discovered, defined, and documented. The result is an initial risk inventory. To map risk tolerance boundaries, selected knowledgeable staff are polled to identify at least five data points that will define the highest acceptable level of risk for cost and value.

Task 3: Identify and Define the Cost Structure

A cost structure is a hierarchy of elements created specifically to accomplish the development of a cost estimate, and is also called a cost element structure (CES).

The most significant objective in the development of a cost structure is to ensure a complete, comprehensive cost estimate and to reduce the risk of missing costs or double counting. An accurate and complete cost estimate is critical for an initiative's success. Incomplete or inaccurate estimates can result in exceeding the budget for implementation, requiring justification for additional funding or a reduction in scope. The cost structure developed in this step is used during Step 2 to estimate the cost for each alternative.

Ideally, a cost structure will be produced early in development, prior to defining alternatives. However, a cost structure can be developed after an alternative has been selected or, in some cases, in the early stage of implementation. Early structuring of costs guides refinement and improvement of the estimate during the progress of planning and implementation.

Task 4: Begin Documentation

Documentation of the elements leading to the selection of a particular alternative above all others is the *audit trail* for the decision. The documentation of assumptions, the analysis, the data, the decisions, and the rationale behind them, are the foundation for the business case and the record of information required to defend a cost estimate or value analysis.

Early documentation will capture the conceptual solution, desired benefits, and attendant global assumptions (e.g., economic factors such as the discount and inflation rates). The documentation also includes project-specific drivers and assumptions, derived from tailoring the structures.

The basis for the estimate, including assumptions and business rules, should be organized in an easy-to-follow manner that links to all other analysis processes and requirements. This will provide easy access to information supporting the course of action, and will also ease the burden associated with preparing investment justification documents. As an initiative evolves through the life cycle, becoming better defined and more specific, the documentation will also mature in specificity and definition.

Step 2. Alternatives Analysis: Estimate Value, Costs, and Risk

An alternatives analysis is an estimation and evaluation of all value, cost, and risk factors (Figure B.4) leading to the selection of the most effective plan of action to address a specific business issue (e.g., service, policy, regulation, business process, or system). An alternative that must be considered is the *base case*. The base case is the alternative where no change is made to current practices or systems. All other alternatives are compared against the base case, as well as to each other.

An alternatives analysis requires a disciplined process to consider the range of possible actions to achieve the desired benefits. The rigor of the process to develop the information on which to base the alternatives evaluation yields the data required to justify an investment or course of action. It also provides the information required to support the completion of the budget justification documents. The process also produces a baseline of anticipated value, costs, and risks to guide the management and ongoing evaluation of an investment.

Defining Risk

In the assessment of an e-Travel initiative, risks were bundled into five categories; cost, technical, schedule, operational, and legal.

The following sample table demonstrates how a single "risk factor" is likely to impact multiple risk categories. Note the level of detail provided in the description. Specificity is critical to distinguish among risks and avoid double counting.

Selected e-Travel Initiative Risks by Risk Category	Cost	Tech	Sch.	Op.	Legal
Different agencies have different levels and quality of security mechanisms, which may leave government data vulnerable. Web-enabled system will have increased points of entry for unauthorized internal or external users and pose greater security risks.	X	X			
The e-Travel concept relies heavily on technology. Although the private sector has reduced travel fees and operational costs by implementing e-Travel services, the commercial sector has not yet widely adopted/developed end-to-end solutions that meet the broad needs (single end-to-end electronic system) articulated by the e-Travel initiative. The technology and applications may not be mature enough to provide all of the functionality sought by the e-Travel initiative managers.	X	X	X	X	
Resistance to change may be partially due to fear of job loss, which may lead to challenges from unions.			X	X	X

Figure B.4 Risk can be bundled across categories.

VMM In Action

Predicting Performance

Example 1: This measure was established for an e-Travel initiative in the Direct User Value Factor.

Value	10	20	30	40	50	60	70	80	90	100
Average # hours from receipt of customer feedback message to response	48.00	44.67	41.33	38.00	34.67	31.33	28.00	24.67	21.33	18.00

Analysts projected the low, expected, and high performance for that measure.

	Low	Expected	High
Average # hours from receipt of customer feedback message to response	38	24	18

The model translated those projections onto the normalized scale.

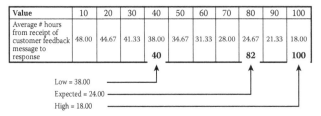

Example 2: This measure was established for Alternative 2 in the Direct User Value Factor. The normalized scale set for this measure was binary.

Normalized Value Scale

Value Points	0	10	20	30	40	50	60	70	80	90	
Duplicative Entry of Data	Yes										NO

Figure B.5 Predicting performance.

An alternatives analysis must consistently assess the value, cost, and risk associated with more than one alternative for a specific initiative. Alternatives must include the base case and accommodate specific parameters of the decision framework. VMM, properly used, is designed to avoid "analysis paralysis."

The estimation of cost and projection of value uses ranges to define the individual elements of each structure. Those ranges are then subject to an uncertainty analysis (see Note 1). The result is a range of expected values and cost. Next, a sensitivity analysis (see Note 2) identifies the variables that have a significant impact on this expected value and cost. The analyses will increase confidence in the accuracy of the cost and predicted performance estimates (Figure B.5). However, a risk analysis is critical to determine the degree to which other factors may drive up expected costs or degrade predicted performance.

An alternatives analysis must be carried out periodically throughout the life cycle of an initiative. The following list provides an overview of how the business value resulting from an alternatives analysis changes depending on where in the life cycle the analysis is conducted.

1. Strategic Planning (predecisional)
   a. How well will each alternative perform against the defined value measures?
   b. What will each alternative cost?
   c. What is the risk associated with each alternative?
   d. What will happen if no investment is made at all (base case)?
   e. What assumptions were used to produce the cost estimates and value projections?
2. Business Modeling and Pilots
   a. What value is delivered by the initiative?
   b. What are the actual costs to date? Do estimated costs need to be re-examined?
   c. Have all risks been addressed and managed?
3. Implementation and Evaluation
   a. Is the initiative delivering the predicted value? What is the level of value delivered?
   b. What are the actual costs to date?
   c. Which risks have been realized, how are they affecting costs and performance, and how are they being managed?

The tasks and outputs involved with conducting an alternatives analysis include:

Tasks
1. Identify and define alternatives.
2. Estimate value and cost.
3. Conduct risk analysis.
4. Ongoing documentation.

Outputs
1. Viable alternatives
2. Cost and value analyses
3. Risk analyses
4. Tailored basis of estimate documenting value, cost, and risk economic factors and assumptions

Task 1: Identify and Define Alternatives

The challenge of this task is to identify viable alternatives that have the potential to deliver an optimum mix of both value and cost efficiency. Decision makers must be given, at a minimum, two alternatives plus the base case to make an informed investment decision.

The starting point for developing alternatives should be the information in the value structure and preliminary drivers identified in the initial basis of the estimate (see Step 1). Using this information will help to ensure that the alternatives and, ultimately, the solution chosen, accurately reflect a balance of performance, priorities, and business imperatives. Successfully identifying and defining alternatives requires cross-functional collaboration and discussion among the stakeholders.

The base case explores the impact of identified drivers on value and cost if an alternative solution is not implemented. That may mean that current processes and systems are kept in place or that organizations will build a patchwork of incompatible disparate solutions. There should always be a base case included in the analysis of alternatives.

Task 2: Estimate Value and Cost

Comparison of alternatives, justification for funding, creation of a baseline against which ongoing performance may be compared, and development of a foundation for more detailed planning require an accurate estimate of an initiative's cost and value. The more reliable the estimated value and cost of the alternatives, the greater confidence one can have in the investment decision.

The first activity to pursue when estimating value and cost is the collection of data. Data sources and detail will vary based on an initiative's stage of development. Organizations should recognize that more detailed information may be available at a later stage in the process and should provide best estimates in the early stages rather than delaying the process by continuing to search for information that is likely not available.

To capture cost and performance data and conduct the VMM analyses, a VMM model should be constructed. The model facilitates the normalization and aggregation of cost and value, as well as the performance of uncertainty, sensitivity, and risk analyses. Analysts populate the model with the dollar amounts for each cost element and projected performance for each measure. These predicted values, or the underlying drivers, will be expressed in ranges (e.g., low, expected, or high). The range between the low and high values will be determined based on the amount of uncertainty associated with the projection. Initial cost and value estimates are rarely accurate. Uncertainty and sensitivity analyses increase confidence that likely cost and value have been identified for each alternative.

Task 3: Conduct Risk Analysis

The only risks that can be managed are those that have been identified and assessed. A risk analysis considers the probability and potential negative impact of specific factors on an organization's ability to realize projected benefits or estimated cost, as shown in Figure B.6.

Even after diligent and comprehensive risk mitigation during the planning stage, some level of residual risk will remain that may lead to increased costs and decreased performance. A rigorous risk analysis will help an organization better understand the probability that a risk will occur and the level of impact the occurrence of the risk will have on both cost and value. Additionally, risk analysis provides a foundation for building a comprehensive risk management plan.

Task 4: Ongoing Documentation

Inherent in these activities is the need to document the assumptions and research that compensate for gaps in information or understanding. For each alternative, the initial documentation of the high-level assumptions and risks will be expanded to include a general description of the alternative being analyzed, a comprehensive list of cost and value assumptions, and assumptions regarding the risks associated with a specific alternative. This often expands the initial risk inventory.

Step 3. Pull Together the Information

As shown in Figure B.7, the estimation of cost, value, and risk provide important data points for investment decision making. However, when analyzing an alternative and making an investment decision, it is critical to understand the relationships among them.

Tasks
1. Aggregate the cost estimate
2. Calculate the return on investment
3. Calculate the value score
4. Calculate the risk scores (cost and value)
5. Compare value, cost, and risk

Outputs
1. Cost estimate
2. Return on investment metrics
3. Value score
4. Risk scores (cost and value)
5. Comparison of cost, value, and risk

VMM In Action

Assessing Probability and Impact

Below are excerpts from tables developed for the risk analysis of an e-Authentication initiative. Note that the impact and probability of risk were assessed for both cost and value.

The probability of a specific risk occurring remains constant throughout the analysis of a specific alternative, regardless of where it impacts the value or cost of a particular alternative

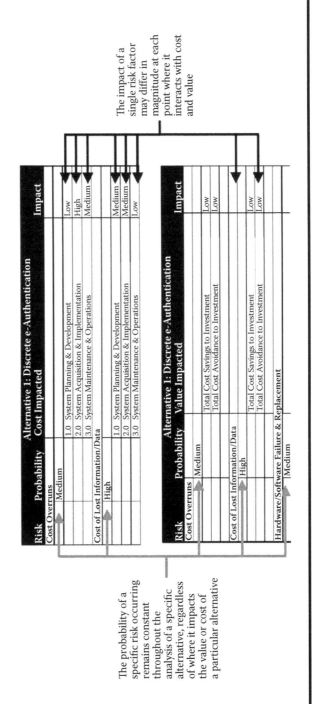

The impact of a single risk factor may differ in magnitude at each point where it interacts with cost and value

Figure B.6   Assessing probability and impact.

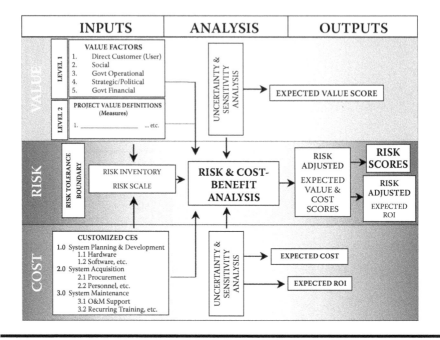

Figure B.7 Risk and cost–benefit analysis.

Task 1: Aggregate the Cost Estimate

A complete and valid cost estimate is critical to determining whether a specific alternative should be selected. It also is used to assess how much funding must be requested. Understating cost estimates to gain approval, or not considering all costs, may create doubt as to the veracity of the entire analysis. An inaccurate cost estimate might lead to cost overruns, create the need to request additional funding, or reduce scope.

The total cost estimate is calculated by aggregating expected values for each cost element.

Task 2: Calculate the Return-on-Investment

Return-on-investment metrics express the relationship between the funds invested in an initiative and the financial benefits the initiative will generate. Simply stated, they express the financial "bang for the buck." Although it is not considered the only measure upon which an investment decision should be made, ROI is, and will continue to be, a critical data point for decision making.

Task 3: Calculate the Value Score

The value score quantifies the full range of value that will be delivered across the five value factors as defined against the prioritized measures within the decision framework. The interpretation of a value score will vary based on the level from which it is being viewed. At the program level, the value score will be viewed as a representation of how alternatives perform against a specific set of measures. They will be used to make an apples-to-apples comparison of the value delivered by multiple alternatives for a single initiative.

For example, the alternative that has a value score of 80 will be preferred over the alternative with a value score of 20, if no other factors are considered. At the organizational or portfolio level, value scores are used as data points in the selection of initiatives to be included in an investment portfolio. Because the objectives and measures associated with each initiative will vary, decision makers at the senior level use value scores to determine what percentage of identified value an initiative will deliver. For example, an initiative with a value score of 75 is providing 75 percent of the possible value the initiative has the potential to deliver. In order to understand what exactly is being delivered, the decision maker will have to look at the measures of the value structure.

Consider the value score as a simple math problem. The scores projected for each of the measures within a value factor should be aggregated according to their established weights. The weighted sum of these scores is a factor's value score. The sum of the factors' value scores, aggregated according to their weights, is the total value score.

Task 4: Calculate the Risk Scores

After considering the probability and potential impact of risks, risk scores are calculated to represent a percentage of overall performance slippage or cost increase. Risk scores provide decision makers with a mechanism to determine the degree to which value and cost will be negatively affected and whether that degree of risk is acceptable based on the risk tolerance boundaries defined by senior staff. If a selected alternative has a high cost or high value risk score, program management is alerted to the need for additional risk mitigation, project definition, or more detailed risk management planning. Actions to mitigate the risk may include establishment of a reserve fund, a reduction of scope, or refinement of the alternative's definition. Reactions to excessive risk may also include reconsideration of whether it is prudent to invest in the project at all, given the potential risks, the probability of their occurrence, and the actions required to mitigate them.

Task 5: Compare Value, Cost, and Risk

Tasks 1 through 4 of this step analyze and estimate the value, cost, and risk associated with an alternative. In isolation, each data point does not provide the depth of information required to ensure sound investment decisions.

Previous to the advent of VMM, only financial benefits could be compared to investment costs through the development of an ROI metric. When comparing alternatives, the consistency of the decision framework allows the determination of how much value will be received for the funds invested. Additionally, the use of risk scores provides insight into how all cost and value estimates are affected by risk.

By performing straightforward calculations, it is possible to model the relationships among value, cost, and risk:

1. The effect risk will have on estimated value and cost.
2. The financial ROI.
3. If comparing alternatives, the value "bang for the buck" (total value returned compared to total required investment).
4. If comparing initiatives to be included in the investment portfolio, senior managers can look deeper into the decision framework, moving beyond overall scores to determine the scope of benefits through an examination of the measures and their associated targets.

Step 4. Communicate and Document

Regardless of the projected merits of an initiative, its success will depend heavily on the ability of its proponents to generate internal support, to gain buy-in from targeted users, and to foster the development of active leadership supporters (champions). Success or failure may depend as much on the utility and efficacy of an initiative as it does on the ability to communicate its value in a manner that is meaningful to stakeholders with diverse definitions of value. The value of an initiative can be expressed to address the diverse definitions of stakeholder value in funding justification documents and in materials designed to inform and enlist support.

Using VMM, the value of a project is decomposed according to the different value factors. This gives project-level managers the tools to customize their value proposition according to the perspective of their particular audience. Additionally, the structure provides the flexibility to respond accurately and quickly to project changes requiring analysis and justification.

The tasks and outputs associated with Step 4 are:

Tasks
1. Communicate value to customers and stakeholders.
2. Prepare budget justification documents.
3. Satisfy ad hoc reporting requirements.
4. Use lessons learned to improve processes.

Outputs
1. Documentation, insight, and support
2. To develop results-based management controls
3. For Exhibit 300 data and analytical needs

4. For communicating initiatives value
5. For improving decision making and performance measurement through lessons learned
6. Change and ad hoc reporting requirements

Task 1: Communicate Value to Customers and Stakeholders

Leveraging the results of VMM analysis can facilitate relations with customers and stakeholders. VMM makes communication to diverse audiences easier by incorporating the perspectives of all potential audience members from the outset of analysis. Because VMM calculates the potential value that an investment could realize for all stakeholders, it provides data pertinent to each of those stakeholder perspectives that can be used to bolster support for the project. It also fosters substantive discussion with customers regarding the priorities and detailed plans of the investment. These stronger relationships not only prove critical to the long-term success of the project, but can also lay the foundation for future improvements and innovation.

Task 2: Prepare Budget Justification Documents

Many organizations require comprehensive analysis and justification to support funding requests. IT initiatives that have not been proven may not be funded. Justification documents should contain:

1. Applicability to executive missions
2. Sound planning
3. Significant benefits
4. Clear calculations and logic justifying the amount of funding requested
5. Adequate risk identification and mitigation efforts
6. A system for measuring effectiveness
7. Full consideration of alternatives
8. Full consideration of how the project fits within the confines of other government entities and current law

After completion of the VMM, one will have data required to complete or support completion of budget justification documents.

Task 3: Satisfy Ad Hoc Reporting Requirements

Once a VMM model is built to assimilate and analyze a set of investment alternatives, it can easily be tailored to support ad hoc requests for information or other reporting requirements. In the current, rapidly changing political and technological environment, there are many instances when project managers need to be able to perform rapid analysis. For example, funding authorities, agency partners, market pricing fluctuations, or portfolio managers might impose modifications on the details (e.g., the weighting factors) of a project investment plan; many of these parties are also likely to request additional investment-related information later in the project life cycle. VMM's customized decision framework makes such adjustments and reporting feasible under short time constraints.

Task 4: Use Lessons Learned to Improve Processes

Lessons learned through the use of VMM can be a powerful tool when used to improve overall organizational decision-making and management processes. For example, in the process of identifying metrics, one might discover that adequate mechanisms are not in place to collect critical performance information. Using this lesson to improve measurement mechanisms would give an organization better capabilities for (1) gauging the project's success and mission fulfillment, (2) demonstrating progress to stakeholders and funding authorities, and (3) identifying shortfalls in performance that could be remedied.

Note 1: Uncertainty Analysis

Conducting an uncertainty analysis requires the following:

1. Identify the variables: Develop a range of values for each variable. This range expresses the level of uncertainty about the projection. For example, an analyst may be unsure whether an Internet application will serve a population of 100 or 100,000. It is important to be aware of this uncertainty and express it when developing the model in order to define the model's reliability in accurately predicting results.
2. Identify the probability distribution for the selected variables: For each variable identified, assign a probability distribution. There are several types of probability distributions. A triangular probability distribution is frequently used for this type of analysis. In addition to establishing the probability distribution for each variable, the analyst must also determine whether the actual amount is likely to be high or low.
3. Run the simulation: Once the variables' level of uncertainty is identified and each one has been assigned a probability distribution, run the Monte Carlo simulation. The simulation provides the analyst with the information required to determine the range (low to high) and "expected" results for both the value projection and cost estimate. As shown in Figure B.8 the output of the Monte Carlo simulation produces a range of possible results and defines the "mean," the point at which there is an equal chance that the actual value or cost will be higher or lower. The analyst then surveys the range and selects the expected value.

VMM In Action

Uncertainty Results

Below is a sample generated by running an automated Monte Carlo simulation on the VMM Model.

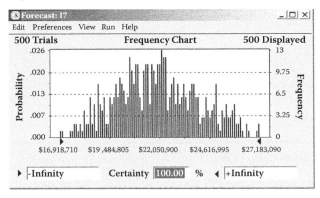

Figure B.8   Output of Monte Carlo simulation.

Note 2: Sensitivity Analysis

Sensitivity analysis is used to identify the business drivers that have the greatest impact on potential variations of an alternative's cost and its returned value. Many of the assumptions made at the beginning of a project's definition phase will be found inaccurate later in the analysis. Therefore, one must consider how sensitive a total cost estimate or value projection is to changes in the data used to produce the result. Insight from this analysis allows stakeholders not only to identify variables that require additional research to reduce uncertainty, but also to justify the cost of that research. The information required to conduct a sensitivity analysis is derived from the same Monte Carlo simulation used for the uncertainty analysis.

Figure B.9 is a sample sensitivity chart. Based on this chart, it is clear that "Build 5/6 Schedule Slip" is the most sensitive variable.

Definitions

Analytic Hierarchy Process (AHP): AHP is a proven methodology that uses comparisons of paired elements (comparing one against the other) to determine mathematically the relative importance of criteria.

Benchmark: A benchmark is a measurement or standard that serves as a point of reference by which process performance is measured.

Benefit: This is a term used to indicate an advantage, profit, or gain attained by an individual or organization.

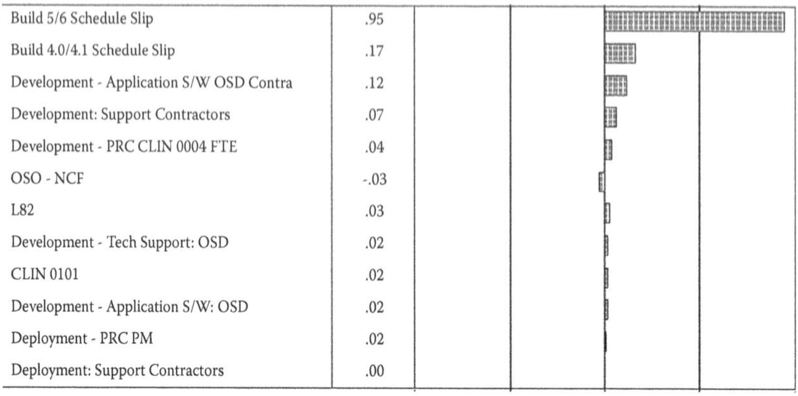

Build 5/6 Schedule Slip	.95	
Build 4.0/4.1 Schedule Slip	.17	
Development - Application S/W OSD Contra	.12	
Development: Support Contractors	.07	
Development - PRC CLIN 0004 FTE	.04	
OSO - NCF	-.03	
L82	.03	
Development - Tech Support: OSD	.02	
CLIN 0101	.02	
Development - Application S/W: OSD	.02	
Deployment - PRC PM	.02	
Deployment: Support Contractors	.00	

Figure B.9 Sensitivity chart.

Benefit to Cost Ratio (BCR) – COST: The computation of the financial benefit/ cost ratio is done within the construct of the following formula: Benefits ÷ Cost.

Cost Element Structure (CES): This is a hierarchical structure created to facilitate the development of a cost estimate. It may include elements that are not strictly products to be developed or produced, such as travel, risk, program management reserve, life cycle phases, and so on. Samples include:

1. System planning and development
   1.1 Hardware
   1.2 Software
       1.2.1 Licensing fees
   1.3 Development support
       1.3.1 Program management oversight
       1.3.2 System engineering architecture design
       1.3.3 Change management and risk assessment
       1.3.4 Requirement definition and data architecture
       1.3.5 Test and evaluation
   1.4 Studies
       1.4.1 Security
       1.4.2 Accessibility
       1.4.3 Data architecture
       1.4.4 Network architecture
   1.5 Other
       1.5.1 Facilities
       1.5.2 Travel
2. System Acquisition and Implementation
   2.1 Procurement

  2.1.1 Hardware
  2.1.2 Software
  2.1.3 Customized software
 2.2 Personnel
 2.3 Training
3. System Maintenance and Operations
 3.1 Hardware
  3.1.1 Maintenance
  3.1.2 Upgrades
  3.1.3 Life-cycle replacement
 3.2 Software
  3.2.1 Maintenance
  3.2.2 Upgrades
  3.2.3 License fees
 3.3 Support
  3.3.1 Helpdesk
  3.3.2 Security
  3.3.3 Training

Cost Estimate: The estimation of a project's life-cycle costs, time-phased by fiscal year, based on the description of a project's or system's technical, programmatic, and operational parameters. A cost estimate may also include related analyses such as cost–risk analyses, cost–benefit analyses, schedule analyses, and trade studies.

Commercial Cost Estimating Tools: PRICE S is a parametric model used to estimate software size, development cost, and schedules, along with software operations and support costs. Software size estimates can be generated for source lines of code, function points, or predictive objective points. Software development costs are estimated based on input parameters reflecting the difficulty, reliability, productivity, and size of the project. These same parameters are used to generate operations and support costs. Monte Carlo risk simulation can be generated as part of the model output. Government agencies (e.g., NASA, IRS, U.S. Air Force, U.S. Army, U.S. Navy, etc.) as well as private companies have used PRICE S.

  PRICE H, HL, M is a suite of hardware parametric cost models used to estimate hardware development, production and operations and support costs. These hardware models provide the capability to generate a total ownership cost to support program management decisions. Monte Carlo risk simulation can be generated as part of the model output. Government Agencies (e.g., NASA, U.S. Air Force, U.S. Army, U.S. Navy, etc.) as well as private companies have used the PRICE suite of hardware models.

  SEER-SEM (System Evaluations and Estimation of Resources-Software Estimating Model) is a parametric modeling tool used to estimate software development costs, schedules, and manpower resource requirements. Based on the input parameters provided, SEER-SEM develops cost, schedule, and resource requirement estimates for a given software development project.

SEER-H (System Evaluations and Estimation of Resources-Hybrid) is a hybrid cost estimating tool that combines analogous and parametric cost-estimating techniques to produce models that accurately estimate hardware development, production, and operations and maintenance cost. SEER-H can be used to support a program manager's hardware life-cycle cost estimate or provide an independent check of vendor quotes or estimates developed by third parties. SEER-H is part of a family of models from Galorath Associates, including SEER SEM (which estimates the development and production costs of software) and SEER-DFM (used to support design for manufacturability analyses).

Data Sources (by phase of development):
1. Strategic planning
   1.1 Strategic and performance plans
   1.2 Subject matter expert input
   1.3 New and existing user surveys
   1.4 Private/public sector best practices, lessons learned, and benchmarks
   1.5 Enterprise architecture
   1.6 Modeling and simulation
   1.7 Vendor market survey
2. Business Modeling and Pilots
   2.1 Subject matter expert input
   2.2 New and existing user surveys
   2.3 Best practices, lessons learned, and benchmarks
   2.4 Refinement of modeling and simulation
3. Implementation and Evaluation
   3.1 Data from phased implementation
   3.2 Actual spending/cost data
   3.3 User group/stakeholder focus groups
   3.4 Other performance measurement

Internal Rate of Return (IRR): The internal rate of return is the discount rate that sets the net present value of the program or project to zero. Although the internal rate of return does not generally provide an acceptable decision criterion, it does provide useful information, particularly when budgets are constrained or there is uncertainty about the appropriate discount rate.

Life-Cycle Costs: The overall estimated cost for a particular program alternative over the time period corresponding to the life of the program, including direct and indirect initial costs plus any periodic or continuing costs of operation and maintenance.

Monte Carlo Simulation: A simulation is any analytical method that is meant to imitate a real-life system, especially when other analyses are too mathematically complex or too difficult to reproduce. Spreadsheet risk analysis uses both a spreadsheet model and simulation to analyze the effect of varying inputs on outputs of the modeled system. One type of spreadsheet simulation is Monte Carlo simulation, which randomly generates values for uncertain variables over and over to simulate a model. (Monte Carlo simulation was named for Monte Carlo, Monaco, where the primary attractions are casinos containing games of chance.) Analysts identify all key assumptions for which the outcome is uncertain. For the life cycle, numerous inputs are each assigned one of several probability distributions. The type of distribution selected depends on the conditions surrounding the variable. During simulation, the value used in the cost model is selected randomly from the defined possibilities.

Net Present Value (NPV): NPV is defined as the difference between the present value of benefits and the present value of costs. The benefits referred to in this calculation must be quantified in cost or financial terms in order to be included.

$$\text{Net Present Value} = [\text{PV(Internal Project Cost Savings, Operational)} + \text{PV(Mission Cost Savings)}] - \text{PV(Initial Investment)}$$

Polling Tools: Option Finder is a real-time polling device, which permits participants, using handheld remotes, to vote on questions and have the results with statistical information such as "degree of variance" displayed immediately and discussed.

Group Systems is a tool that allows participants to answer questions using individual laptops. The answers to these questions are then displayed to all participants anonymously, in order to spur discussion and the free-flowing exchange of ideas. Group Systems also has a polling device.

Return-on-Investment (ROI): This is a financial management approach used to explain how well a project delivers benefits in relationship to its cost. Several methods are used to calculate a return on investment. Refer to Internal Rate of Return (IRR), Net Present Value (NPV), and Savings to Investment Ratio (SIR)

Risk: This is a term used to define the class of factors that (1) have a measurable probability of occurring during an investment's life cycle, (2) have an associated cost or effect on the investment's output or outcome (typically an adverse effect that jeopardizes the success of an investment), and (3) have alternatives from which the organization may choose.

Risk Categories:

1. Project Resources/Financial: Risk associated with "cost creep," misestimation of life-cycle costs, reliance on a small number of vendors without cost controls, and (poor) acquisition planning.
2. Technical/Technology: Risk associated with immaturity of commercially available technology; reliance on a small number of vendors; risk of technical problems/failures with applications and the ability to provide planned and desired technical functionality.
3. Business/Operational: Risk associated with business goals; risk that the proposed alternative fails to result in process efficiencies and streamlining; risk that business goals of the program or initiative will not be achieved; risk that the program effectiveness targeted by the project will not be achieved.
4. Organizational and Change Management: Risk associated with organizational/agency/governmentwide cultural resistance to change and standardization; risk associated with bypassing; lack of use or improper use or adherence to new systems and processes due to organizational structure and culture; inadequate training or planning.
5. Data/Information: Risk associated with the loss/misuse of data or information; risk of increased burdens on citizens and businesses due to data collection requirements if the associated business processes or the project requires access to data from other sources (federal, state, or local agencies).
6. Security: Risk associated with the security/vulnerability of systems, Web sites, information and networks; risk of intrusion and connectivity to other (vulnerable) systems; risk associated with the misuse (criminal/fraudulent) of information; must include level of risk (high, medium, basic) and what aspect of security determines the level of risk, for example, need for confidentiality of information associated with the project or system, availability of the information or system, or reliability of the information or system.
7. Strategic: Risk that the proposed alternative fails to result in the achievement of those goals or in making contributions to them.
8. Privacy: Risk associated with the vulnerability of information collected on individuals, or risk of vulnerability of proprietary information on businesses.

Risk Analysis: This is a technique to identify and assess factors that may jeopardize the success of a project or achieving a goal. This technique also helps define preventive measures to reduce the probability of these factors from occurring and identify countermeasures to successfully deal with these constraints when they develop.

Savings to Investment Ratio (SIR): SIR represents the ratio of savings to investment. The "savings" in the SIR computation are generated by internal operational savings and mission cost savings. The flow of costs and cost savings into the SIR formula is as shown in Figure B.10.

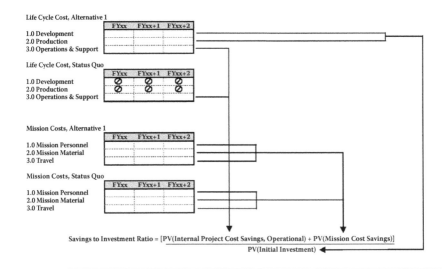

Figure B.10   Savings to investment ratio.

Sensitivity Analysis: This is an analysis of how sensitive outcomes are to changes in the assumptions. The assumptions that deserve the most attention should depend largely on the dominant benefit and cost elements and the areas of greatest uncertainty of the program or process being analyzed.

Stakeholder: This is an individual or group with an interest in the success of an organization in delivering intended results and maintaining the viability of the organization's products and services. Stakeholders influence programs, products, and services.

Note: This appendix is based on the *Value Measuring Methodology – How-To-Guide.* The U.S. Chief Information Officers Council. http://www.cio.gov/archive/ValueMeasuring_Methodology_HowToGuide_Oct_2002.pdf

Appendix C: Establishing a Measurement Program

The following four steps illustrate a comprehensive process for establishing a measurement program.

Step 1: Adopt a Measurement Program Model.

1. Identify resources, processes, products
2. Derive core measurement views

Step 2: Use a Process Improvement Model.

1. Establish a baseline assessment of the project/organization
2. Set and prioritize measurable goals for improvement
3. Establish action plan with measures
4. Accomplish actions and analyze results
5. Leverage improvements through measurement

Step 3: Identify a Goal-Question-Metric (GQM) Structure.

1. Link project goals with corporate goals
2. Derive measures from attribute questions
3. Establish success criteria for measurement

Step 4: Develop a Measurement Plan and Case.

1. Plan: What, why, who, how, when
2. Case: Measurement evidence and analysis results

An organization may decide to implement a subset of these activities. Organizations should tailor their use of the activities as necessary to meet

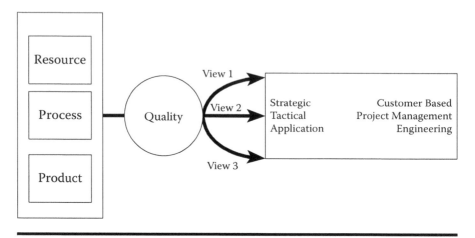

Figure C.1   Measurement program model.

organization and project goals and objectives. Each of these four major activities is described in the following subsections.

An organization or a project manager must understand what to measure, who is interested in the results, and why. To assist this understanding, it is recommended that a measurement program model be adopted such as that illustrated in Figure C.1.

The measurement program model provides a simple framework for specifically identifying what attributes are of potential interest to measure, who the various customers of measurement results might be, and why such measurement results are of interest to those customers. The measurement program model includes the general objects of measurement interest such as resources, processes, and products. The measurement customers include the end-use customer, organization, and project management. These customers need measures for different reasons. Their viewpoints drive the eventual measurement selection priorities and must be integrated and consistent to be most effective.

To establish a successful measurement program (e.g., one that is used for organization or project decision making and lasts more than two years), it is necessary to have a basic understanding of measurement.

Resources, Products, Processes

Objects such as resources, products, and processes have attributes that characterize projects and are therefore of interest to measure. A *measure* is an objective assignment of a number (or symbol) to an object to characterize a specific attribute (Fenton, 1991).

Resources are inputs to processes. Such inputs specifically include personnel, materials, tools, and methods. Resources for some processes are products of other processes. An attribute of great interest that is relevant to all of these types of resources is *cost*. Cost is dependent on the number of resources and the market price of each resource. For personnel, the cost is dependent upon the effort expended during the process and the market price value of each person assigned to the process.

Processes normally have time and effort as attributes of interest, as well as the number of incidents of a specified type arising during the process. Certain incidents may be considered to be defects in the process and may result in defects or faults in products. Products are any artifacts, deliverables, or documents that are produced by processes. Products normally have size and inherent defects as attributes of interest.

Direct and Indirect Measurement

Direct measurement of an attribute does not depend on the measurement of any other attribute. Measures that involve counting, such as number of staff hours expended on a process, are examples of a direct measure.

Indirect or derived measurement involves more than one attribute. Rates are typically indirect measures because they involve the computation of a ratio of two other measures. For example, failure rate is computed by dividing the count of the failures observed during execution by the execution time. Productivity is also an indirect measure because it depends on the amount of product produced divided by the amount of effort or time expended.

Two other very important aspects of the measurement assignment are preservation of attribute properties and mapping uniqueness. The mapping should preserve natural attribute properties (e.g., such as order and interval size). If another assignment mapping of the attribute is identified, there should be a unique relationship between the first mapping and the second mapping. It is very difficult to ensure that measures satisfy these preservation and uniqueness properties. We do not consider these issues here in any detail.

Views of Core Measures

The three views (strategic, tactical, application) of the core measures illustrated in Figure C.1 identify important attributes from the viewpoints of the customer, project management, or applications engineers, respectively. It is extremely important for the measurement program to be consistent across the three views of core measures. There must be agreement and consistency on what measures mean, what measures are important, and how measures across the three views relate to and support each other.

Strategic View

This view is concerned with measurement for the long-term needs of the organization and its customers. Important measures include product cost (effort), time to market (schedule), and the trade-offs among such quality measures as functionality, reliability, usability, and product support. It may be critical to an organization to establish new customers and solidify old customers through new product capabilities, with limited reliability and usability, but with a well-planned support program. Time to market is usually a critical measure, and may become one of upper management's most important measures.

Tactical View

This view is concerned with short- and long-term needs of each individual project's management goals. The project measures that support the tactical view should be able to be aggregated to show a relationship to the organization's strategic goals. If not, then individual projects will appear to be "out of sync" with the organization. The primary measures of interest to project management are schedule progress and labor cost.

Application View

This view is concerned with the immediate resource, process, and product engineering needs of the project. Resources (e.g., personnel and support equipment) are of some interest in this view, but the engineer is primarily interested in the process activities to produce a high-quality product. The engineering definitions of process and product quality should be consistent with project management or upper-level organization management understanding. Product size, complexity, reliability, and inherent defect measures are important to the engineers because they indicate achievement of functional and performance requirements.

Use a Process Improvement Model

In order for a measurement program to be successful, the measurement activities should be conducted within the environment of continuous process improvement. Without such an environment, measures will not be seen as value-added and the measurement program will not be sustainable. Two models are important to a process improvement initiative and the integration of measurement, as illustrated in Figure C.2. The IDEAL model (McFeeley, 1996) provides an organization with an approach to continuous improvement. The Capability Maturity Model (Paulk et al., 1993) can be used to establish a measurement baseline.

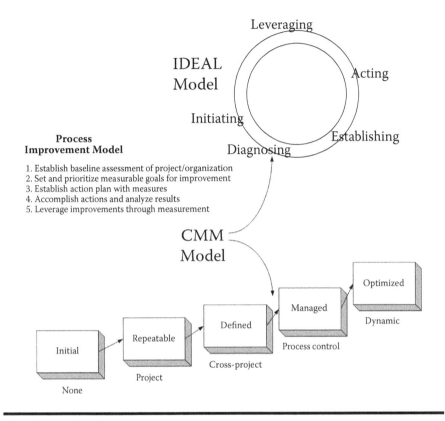

Figure C.2   Process improvement models.

The IDEAL model (McFeeley, 1996) provides a framework for conducting process improvement activities at the organization and project levels. The IDEAL model is similar to the Plan/Do/Check/Act model identified in Deming (1986).

Organization Measurement

During the initiate stage, the organization's goals and measures for the improvement are defined along with success criteria. The diagnose stage includes baselining the organization's current process capability (e.g., using the SEI CMM during a process assessment) in accordance with the measures inherent in the assessment process. The establish stage provides focus on identifying specific improvements that will be accomplished by action teams and the measures for those improvements. Prioritized improvement actions are determined and action teams are formed to develop specific plans that address the high-priority improvements. The act stage includes implementation of the action team plan including collection of measurements to determine if the improvement has been (or can be) accomplished. The leverage stage includes documenting the results of the improvement effort and leveraging the improvement across all applicable organization projects.

Project Measurement

During the initiate stage, the project goals and measures for success are defined along with success criteria. A project measurement plan should be developed or included as part of the project management information. The diagnose stage includes documenting and analyzing the project's measures as a measurement case during the project life cycle in accordance with the measures in the measurement plan. The establish stage provides focus on identifying specific project or organization improvements that might be accomplished. Prioritized improvement actions are determined and assigned to the project or organization level, as appropriate.

For more mature organizations, project teams can accomplish the improvements during the project. For less mature organizations, the identified improvements will serve as lessons learned for future projects. Action teams are formed (by the project or organization) and a plan developed to address the high-priority improvements. The act and leverage stages for the project are limited to making mid-course project corrections based on the measurement information. Such measurement data and the actions taken are recorded in the measurement case. The project's measurement case then becomes the complete documentation of the project management and engineering measures, any changes to project direction based on measurement analysis, and lessons learned for future projects.

SEI CMM

The SEI CMM serves as a guide for determining what to measure first and how to plan an increasingly comprehensive improvement program. The measures suggested for different levels of the CMM are illustrated in Table C.1. The set of core measures described in this document primarily address Level 1, 2, and 3 issues.

Level 1 measures provide baselines for comparison as an organization seeks to start improving. Measurement occurs at a project level without good organizational control, or perhaps on a pilot project with better controls.

Level 2 measures focus on project planning and tracking. Applicable core measures are the staff effort and schedule progress. Size and defect data are necessary to understand measurement needs for Levels 3 and 4 and to provide a database for future evaluations. Individual projects can use the measurement data to set process entry and exit criteria.

Level 3 measures become increasingly directed toward measuring and comparing the intermediate and final products produced across multiple projects. The measurement data for all core measures are collected for each project and compared to organization project standards.

Table C.1   Relationship of Measures to Process Maturity

Maturity Level	Measurement Focus	Applicable Core Measures
1	Establish baselines for planning and estimating project resources and tasks	Effort, schedule progress (Pilot or selected projects)
2	Track and control project resources and tasks	Effort, schedule progress (Project-by-project basis)
3	Define and quantify products and processes within and across projects	Products: Size, defects Processes: Effort, schedule (Compare above across projects)
4	Define, quantify, and control subprocesses and elements	Set upper and lower statistical control boundaries for core measures. Use estimated versus actual comparisons for projects and compare across projects.
5	Dynamically optimize at the project level and improve across projects	Use statistical control results dynamically within the project to adjust processes and products for improved success.

Level 4 measures capture characteristics of the development process to allow control of the individual activities of the process. This is usually done through techniques such as statistical process control, where upper and lower bounds are set for all core measures (and any useful derived measures). Actual measure deviation from the estimated values is tracked to determine whether the attributes being measured are within the statistically allowed control bounds. A decision process is put into place to react to projects that do not meet the statistical control boundaries. Process improvements can be identified based on the decision process.

Level 5 processes are mature enough and managed carefully enough that the statistical control process measurements from Level 4 provide immediate feedback to individual projects based on integrated decisions across multiple projects. Decisions concerning dynamically changing processes across multiple projects can then be optimized while the projects are being conducted.

Identify a Goal-Question-Metric (GQM) Structure

One of the organization's or project's most difficult tasks is to decide what to measure. The key is to relate any measurement to organization and project goals. One method for doing this is to use Basili and Weiss's (1984) Goal-Question-Metric (GQM) paradigm, illustrated in Figure C.3 with a partial example related to reliability.

This method links project goals to corporate goals and derives the specific measures that provide evidence of whether the goals are met. Because such measures are linked directly to organization goals, it is much easier to show the value of the measurement activity and establish success criteria for measurement.

The GQM method of measurement uses a top-down approach with the following steps:

1. Determine the goals of the organization or project in terms of what is wanted, who wants it, why it is wanted, and when it is wanted.
2. Refine the goals into a set of questions that require quantifiable answers.

GOAL   QUESTION   METRIC

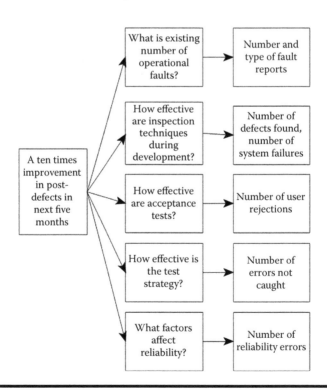

Figure C.3   Goal-question-metric (GQM) paradigm.

3. Refine the questions into a set of measurable attributes (measures for data collection) that attempt to answer the question.
4. Develop models relating each goal to its associated set of measurable attributes.

Some attributes of product development, such as productivity, are dependent on many factors that are specific to a particular environment. The GQM method does not rely on any standard measures and the method can cope with any environment.

This activity may be conducted concurrently with any other measurement activities and may be used to iteratively refine the measurement program model, core measurement views, and process improvement efforts.

Develop a Measurement Plan and Case

The measurement program activities provide organization and project-specific planning information and a variety of measurement data and analysis results. These plans, data, and results should be documented through use of a measurement plan and measurement case.

A measurement plan defines:

■ What measurement data are to be collected
■ How the data are to be analyzed to provide the desired measures
■ The representation forms that will describe the measurement results

Such a plan also provides information as to who is responsible for the measurement activities and when the measurement activities are to be conducted. A measurement plan should be developed at an organization level to direct all measurement activity and at a project level to direct specific project activity. In most cases a project's measurement plan can be a simple tailoring of the organizational plan. The organization's measurement plan can be a separate document or might be an integrated part of the organization's management plan or quality plan.

A measurement plan at either the organization or project level should relate goals to specific measures of the resource, process, and product attributes that are to be measured. The GQM method can be used to identify such measures. Improvement in accordance with the SEI CMM key process areas should be an integrated part of the derivation. The identified measures may be a core measure or derived from one or more core measures.

The following activities are key to developing a measurement plan:

1. Establish Program Commitment. Define why the program is needed, obtain management approval, and identify ownership.

2. Determine Goals and Expected Results. Use process assessment results to set the improvement context.
3. Select Project Measurements. Apply the GQM method to derive project measures.
4. Develop Measurement Plan. Document the measures to be collected; data collection, analysis and presentation methods; and relationship to an overall improvement program.

The measurement case documents the actual data, analysis results, lessons learned, and presentations of information identified in an associated measurement plan. The following activities are key to developing a measurement case:

1. Implement Measurement Plan. Collect and analyze data, provide project feedback, and modify project/program as necessary.
2. Analyze Measurement Results. Store project measurement results; analyze results against historical project results.
3. Provide Measurement Feedback. Report results of analysis as project lessons learned, update measurement and process improvement programs, and repeat the process of developing/updating a measurement plan and case.

Example Measurement Plan Standard

Abstract

This document contains an example of a standard defining the contents and structure of a Measurement Plan for each project of an organization. The term Measurement Plan is used throughout.

Table of Contents

1 Introduction

This standard provides guidance on the production of a Measurement Plan for individual projects.

1.1 Scope

This standard is mandatory for all projects. Assistance in applying it to existing projects will be given by the Organization Measures Coordinator.

2 Policy

It is policy to collect measures to assist in the improvement of:

- The accuracy of cost estimates
- Project productivity
- Product quality
- Project monitoring and control

In particular, each project will be responsible for identifying and planning all activities associated with the collection of these measures. The project is responsible for the definition of the project's objectives for collecting measures, analyzing the measures to provide the required presentation results, and documenting the approach in an internally approved Measurement Plan. The project is also responsible for capturing the actual measurement information and analysis results. The form of this actual measurement information could be appended to the Measurement Plan or put in a separate document called a Measurement Case.

3 Responsibility and Authorities

The Project Leader/Manager shall be responsible for the production of the project Measurement Plan at the start of the project. Advice and assistance from the Organization Measures Coordinator shall be sought when needed.

The Measurement Plan shall be approved by the Project Leader/Manager (if not the author), Product Manager, Organization Measures Coordinator, and Project Quality Manager.

4 General Information

4.1 Overview of Project Measures Activities

The collection and use of measures must be defined and planned into a project during the start-up phase. The haphazard collection of measures is more likely to result in the collection of a large amount of inconsistent data that will provide little useful information to the project management team, or for future projects.

The following activities shall be carried out at the start of the project:

- Define the project's objectives for collecting measures.
- Identify the users of the measures' derived information, as well as any particular requirements they may have.
- Identify the measures to meet these objectives or provide the information. Most, if not all, of these should be defined at the Organization level.
- Define the project task structure, for example, work breakdown structure (WBS).
- Define when each measure is to be collected, in terms of the project task structure.
- Define how each measure is to be collected (in terms of preprinted forms or tools), who will collect it, and where or how it will be stored.
- Define how the data will be analyzed to provide the required information, including the specification of any necessary algorithms, and the frequency with which this will be done.
- Define the organization, including the information flow, within the project required to support the measures collection and analyses activities.
- Identify the standards and procedures to be used.
- Define which measures will be supplied to the organization.

4.2 Purpose of the Measurement Plan

The project's Measurement Plan is produced as one of the start-up documents to record the project's objectives for measures collection and how it intends to carry out the program. The plan also:

- Ensures that activities pertinent to the collection of project measures are considered early in the project and are resolved in a clear and consistent manner
- Ensures that project staff are aware of the measures activities and provides an easy reference to them

The Measurement Plan complements the project's Quality and Project Plans, highlighting matters specifically relating to measures. The Measurement Plan information can be incorporated into the Quality or Project Plans. Information and instructions shall not be duplicated in these plans.

4.3 Format

Section 5 defines a format for the Measurement Plan in terms of a set of headings that are to be used, and the information required to be given under each heading. The front pages shall be the minimum requirements for a standard configurable document.

4.4 Document Control

The Measurement Plan shall be controlled as a configurable document.

4.5 Filing

The Measurement Plan shall be held in the project filing system.

4.6 Updating

The Measurement Plan may require updating during the course of the project. Updates shall follow any changes in requirements for collecting measures or any change to the project that results in change to the project WBS. The Project Leader/Manager shall be responsible for such updates or revisions.

5 Contents of Measurement Plan

This section details what is to be included in the project's Measurement Plan. Wherever possible, the Measurement Plan should point to existing Organization standards and the like, rather than duplicating the information. The information required in the Plan is detailed below under appropriate headings.

For small projects, the amount of information supplied under each topic may amount to only a paragraph or so and may not justify the production of the Measurement Plan as a separate document. Instead, the information may form a separate chapter in the Quality plan, with the topic headings forming the sections or paragraphs in that chapter. On larger projects a separate document will be produced, with each topic heading becoming a section in its own right.

Thematic Outline for a Measurement Plan

Section 1. Objectives for Collecting Measures

The project's objectives for collecting measures shall be described here. These will also include the relevant Organization objectives. Where the author of the Measurement Plan is not the Project Leader/Manager, Project Management agreement to these objectives will be demonstrated by the fact that the Project Manager is a signatory to the Plan.

Section 2.   Use and Users of Information

Provide information that includes:

- Who will be the users of the information to be derived from the measures
- Why the information is needed
- Required frequency of the information

Section 3.   Measures to Be Collected

This section describes the measures to be collected by the project. As far as possible, the measures to be collected should be a derivative of the Core Measures. If Organization standards are not followed, justification for the deviation should be provided. Project-specific measures shall be defined in full here in terms of the project tasks.

A Goal-Question-Metric approach should be used to identify the measures from the stated project objectives. The results of the GQM approach should also be documented.

Section 4.   Collection of Measures

Provide information that includes:

- Who will collect each measure
- The level within the project task against which each measure is to be collected
- When each measure is to be collected in terms of initial estimate, re-estimates and actual measurement
- How the measures are to be collected, with reference to proformas, tools, and procedures as appropriate
- Validation to be carried out, including details of the project-specific techniques if necessary, and by whom
- How and where the measures are to be stored, including details of electronic database/spreadsheet/filing cabinet as appropriate, how the data is amalgamated and when it is archived, who is responsible for setting up the storage process, and who is responsible for inserting the data into the database
- When, how, and which data are provided to the Organization Measures database

Section 5. Analysis of Measures

Provide information that includes:

- How the data is to be analyzed, giving details of project specific techniques if necessary, any tools required and how frequently it is to be carried out
- The information to be provided by the analysis
- Who will carry out the analysis

▪ Details of project specific reports, frequency of generation, how they are generated and by whom

Section 6. Project Organization

Describe the organization within the project that is required to support the measurement activities. Identify roles and the associated tasks and responsibilities. These roles may be combined with other roles within the project to form complete jobs for individual people.

The information flow between these roles and the rest of the project should also be described.

Section 7. Project Task Structure

Describe or reference the project task structure. It should be noted that the project's measurement activities should be included in the project task structure.

Section 8. Standards

The measurement standards and procedures to be used by the project must be given, indicating which are Organization standards and which are project specific. These standards will have been referenced throughout the plan, as necessary. If it is intended not to follow any of the Organization standards in full, this must be clearly indicated in the relevant section of the Measurement Plan, and a note made in this section.

Note: This appendix has been adapted from: Software Quality Assurance Subcommittee of the Nuclear Weapons Complex Quality Managers. United States Department of Energy Albuquerque Operations Office. (1997, April). *Guidelines for Software Measurement, Quality Report SAQS97-001.* http://cio.doe.gov/ITReform/sqse/download/sqas97_1.doc

References

Basili, V. and D.M. Weiss. 1984. A methodology for collecting valid software engineering data, *IEEE Transactions on Software Engineering*, SE-10(6, November) pp 728–738.

Deming, W.E. 1986. *Out of the Crisis,* Cambridge, MA: MIT Press.

Fenton, N.E. 1991. *Software Metrics A Rigorous Approach*, London: Chapman & Hall.

McFeeley, B. 1996. *IDEAL: A User's Guide for Software Process Improvement* (CMU/SEI-96-HB-001), February, Pittsburgh, PA: Software Engineering Institute.

Paulk, M.C., B. Curtis, M.B. Chrissis, and C.V. Weber. 1993. *Capability Maturity Model for Software, Version 1.1* (CMU/SEI-93-TR-024), Pittsburgh, PA: Software Engineering Institute.

Appendix D: Selected Performance Metrics

Types of Performance Measures

Process Metrics	Increase capability level (i.e., SEI-CMM levels)
	Do more with less (shorter schedule, less resources)
	Improve quality (fewer defects, less rework)
Project Metrics	Track project progress
	Assess project status
	Award contract fees
Product Metrics	Determine product quality
	Identify defect rates
	Ensure product performance

Typical Metric Categories

Schedule	Actual versus planned:
	• Schedule and progress
Budget	Actual versus planned:
	• Resources and cost
Functionality	Delivered versus planned:
	• Product characteristics
	• Technology effectiveness
	• Process performance
	• Customer satisfaction

Measures Versus Indicators. Example: Finding Defects in Products (e.g., a Requirements Document)

Basic Measures:	Indicators: Efficiency
• Number of requirements reviewed	• Number reviewed/effort
• Number of reviewers involved	• Number reviewed/time
• Number of defects found	• Number found per effort, time
• Effort expended	Indicators: Effectiveness:
	• Percentage found of those expected
	• Percentage escaped

Examples of Quality Metrics

Metric	Description	Source	Frequency	Report/ Location
Deliverable status	Late versus on time	Project Control Office	Monthly, as document deliverables are identified	QAS and QM Metrics Report in Lotus Notes
Process audit status	Planned versus completed ARs written, awaiting response, closed, past due	Quality Activity Schedule and Status Report	Monthly	QAS and QM Metrics Report in Lotus Notes
Product review status	Planned versus completed Number of defects by type	QM Measurements Report Product Review Artifacts	Monthly	QAS and QM Metrics Report in Lotus Notes
Unplanned product reviews	Total number unplanned reviews Percentage unplanned versus planned	Quality Activity Schedule Product Review Artifacts	Monthly	QAS and QM Metrics Report in Lotus Notes

Average number of PRs to CCR	Total number of PRs for the release divided by the total number of CCRs in the release	Release Report	Release	QM Measurements Report in the CLASS Document Repository
Percentage of reviews completed	Percentage of review types by release	QM Measurements Report	Release	QM Measurements Report in the CLASS Document Repository
Average errors by review type	Calculated average of errors by review type	QM Measurements Report	Release	QM Measurements Report in the CLASS Document Repository

Examples of Performance Measures

Table D.1 provides examples of performance measures that are typical for many IT projects. Although the Category and Metrics columns are fairly representative of those used in IT projects in general, the Measure of Success will vary greatly and should be established for each individual project, as appropriate.

The following set of questions is intended to assist in stimulating the thought process to determine performance measures that are appropriate for a given project or organization.

Project/Process Measurement Questions

- What options are available if the schedule is accelerated by four months to meet a tight market window?
- How many people must be added to get two months of schedule compression and how much will it cost?
- How many defects are still in the product and when will it be good enough so that we can ship a reliable product and have satisfied customers?
- How much impact does requirements growth have on schedule, cost, and reliability?
- Is the current forecast consistent with our company's historical performance?

Table D.1 Examples of Performance Measures

Category	Focus	Purpose	Measure of Success
Schedule performance	Tasks completed versus tasks planned at a point in time.	Assess project progress. Apply project resources.	100 percent completion of tasks on critical path; 90 percent all others.
	Major milestones met versus planned.	Measure time efficiency.	90 percent of major milestones met.
	Revisions to approved plan.	Understand and control project "churn."	All revisions reviewed and approved.
	Changes to customer requirements.	Understand and manage scope and schedule.	All changes managed through approved change process.
	Project completion date.	Award or penalize (depending on contract type).	Project completed on schedule (per approved plan).
Budget performance	Revisions to cost estimates.	Assess and manage project cost.	100 percent of revisions are reviewed and approved.
	Dollars spent versus dollars budgeted.	Measure cost efficiency.	Project completed within approved cost parameters.
	Return on investment (ROI).	Track and assess performance of project investment portfolio.	ROI (positive cash flow) begins according to plan.
	Acquisition cost control.	Assess and manage acquisition dollars.	All applicable acquisition guidelines followed.

Table D.1   Examples of Performance Measures (Continued)

Category	Focus	Purpose	Measure of Success
Product quality	Defects identified through quality activities.	Track progress in, and effectiveness of, defect removal.	90 percent of expected defects identified (e.g., via peer reviews, inspections).
	Test case failures versus number of cases planned.	Assess product functionality and absence of defects.	100 percent of planned test cases execute successfully.
	Number of service calls.	Track customer problems.	75 percent reduction after three months of operation.
	Customer satisfaction index.	Identify trends.	95 percent positive rating.
	Customer satisfaction trend.	Improve customer satisfaction.	5 percent improvement each quarter.
	Number of repeat customers.	Determine if customers are using the product multiple times (could indicate satisfaction with the product).	"X" percent of customers use the product "X" times during a specified time period.
	Number of problems reported by customers.	Assess quality of project deliverables.	100 percent of reported problems addressed within 72 hours.
Compliance	Compliance with enterprise architecture model requirements.	Track progress toward departmentwide architecture model.	Zero deviations without proper approvals.

(continued)

Table D.1 Examples of Performance Measures (Continued)

Category	Focus	Purpose	Measure of Success
	Compliance with interoperability requirements.	Track progress toward system interoperability.	Product works effectively within system portfolio.
	Compliance with standards.	Alignment, interoperability, consistency.	No significant negative findings during architect assessments.
	For Web site projects, compliance with style guide.	To ensure standardization of Web site.	All Web sites have the same "look and feel."
	Compliance with Section 508.	To meet regulatory requirements.	Persons with disabilities may access and utilize the functionality of the system.
Redundancy	Elimination of duplicate or overlapping systems.	Ensure return on investment.	Retirement of 100 percent of identified systems.
	Decreased number of duplicate data elements.	Reduce input redundancy and increase data integrity.	Data elements are entered once and stored in one database.
	Consolidate help desk functions.	Reduce money spent on help desk support.	Approved consolidation plan by June 30, 2010.
Cost avoidance	System is easily upgraded.	Take advantage of, for example, COTS upgrades.	Subsequent releases do not require major "glue code" project to upgrade.
	Avoid costs of maintaining duplicate systems.	Reduce IT costs.	100 percent of duplicate systems have been identified and eliminated.

Table D.1   Examples of Performance Measures (Continued)

Category	*Focus*	*Purpose*	*Measure of Success*
	System is maintainable.	Reduce maintenance costs.	New version (of COTS) does not require "glue code."
Customer satisfaction	System availability (up time).	Measure system availability.	100 percent of requirement is met. (e.g., 99 percent M–F, 8 a.m. to 6 p.m., and 90 percent S and S, 8 a.m. to 5 p.m.).
	System functionality (meets customer's/user's needs).	Measure how well customer needs are being met.	Positive trend in customer satisfaction survey(s).
	Absence of defects (that affect customer).	Number of defects removed during project life cycle.	90 percent of defects expected were removed.
	Ease of learning and use.	Measure time to becoming productive.	Positive trend in training survey(s).
	Time it takes to answer calls for help.	Manage/reduce response times.	95 percent of severity one calls answered within three hours.
	Rating of training course.	Assess effectiveness and quality of training.	90 percent of responses of "good" or better.
Business goals/ mission	Functionality tracks reportable inventory.	Validate system supports program mission.	All reportable inventory is tracked in system.

(continued)

Table D.1 Examples of Performance Measures (Continued)

Category	Focus	Purpose	Measure of Success
	Turnaround time in responding to queries.	Improve customer satisfaction.	Improve turnaround time from two days to four hours.
	Maintenance costs.	Track reduction of costs to maintain system.	Reduce maintenance costs by 2/3 over three-year period.
	Standard desktop platform.	Reduce costs associated with upgrading user's systems.	Reduce upgrade costs by 40 percent.
Productivity	Time taken to complete tasks.	To evaluate estimates.	Completions are within 90 percent of estimates.
	Number of deliverables produced.	Assess capability to deliver products.	Improve product delivery 10 percent in each of the next three years.

Organizational Measurement Questions

- What is the current typical cycle time and cost of our organization's development process?
- What is the quality of the products our organization produces?
- Is our organization's development process getting more or less effective and efficient?
- How does our organization stack up against the competition?
- How does our organization's investment in process improvement compare with the benefits we have achieved?
- What impact are environmental factors such as requirements volatility and staff turnover having on our process productivity?
- What level of process productivity should we assume for our next development project?

Software Testing

- Number of projects completed.
- Number of projects cancelled during testing.
- Number of defects found. This is further broken down into categories of defects, such as major defects (software won't install or causes blue screen) and minor/cosmetic defects (e.g., text in message box is missing). These numbers are put into a calculation that shows how much money we saved the company by catching defects before they were found in production.
- Number of new projects started. (Shows expected workload for next month.)
- Number of projects not completed or carried over to next month. (This shows if we are staying current with work. For example, if we started 50 new projects this month, and completed 20, we are carrying 30 projects to next month. Typically, this number is constant each month, but will increase if we encounter a number of difficult projects. The value of this metric is only meaningful compared to the number of new requests, number of projects completed, and number of requests carried forward in previous months.)

Enterprise Resource Planning

Reduction of operational problems:

- Number of problems with customer order processing
- Percentage of problems with customer order processing
- Number of problems with warehouse processes
- Number of problems with standard reports
- Number of problems with reports on demand

Availability of the ERP system:

- Average system availability
- Average downtime
- Maximum downtime

Avoidance of operational bottlenecks:

- Average response time in order processing
- Average response time in order processing during peak time
- Average number of OLTP transactions
- Maximum number of OLTP transactions

Actuality of the system:

■ Average time to upgrade the system release levels behind the actual level

Improvement in system development:

■ Punctuality index of system delivery
■ Quality index

Avoidance of developer bottlenecks:

■ Average workload per developer
■ Rate of sick leave per developer
■ Percent of modules covered by more than two developers

Project Management

Category	Measurement (How)	Metric (What)
Costs	Actual versus budget	• Labor (costs) • Materials (hardware/software) • Other (office space, telcom)
Schedule	Actual versus planned	• Key deliverables completed • Key deliverables not completed • Milestones met • Milestones not met
Risks	Anticipated versus actual	• Event (actual occurrence) • Impact (effect on project)
Quality	Actual versus planned activities	• Number of reviews (peer, structured walkthrough) • Number of defects (code, documentation) • Type defect (major/minor) • Origin of defect (coding, testing, documentation)

Software Maintenance

Software Maintenance

	Problem Identification Stage	Analysis Stage	Design Stage	Programming Stage	System Test Stage	Acceptance Stage	Delivery Stage
Factors	Correctness Maintainability	Flexibility Traceability Usability Reusability Maintainability Comprehensibility	Flexibility Traceability Reusability Testability Maintainability Comprehensibility Reliability	Flexibility Traceability Maintainability Comprehensibility Reliability	Flexibility Traceability Verifiability Testability Interoperability Comprehensibility Reliability	Flexibility Traceability Interoperability Testability Comprehensibility Reliability	Completeness Reliability
Metrics	Number of omissions on modification request (MR) Number of MR submittals Number of duplicate MRs Time expended for problem validation	Requirement changes Documentation error rates Effort per function area (e.g., SQA) Elapsed time (schedule) Error rates, by priority and type	S/W complexity Design changes Effort per function area Elapsed time Test plans and procedure changes Error rates, by priority and type Number of lines of code, added, deleted, modified, tested	Volume/ functionality (function points or lines of code) Error rates, by priority and type	Error rates, by priority and type Generated Corrected	Error rates, by priority and type Generated Corrected	Documentation changes (i.e., version description documents, training manuals, operation guidelines)

Note: Adapted from "Basic Performance Measures for Information Technology Projects." 2002. Department of Energy (DOE). Retrieved December 15, 2009, from cio.energy.gov/PE-WI-V3-011502.doc.

Appendix E: The Malcolm Baldrige National Quality Award Program

For 16 years, the Baldrige criteria have been used by thousands of U.S. organizations to stay abreast of ever-increasing competition and to improve performance. For today's business environment, the criteria help organizations respond to current challenges: openness and transparency in governance and ethics, the need to create value for customers and the business, and the challenges of rapid innovation and capitalizing on your knowledge assets. Whether your business is small or large, is involved in service or manufacturing, or has one office or multiple sites across the globe, the criteria provide a valuable framework that can help you plan in an uncertain environment. Use the criteria to assess performance on a wide range of key business indicators: customer, product and service, financial, human resource, and operational. The criteria can help you align resources and approaches, such as ISO 9000, Lean Enterprise, Balanced Scorecard, and Six Sigma; improve communication, productivity, and effectiveness; and achieve strategic goals.

Criteria

The criteria are the basis for organizational self-assessments, for making awards, and for giving feedback to applicants. In addition, the criteria have three important roles in strengthening U.S. competitiveness:

- To help improve organizational performance practices, capabilities, and results
- To facilitate communication and sharing of best practices information among U.S. organizations of all types
- To serve as a working tool for understanding and managing performance and for guiding organizational planning and opportunities for learning

Core Values and Concepts

The Criteria are built upon the following set of interrelated Core Values and Concepts:

- Visionary leadership
- Customer-driven excellence
- Organizational and personal learning
- Valuing employees and partners
- Agility
- Focus on the future
- Managing for innovation
- Management by fact
- Social responsibility
- Focus on results and creating value
- Systems perspective

These values and concepts, described below, are embedded beliefs and behaviors found in high-performing organizations. They are the foundation for integrating key business requirements within a results-oriented framework that creates a basis for action and feedback.

Visionary Leadership

Your organization's senior leaders should set directions and create a customer focus, clear and visible values, and high expectations. The directions, values, and expectations should balance the needs of all your stakeholders. Your leaders should ensure the creation of strategies, systems, and methods for achieving excellence, stimulating innovation, and building knowledge and capabilities. The values and strategies should help guide all activities and decisions of your organization. Senior leaders should inspire and motivate your entire workforce and should encourage all employees to contribute, to develop and learn, to be innovative, and to be creative. Senior leaders should be responsible to your organization's governance body for their actions and performance. The governance body should be responsible ultimately to all your stakeholders for the ethics, vision, actions, and performance of your organization and its senior leaders.

Senior leaders should serve as role models through their ethical behavior and their personal involvement in planning, communications, coaching, development of future leaders, review of organizational performance, and employee recognition. As role models, they can reinforce ethics, values, and expectations while building leadership, commitment, and initiative throughout your organization.

Customer-Driven Excellence

Quality and performance are judged by an organization's customers. Thus, your organization must take into account all product and service features and characteristics as well as all modes of customer access that contribute value to your customers. Such behavior leads to customer acquisition, satisfaction, preference, referral, retention and loyalty, and business expansion. Customer-driven excellence has both current and future components: understanding today's customer desires and anticipating future customer desires and marketplace potential.

Value and satisfaction may be influenced by many factors throughout your customers' overall purchase, ownership, and service experiences. These factors include your organization's relationships with customers, which help to build trust, confidence, and loyalty.

Customer-driven excellence means much more than reducing defects and errors, merely meeting specifications, or reducing complaints. Nevertheless, reducing defects and errors and eliminating causes of dissatisfaction contribute to your customers' view of your organization and thus are also important parts of customer-driven excellence. In addition, your organization's success in recovering from defects and mistakes ("making things right for your customer") is crucial to retaining customers and building customer relationships.

Customer-driven organizations address not only the product and service characteristics that meet basic customer requirements but also those features and characteristics that differentiate products and services from competing offerings. Such differentiation may be based upon new or modified offerings, combinations of product and service offerings, customization of offerings, mutiple access mechanisms, rapid response, or special relationships.

Customer-driven excellence is thus a strategic concept. It is directed toward customer retention and loyalty, market share gain, and growth. It demands constant sensitivity to changing and emerging customer and market requirements and to the factors that drive customer satisfaction and loyalty. It demands listening to your customers. It demands anticipating changes in the marketplace. Therefore, customer-driven excellence demands awareness of developments in technology and competitors' offerings, as well as rapid and flexible response to customer and market changes.

Organizational and Personal Learning

Achieving the highest levels of business performance requires a well-executed approach to organizational and personal learning. Organizational learning includes both continuous improvement of existing approaches and adaptation to change, leading to new goals or approaches. Learning needs to be embedded in the way your organization operates. This means that learning (1) is a regular part of daily work; (2) is practiced at personal, work unit, and organizational levels; (3) results in solving problems at their source ("root cause"); (4) is focused on building and sharing knowledge throughout your organization; and (5) is driven by opportunities to effect significant meaningful change. Sources for learning include employees' ideas, research and development (R&D), customers' input, best practice sharing, and benchmarking.

Organizational learning can result in (1) enhancing value to customers through new and improved products and services; (2) developing new business opportunities; (3) reducing errors, defects, waste, and related costs; (4) improving responsiveness and cycle time performance; (5) increasing productivity and effectiveness in the use of all resources throughout your organization; and (6) enhancing your organization's performance in fulfilling its societal responsibilities and its service to your community as a good citizen.

Employees' success depends increasingly on having opportunities for personal learning and practicing new skills. Organizations invest in employees' personal learning through education, training, and other opportunities for continuing growth. Such opportunities might include job rotation and increased pay for demonstrated knowledge and skills. On-the-job training offers a cost-effective way to train and to better link training to your organizational needs and priorities. Education and training programs may benefit from advanced technologies such as computer- and Internet-based learning and satellite broadcasts.

Personal learning can result in (1) more satisfied and versatile employees who stay with your organization, (2) organizational cross-functional learning, (3) building the knowledge assets of your organization, and (4) an improved environment for innovation. Thus, learning is directed not only toward better products and services but also toward being more responsive, adaptive, innovative, and efficient, giving your organization marketplace sustainability and performance advantages and giving your employees satisfaction and motivation to excel.

Valuing Employees and Partners

An organization's success depends increasingly on the diverse knowledge, skills, creativity, and motivation of all its employees and partners. Valuing employees means committing to their satisfaction, development, and well-being. Increasingly, this involves more flexible, high-performance work practices tailored to employees with diverse workplace and home life needs. Major challenges in the area of valuing employees include: (1) demonstrating your leaders' commitment to your employees' success, (2) recognition that goes beyond the regular compensation system, (3) development and progression within your organization, (4) sharing your organization's knowledge so your employees can better serve your customers and contribute to achieving your strategic objectives, and (5) creating an environment that encourages risk taking and innovation.

Organizations need to build internal and external partnerships to better accomplish overall goals. Internal partnerships might include labor–management cooperation, such as agreements with unions. Partnerships with employees might entail employee development, cross-training, or new work organizations, such as high-performance work teams. Internal partnerships also might involve creating network relationships among your work units to improve flexibility, responsiveness, and knowledge sharing.

External partnerships might be with customers, suppliers, and education organizations. Strategic partnerships or alliances are increasingly important kinds of external partnerships. Such partnerships might offer entry into new markets or a basis for new products or services. Also, partnerships might permit the blending of your organization's core competencies or leadership capabilities with the complementary strengths and capabilities of partners.

Successful internal and external partnerships develop longer-term objectives, thereby creating a basis for mutual investments and respect. Partners should address the key requirements for success, means for regular communication, approaches to evaluating progress, and means for adapting to changing conditions. In some cases, joint education and training could offer a cost-effective method for employee development.

Agility

Success in globally competitive markets demands agility: a capacity for rapid change and flexibility. E-business requires and enables more rapid, flexible, and customized responses. Businesses face ever-shorter cycles for the introduction of new or improved products and services, as well as for faster and more flexible response to customers. Major improvements in response time often require simplification of work units and processes or the ability for rapid changeover from one process to another. Cross-trained and empowered employees are vital assets in such a demanding environment.

A major success factor in meeting competitive challenges is the design-to-introduction (product or service initiation) or innovation cycle time. To meet the demands of rapidly changing global markets, organizations need to carry out stage-to-stage integration (such as concurrent engineering) of activities from research or concept to commercialization.

All aspects of time performance now are more critical, and cycle time has become a key process measure. Other important benefits can be derived from this focus on time; time improvements often drive simultaneous improvements in organization, quality, cost, and productivity.

Focus on the Future

In today's competitive environment, a focus on the future requires understanding the short- and longer-term factors that affect your business and marketplace. Pursuit of sustainable growth and market leadership requires a strong future

orientation and a willingness to make long-term commitments to key stakeholders: your customers, employees, suppliers and partners, stockholders, the
public, and your community. Your organization's planning should anticipate
many factors, such as customers' expectations, new business and partnering
opportunities, employee development and hiring needs, the increasingly global
marketplace, technological developments, the evolving e-business environment,
new customer and market segments, evolving regulatory requirements, community and societal expectations, and strategic moves by competitors. Strategic
objectives and resource allocations need to accommodate these influences. A
focus on the future includes developing employees and suppliers, doing effective succession planning, creating opportunities for innovation, and anticipating
public responsibilities.

Managing for Innovation

Innovation means making meaningful change to improve an organization's products, services, and processes and to create new value for the organization's stakeholders. Innovation should lead your organization to new dimensions of performance.
Innovation is no longer strictly the purview of research and development departments; innovation is important for all aspects of your business and all processes.
Organizations should be led and managed so that innovation becomes part of the
learning culture and is integrated into daily work.

Innovation builds on the accumulated knowledge of your organization and its
employees. Therefore, the ability to capitalize on this knowledge is critical to managing for innovation.

Management by Fact

Organizations depend on the measurement and analysis of performance. Such measurements should derive from business needs and strategy, and they should provide
critical data and information about key processes, outputs, and results. Many types
of data and information are needed for performance management. Performance
measurement should include customer, product, and service performance; comparisons of operational, market, and competitive performance; and supplier, employee,
and cost and financial performance. Data should be segmented by, for example,
markets, product lines, and employee groups to facilitate analysis.

Analysis refers to extracting larger meaning from data and information to support evaluation, decision making, and improvement. Analysis entails using data
to determine trends, projections, and cause and effect that might not otherwise be
evident. Analysis supports a variety of purposes, such as planning, reviewing your
overall performance, improving operations, change management, and comparing
your performance with competitors' or with "best practices" benchmarks.

A major consideration in performance improvement and change management involves the selection and use of performance measures or indicators. The measures or indicators you select should best represent the factors that lead to improved customer, operational, and financial performance. A comprehensive set of measures or indicators tied to customer or organizational performance requirements represents a clear basis for aligning all processes with your organization's goals.

Through the analysis of data from your tracking processes, your measures or indicators themselves may be evaluated and changed to better support your goals.

Social Responsibility

An organization's leaders should stress responsibilities to the public, ethical behavior, and the need to practice good citizenship. Leaders should be role models for your organization in focusing on business ethics and protection of public health, safety, and the environment. Protection of health, safety, and the environment includes your organization's operations, as well as the life cycles of your products and services. Also, organizations should emphasize resource conservation and waste reduction at the source. Planning should anticipate adverse impacts from production, distribution, transportation, use, and disposal of your products. Effective planning should prevent problems, provide for a forthright response if problems occur, and make available information and support needed to maintain public awareness, safety, and confidence.

For many organizations, the product design stage is critical from the point of view of public responsibility. Design decisions affect your production processes and often the content of municipal and industrial waste. Effective design strategies should anticipate growing environmental concerns and responsibilities.

Organizations should not only meet all local, state, and federal laws and regulatory requirements, but they should treat these and related requirements as opportunities for improvement "beyond mere compliance." Organizations should stress ethical behavior in all stakeholder transactions and interactions. Highly ethical conduct should be a requirement of and should be monitored by the organization's governance body.

Practicing good citizenship refers to leadership and support—within the limits of an organization's resources—of publicly important purposes. Such purposes might include improving education and health care in your community, environmental excellence, resource conservation, community service, improving industry and business practices, and sharing nonproprietary information. Leadership as a corporate citizen also entails influencing other organizations, private and public, to partner for these purposes. For example, your organization might lead or participate in efforts to help define the obligations of your industry to its communities. Managing social responsibility requires the use of appropriate measures and leadership responsibility for those measures.

Focus on Results and Creating Value

An organization's performance measurements need to focus on key results. Results should be used to create and balance value for your key stakeholders: customers, employees, stockholders, suppliers and partners, the public, and the community. By creating value for your key stakeholders, your organization builds loyalty and contributes to growing the economy. To meet the sometimes conflicting and changing aims that balancing value implies, organizational strategy should explicitly include key stakeholder requirements. This will help ensure that plans and actions meet differing stakeholder needs and avoid adverse impacts on any stakeholders. The use of a balanced composite of leading and lagging performance measures offers an effective means to communicate short- and longer-term priorities, monitor actual performance, and provide a clear basis for improving results.

Systems Perspective

The Baldrige criteria provide a systems perspective for managing your organization and its key processes to achieve results: performance excellence. The seven Baldrige categories and the core values form the building blocks and the integrating mechanism for the system. However, successful management of overall performance requires organization-specific synthesis, alignment, and integration. Synthesis means looking at your organization as a whole and builds upon key business requirements, including your strategic objectives and action plans. Alignment means using the key linkages among requirements given in the Baldrige categories to ensure consistency of plans, processes, measures, and actions. Integration builds on alignment so that the individual components of your performance management system operate in a fully interconnected manner.

A systems perspective includes your senior leaders' focus on strategic directions and on your customers. It means that your senior leaders monitor, respond to, and manage performance based on your business results. A systems perspective also includes using your measures, indicators, and organizational knowledge to build your key strategies. It means linking these strategies with your key processes and aligning your resources to improve overall performance and satisfy customers. Thus, a systems perspective means managing your whole organization, as well as its components, to achieve success.

Criteria for Performance Excellence Framework

The core values and concepts are embodied in seven categories, as follows:

1. Leadership
2. Strategic planning

3. Customer and market focus
4. Measurement, analysis, and knowledge management
5. Human resource focus
6. Process management
7. Business results

The criteria can be thought of within the context of a framework consisting of the following.

Organizational Profile

Your organizational profile sets the context for the way your organization operates. Your environment, key working relationships, and strategic challenges serve as an overarching guide for your organizational performance management system.

System Operations

System operations are composed of the six Baldrige categories that define your business results. Leadership (Category 1), Strategic Planning (Category 2), and Customer and Market Focus (Category 3) represent the leadership triad. These categories are placed together to emphasize the importance of a leadership focus on strategy and customers. Senior leaders set your organizational direction and seek future opportunities for your organization. Human Resource Focus (Category 5), Process Management (Category 6), and Business Results (Category 7) represent the results triad. Your organization's employees and key processes accomplish the work of the organization that yields your business results. All actions point toward business results: a composite of customer, product and service, financial, and internal operational performance results, including human resource, governance, and social responsibility results.

System Foundation

Measurement, Analysis, and Knowledge Management (Category 4) are critical to the effective management of your organization and to a fact-based, knowledge-driven system for improving performance and competitiveness. Measurement, analysis, and knowledge management serve as a foundation for the performance management system.

Criteria Structure

The seven Criteria categories are subdivided into Items and Areas to Address. There are 19 items, each focusing on a major requirement. Items consist of one or more

Areas to Address (Areas). Organizations should address their responses to the specific requirements of these Areas.

1. The Criteria focus on business results.
2. The Criteria support a systems perspective to maintaining organizationwide goal alignment.
3. The Criteria are nonprescriptive and adaptable. The Criteria are made up of results-oriented requirements. However, the Criteria do not prescribe that your organization should or should not have departments for quality, planning, or other functions; how your organization should be structured; or that different units in your organization should be managed in the same way.
   a. The focus is on results, not on procedures, tools, or organizational structure. Organizations are encouraged to develop and demonstrate creative, adaptive, and flexible approaches for meeting requirements. Nonprescriptive requirements are intended to foster incremental and major ("breakthrough") improvements, as well as basic change.
   b. The selection of tools, techniques, systems, and organizational structure usually depends on factors such as business type and size, organizational relationships, your organization's stage of development, and employee capabilities and responsibilities.
   c. A focus on common requirements, rather than on common procedures, fosters understanding, communication, sharing, and alignment, while supporting innovation and diversity in approaches.

Alignment in the Criteria is built around connecting and reinforcing measures derived from your organization's processes and strategy. These measures tie directly to customer value and to overall performance. The use of measures thus channels different activities in consistent directions with less need for detailed procedures, centralized decision making, or overly complex process management. Measures thereby serve both as a communications tool and a basis for deploying consistent overall performance requirements. Such alignment ensures consistency of purpose while also supporting agility, innovation, and decentralized decision making.

A systems perspective to goal alignment, particularly when strategy and goals change over time, requires dynamic linkages among Criteria Items. In the Criteria, action-oriented cycles of learning take place via feedback between processes and results.

The learning cycles have four clearly defined stages:

1. Planning, including design of processes, selection of measures, and deployment of requirements
2. Executing plans
3. Assessing progress and capturing new knowledge, taking into account internal and external results

4. Revising plans based upon assessment findings, learning, new inputs, and new requirements

The Criteria support goal-based diagnosis. The Criteria and the Scoring Guidelines make up a two-part diagnostic (assessment) system. The Criteria are a set of 19 performance-oriented requirements. The Scoring Guidelines spell out the assessment dimensions—Process and Results—and the key factors used to assess each dimension. An assessment thus provides a profile of strengths and opportunities for improvement relative to the 19 performance-oriented requirements. In this way, assessment leads to actions that contribute to performance improvement in all areas. This diagnostic assessment is a useful management tool that goes beyond most performance reviews and is applicable to a wide range of strategies and management systems.

Preface: Organizational Profile

The organizational profile is a snapshot of your organization, the key influences on how you operate, and the key challenges you face.

P.1 Organizational Description

Describe your organization's business environment and your key relationships with customers, suppliers, and other partners.

Within your response, include answers to the following questions:

a. Organizational Environment
   1. What are your organization's main products and services? What are the delivery mechanisms used to provide your products and services to your customers?
   2. What is your organizational culture? What are your stated purpose, vision, mission, and values?
   3. What is your employee profile? What are your employees' educational levels? What are your organization's workforce and job diversity, organized bargaining units, use of contract employees, and special health and safety requirements?
   4. What are your major technologies, equipment, and facilities?
   5. What is the regulatory environment under which your organization operates? What are the applicable occupational health and safety regulations; accreditation, certification, or registration requirements; and environmental, financial, and product regulations?

b. Organizational Relationships

1. What is your organizational structure and governance system? What are the reporting relationships among your board of directors, senior leaders, and your parent organization, as appropriate?
2. What are your key customer groups and market segments, as appropriate? What are their key requirements and expectations for your products and services? What are the differences in these requirements and expectations among customer groups and market segments?
3. What role do suppliers and distributors play in your value creation processes? What are your most important types of suppliers and distributors? What are your most important supply chain requirements?
4. What are your key supplier's and customers' partnering relationships and communication mechanisms?

P.2 Organizational Challenges

Describe your organization's competitive environment, your key strategic challenges, and your system for performance improvement.

Within your response, include answers to the following questions:

a. Competitive Environment

1. What is your competitive position? What is your relative size and growth in your industry or markets served? What are the numbers and types of competitors for your organization?
2. What are the principal factors that determine your success relative to your competitors? What are any key changes taking place that affect your competitive situation?
3. What are your key available sources of comparative and competitive data from within your industry? What are your key available sources of comparative data for analogous processes outside your industry? What limitations, if any, are there in your ability to obtain these data?

b. Strategic Challenges

1. What are your key business, operational, and human resource strategic challenges?
2. What is the overall approach you use to maintain an organizational focus on performance improvement and to guide systematic evaluation and improvement of key processes?
3. What is your overall approach to organizational learning and sharing your knowledge assets within the organization?

1 Leadership (120 points)

The Leadership category examines how your organization's senior leaders address values, directions, and performance expectations, as well as a focus on customers and other stakeholders, empowerment, innovation, and learning. Also examined are your organization's governance and how your organization addresses its public and community responsibilities.

1.1 Organizational Leadership (70 points) Process

Describe how senior leaders guide your organization. Describe your organization's governance system. Describe how senior leaders review organizational performance.
   Within your response, include answers to the following questions:

a. Senior Leadership Direction
1. How do senior leaders set and deploy organizational values, short- and longer-term directions, and performance expectations? How do senior leaders include a focus on creating and balancing value for customers and other stakeholders in their performance expectations? How do senior leaders communicate organizational values, directions, and expectations through your leadership system to all employees and to key suppliers and partners? How do senior leaders ensure two-way communication on these topics?
2. How do senior leaders create an environment for empowerment, innovation, and organizational agility? How do they create an environment for organizational and employee learning? How do they create an environment that fosters and requires legal and ethical behavior?

b. Organizational Governance
1. How does your organization address the following key factors in your governance system?
   a. Management accountability for the organization's actions
   b. Fiscal accountability
   c. Independence in internal and external audits
   d. Protection of stockholder and stakeholder interests, as appropriate

c. Organizational Performance Review
1. How do senior leaders review organizational performance and capabilities? How do they use these reviews to assess organizational success, competitive performance, and progress relative to short- and longer-term goals? How do they use these reviews to assess your organizational ability to address changing organizational needs?
2. What are the key performance measures regularly reviewed by your senior leaders? What are your key recent performance review findings?

3. How do senior leaders translate organizational performance review findings into priorities for continuous and breakthrough improvement of key business results and into opportunities for innovation? How are these priorities and opportunities deployed throughout your organization? When appropriate, how are they deployed to your suppliers and partners to ensure organizational alignment?

4. How do you evaluate the performance of your senior leaders, including the chief executive? How do you evaluate the performance of members of the board of directors, as appropriate? How do senior leaders use organizational performance review findings to improve both their own leadership effectiveness and that of your board and leadership system, as appropriate?

1.2 Social Responsibility (50 points) Process

Describe how your organization addresses its responsibilities to the public, ensures ethical behavior, and practices good citizenship.

Within your response, include answers to the following questions:

a. Responsibilities to the Public
   1. How do you address the impacts on society of your products, services, and operations? What are your key compliance processes, measures, and goals for achieving and surpassing regulatory and legal requirements, as appropriate? What are your key processes, measures, and goals for addressing risks associated with your products, services, and operations?
   2. How do you anticipate public concerns with current and future products, services, and operations? How do you prepare for these concerns in a proactive manner?

b. Ethical Behavior
   1. How do you ensure ethical behavior in all stakeholder transactions and interactions? What are your key processes and measures or indicators for monitoring ethical behavior throughout your organization, with key partners, and in your governance structure?

c. Support of Key Communities
   1. How does your organization actively support and strengthen your key communities? How do you identify key communities and determine areas of emphasis for organizational involvement and support? What are your key communities? How do your senior leaders and your employees contribute to improving these communities?

2 Strategic Planning (85 points)

The Strategic Planning category examines how your organization develops strategic objectives and action plans. Also examined are how your chosen strategic objectives and action plans are deployed and how progress is measured.

2.1 Strategy Development (40 points) Process

Describe how your organization establishes its strategic objectives, including how it enhances its competitive position, overall performance, and future success.

Within your response, include answers to the following questions:

a. Strategy Development Process
1. What is your overall strategic planning process? What are the key steps? Who are the key participants? What are your short- and longer-term planning time horizons? How are these time horizons set? How does your strategic planning process address these time horizons?
2. How do you ensure that strategic planning addresses the key factors listed below? How do you collect and analyze relevant data and information to address these factors as they relate to your strategic planning:
   - Your customers and market needs, expectations, and opportunities
   - Your competitive environment and your capabilities relative to competitors
   - Technological and other key innovations or changes that might affect your products and services and how you operate
   - Your strengths and weaknesses, including human and other resources
   - Your opportunities to redirect resources to higher priority products, services, or areas
   - Financial, societal and ethical, regulatory, and other potential risks
   - Changes in the national or global economy
   - Factors unique to your organization, including partner and supply chain needs, strengths, and weaknesses

b. Strategic Objectives
1. What are your key strategic objectives and your timetable for accomplishing them? What are your most important goals for these strategic objectives?
2. How do your strategic objectives address the challenges identified in response to P.2 in your organizational profile? How do you ensure that your strategic objectives balance short- and longer-term challenges and opportunities? How do you ensure that your strategic objectives balance the needs of all key stakeholders?

2.2 Strategy Deployment (45 points) Process

Describe how your organization converts its strategic objectives into action plans. Summarize your organization's action plans and related key performance measures or indicators. Project your organization's future performance on these key performance measures or indicators.

Within your response, include answers to the following questions:

a. Action Plan Development and Deployment

1. How do you develop and deploy action plans to achieve your key strategic objectives? How do you allocate resources to ensure accomplishment of your action plans? How do you ensure that the key changes resulting from action plans can be sustained?

2. What are your key short- and longer-term action plans? What are the key changes, if any, in your products and services, your customers and markets, and how you will operate?

3. What are your key human resource plans that derive from your short- and longer-term strategic objectives and action plans?

4. What are your key performance measures or indicators for tracking progress on your action plans? How do you ensure that your overall action plan measurement system reinforces organizational alignment? How do you ensure that the measurement system covers all key deployment areas and stakeholders?

b. Performance Projection

For the key performance measures or indicators identified in 2.2a(4), what are your performance projections for both your short- and longer-term planning time horizons? How does your projected performance compare with competitors' projected performance? How does it compare with key benchmarks, goals, and past performance, as appropriate?

3 Customer and Market Focus (85 points)

The Customer and Market Focus category examines how your organization determines requirements, expectations, and preferences of customers and markets. Also examined is how your organization builds relationships with customers and determines the key factors that lead to customer acquisition, satisfaction, loyalty and retention, and to business expansion.

3.1 Customer and Market Knowledge (40 points) Process

Describe how your organization determines requirements, expectations, and preferences of customers and markets to ensure the continuing relevance of your products and services and to develop new opportunities.

Within your response, include answers to the following questions:

a. Customers and Market Knowledge
   1. How do you determine or target customers, customer groups, and market segments? How do you include customers of competitors and other potential customers and markets in this determination?
   2. How do you listen and learn to determine key customer requirements and expectations (including product and service features) and their relative importance to customers' purchasing decisions? How do determination methods vary for different customers or customer groups? How do you use relevant information from current and former customers, including marketing and sales information, customer loyalty and retention data, win/loss analysis, and complaints? How do you use this information for purposes of product and service planning, marketing, process improvements, and other business development?
   3. How do you keep your listening and learning methods current with business needs and directions?

3.2 Customer Relationships and Satisfaction
(45 points) Process

Describe how your organization builds relationships to acquire, satisfy, and retain customers, to increase customer loyalty, and to develop new opportunities. Also describe how your organization determines customer satisfaction.

Within your response, include answers to the following questions:

a. Customer Relationship Building
   1. How do you build relationships to acquire customers, to meet and exceed their expectations, to increase loyalty and repeat business, and to gain positive referrals?
   2. What are your key access mechanisms for customers to seek information, conduct business, and make complaints? How do you determine key customer contact requirements for each mode of customer access? How do you ensure that these contact requirements are deployed to all people and processes involved in the customer response chain?
   3. What is your complaint management process? How do you ensure that complaints are resolved effectively and promptly? How are complaints

aggregated and analyzed for use in improvement throughout your organization and by your partners?

4. How do you keep your approaches to building relationships and providing customer access current with business needs and directions?

b. Customer Satisfaction Determination

1. How do you determine customer satisfaction and dissatisfaction? How do these determination methods differ among customer groups? How do you ensure that your measurements capture actionable information for use in exceeding your customers' expectations, securing their future business, and gaining positive referrals? How do you use customer satisfaction and dissatisfaction information for improvement?

2. How do you follow up with customers on products, services, and transaction quality to receive prompt and actionable feedback?

3. How do you obtain and use information on your customers' satisfaction relative to customers' satisfaction with your competitors or industry benchmarks?

4. How do you keep your approaches to determining satisfaction current with business needs and directions?

4 Measurement, Analysis, and Knowledge Management (90 points)

The Measurement, Analysis, and Knowledge Management category examines how your organization selects, gathers, analyzes, manages, and improves its data, information, and knowledge assets.

4.1 Measurement and Analysis of Organizational Performance (45 points) Process

Describe how your organization measures, analyzes, aligns, and improves its performance data and information at all levels and in all parts of your organization.

Within your response, include answers to the following questions:

a. Performance Measurement

1. How do you select, collect, align, and integrate data and information for tracking daily operations and for tracking overall organizational performance? How do you use this data and information to support organizational decision making and innovation?

2. How do you select and ensure the effective use of key comparative data and information to support operational and strategic decision making and innovation?

3. How do you keep your performance measurement system current with business needs and directions? How do you ensure that your performance measurement system is sensitive to rapid or unexpected organizational or external changes?

b. Performance Analysis

1. What analyses do you perform to support your senior leaders' organizational performance review? What analyses do you perform to support your organization's strategic planning?

2. How do you communicate the results of organizational-level analyses to work group and functional-level operations to enable effective support for their decision making?

4.2 Information and Knowledge Management (45 points) Process

Describe how your organization ensures the quality and availability of needed data and information for employees, suppliers, partners, and customers. Describe how your organization builds and manages its knowledge assets.

Within your response, include answers to the following questions:

a. Data and Information Availability

1. How do you make needed data and information available? How do you make it accessible to employees, suppliers, partners, and customers, as appropriate?

2. How do you ensure that hardware and software are reliable, secure, and user friendly?

3. How do you keep your data and information availability mechanisms, including your software and hardware systems, current with business needs and directions?

b. Organizational Knowledge

1. How do you manage organizational knowledge to accomplish:
   - The collection and transfer of employee knowledge
   - The transfer of relevant knowledge from customers, suppliers, and partners
   - The identification and sharing of best practices

2. How do you ensure the following properties of your data, information, and organizational knowledge:
   - Integrity
   - Timeliness
   - Reliability
   - Security
   - Accuracy
   - Confidentiality

5 Human Resource Focus (85 points)

The Human Resource Focus category examines how your organization's work systems and employee learning and motivation enable employees to develop and utilize their full potential in alignment with your organization's overall objectives and action plans. Also examined are your organization's efforts to build and maintain a work environment and employee support climate conducive to performance excellence and to personal and organizational growth.

5.1 Work Systems (35 points) Process

Describe how your organization's work and jobs enable employees and the organization to achieve high performance. Describe how compensation, career progression, and related workforce practices enable employees and the organization to achieve high performance.

Within your response, include answers to the following questions:

a. Organization and Management of Work
1. How do you organize and manage work and jobs to promote cooperation, initiative, empowerment, innovation, and your organizational culture? How do you organize and manage work and jobs to achieve the agility to keep current with business needs?
2. How do your work systems capitalize on the diverse ideas, cultures, and thinking of your employees and the communities with which you interact (your employee hiring and your customers' communities)?
3. How do you achieve effective communication and skill sharing across work units, jobs, and locations?
b. Employee Performance Management System
1. How does your employee performance management system, including feedback to employees, support high-performance work? How does your employee performance management system support a customer and business focus? How do your compensation, recognition, and related reward and incentive practices reinforce high-performance work and a customer and business focus?
c. Hiring and Career Progression
1. How do you identify characteristics and skills needed by potential employees?
2. How do you recruit, hire, and retain new employees? How do you ensure that the employees represent the diverse ideas, cultures, and thinking of your employee hiring community?
3. How do you accomplish effective succession planning for leadership and management positions, including senior leadership? How do you

manage effective career progression for all employees throughout the organization?

5.2 Employee Learning and Motivation (25 points) Process

Describe how your organization's employee education, training, and career development support the achievement of your overall objectives and contribute to high performance. Describe how your organization's education, training, and career development build employee knowledge, skills, and capabilities.

Within your response, include answers to the following questions:

a. Employee Education, Training, and Development
   1. How do employee education and training contribute to the achievement of your action plans? How do your employee education, training, and development address your key needs associated with organizational performance measurement, performance improvement, and technological change? How does your education and training approach balance short- and longer-term organizational objectives with employee needs for development, learning, and career progression?
   2. How do employee education, training, and development address your key organizational needs associated with new employee orientation, diversity, ethical business practices, and management and leadership development? How do employee education, training, and development address your key organizational needs associated with employee, workplace, and environmental safety?
   3. How do you seek and use input from employees and their supervisors and managers on education and training needs? How do you incorporate your organizational learning and knowledge assets into your education and training?
   4. How do you deliver education and training? How do you seek and use input from employees and their supervisors and managers on options for the delivery of education and training? How do you use both formal and informal delivery approaches, including mentoring and other approaches, as appropriate?
   5. How do you reinforce the use of new knowledge and skills on the job?
   6. How do you evaluate the effectiveness of education and training, taking into account individual and organizational performance?
b. Motivation and Career Development
   1. How do you motivate employees to develop and utilize their full potential? How does your organization use formal and informal mechanisms to help employees attain job- and career-related development and learning objectives? How do managers and supervisors help employees attain job- and career-related development and learning objectives?

5.3 *Employee Well-Being and Satisfaction (25 points) Process*

Describe how your organization maintains a work environment and an employee support climate that contribute to the well-being, satisfaction, and motivation of all employees.

Within your response, include answers to the following questions:

a. Work Environment
1. How do you improve workplace health, safety, security, and ergonomics? How do employees take part in improving them? What are your performance measures or targets for each of these key workplace factors? What are the significant differences in workplace factors and performance measures or targets if different employee groups and work units have different work environments?
2. How do you ensure workplace preparedness for emergencies or disasters? How do you seek to ensure business continuity for the benefit of your employees and customers?

b. Employee Support and Satisfaction
1. How do you determine the key factors that affect employee well-being, satisfaction, and motivation? How are these factors segmented for a diverse workforce and for different categories and types of employees?
2. How do you support your employees via services, benefits, and policies? How are these tailored to the needs of a diverse workforce and different categories and types of employees?
3. What formal and informal assessment methods and measures do you use to determine employee well-being, satisfaction, and motivation? How do these methods and measures differ across a diverse workforce and different categories and types of employees? How do you use other indicators, such as employee retention, absenteeism, grievances, safety, and productivity, to assess and improve employee well-being, satisfaction, and motivation?
4. How do you relate assessment findings to key business results to identify priorities for improving the work environment and employee support climate?

6 Process Management (85 points)

The Process Management category examines the key aspects of your organization's process management, including key product, service, and business processes for creating customers and organizational value and key support processes. This category encompasses all key processes and all work units.

6.1 Value Creation Processes (50 points) Process

Describe how your organization identifies and manages its key processes for creating customer value and achieving business success and growth.

Within your response, include answers to the following questions:

a. Value Creation Processes
1. How does your organization determine its key value creation processes? What are your organization's key product, service, and business processes for creating or adding value? How do these processes create value for the organization, your customers, and your other key stakeholders? How do they contribute to profitability and business success?
2. How do you determine key value creation process requirements, incorporating input from customers, suppliers, and partners, as appropriate? What are the key requirements for these processes?
3. How do you design these processes to meet all the key requirements? How do you incorporate new technology and organizational knowledge into the design of these processes? How do you incorporate cycle time, productivity, cost control, and other efficiency and effectiveness factors into the design of these processes? How do you implement these processes to ensure they meet design requirements?
4. What are your key performance measures or indicators used for the control and improvement of your value creation processes? How does your day-to-day operation of these processes ensure meeting key process requirements? How are in-process measures used in managing these processes? How are customer, supplier, and partner input used in managing these processes, as appropriate?
5. How do you minimize overall costs associated with inspections, tests, and process or performance audits, as appropriate? How do you prevent defects and rework, and minimize warranty costs, as appropriate?
6. How do you improve your value creation processes to achieve better performance, to reduce variability, to improve products and services, and to keep the processes current with business needs and directions? How are improvements shared with other organizational units and processes?

6.2 Support Processes (35 points) Process

Describe how your organization manages its key processes that support your value creation processes.

Within your response, include answers to the following questions:

a. Support Processes

1. How does your organization determine its key support processes? What are your key processes for supporting your value creation processes?

2. How do you determine key support process requirements, incorporating input from internal and external customers, and suppliers and partners, as appropriate? What are the key requirements for these processes?

3. How do you design these processes to meet all the key requirements? How do you incorporate new technology and organizational knowledge into the design of these processes? How do you incorporate cycle time, productivity, cost control, and other efficiency and effectiveness factors into the design of the processes? How do you implement these processes to ensure they meet design requirements?

4. What are your key performance measures or indicators used for the control and improvement of your support processes? How does your day-to-day operation of key support processes ensure meeting key performance requirements? How are in-process measures used in managing these processes? How are customer, supplier, and partner input used in managing these processes, as appropriate?

5. How do you minimize overall costs associated with inspections, tests, and process or performance audits, as appropriate? How do you prevent defects and rework?

6. How do you improve your support processes to achieve better performance, to reduce variability, and to keep the processes current with business needs and directions? How are improvements shared with other organizational units and processes?

7 Business Results (450 points)

The Business Results category examines your organization's performance and improvement in key business areas: customer satisfaction, product and service performance, financial and marketplace performance, human resource results, operational performance, and governance and social responsibility. Also examined are performance levels relative to those of competitors.

7.1 Customer-Focused Results (75 points)

Summarize your organization's key customer-focused results, including customer satisfaction and customer perceived value. Segment your results by customer groups and market segments, as appropriate. Include appropriate comparative data.

Provide data and information to answer the following questions:

a. Customer-Focused Results

1. What are your current levels and trends in key measures or indicators of customer satisfaction and dissatisfaction? How do these compare with competitors' levels of customer satisfaction?

2. What are your current levels and trends in key measures or indicators of customer-perceived value, including customer loyalty and retention, positive referral, and other aspects of building relationships with customers, as appropriate?

7.2 Product and Service Results (75 points)

Summarize your organization's key product and service performance results. Segment your results by product groups, customer groups, and market segments, as appropriate. Include appropriate comparative data.

Provide data and information to answer the following question:

a. Product and Service Results

1. What are your current levels and trends in key measures or indicators of product and service performance that are important to your customers? How do these results compare with your competitors' performance?

7.3 Financial and Market Results (75 points)

Summarize your organization's key financial and marketplace performance results by market segments, as appropriate. Include appropriate comparative data.

Provide data and information to answer the following questions:

a. Financial and Market Results

1. What are your current levels and trends in key measures or indicators of financial performance, including aggregate measures of financial return and economic value, as appropriate?

2. What are your current levels and trends in key measures or indicators of marketplace performance, including market share or position, business growth, and new markets entered, as appropriate?

7.4 Human Resource Results (75 points)

Summarize your organization's key human resource results, including work system performance and employee learning, development, well-being, and satisfaction. Segment your results to address the diversity of your workforce and the different types and categories of employees, as appropriate. Include appropriate comparative data.

Provide data and information to answer the following questions:

a. Human Resource Results
   1. What are your current levels and trends in key measures or indicators of work system performance and effectiveness?
   2. What are your current levels and trends in key measures of employee learning and development?
   3. What are your current levels and trends in key measures or indicators of employee well-being, satisfaction, and dissatisfaction?

7.5 Organizational Effectiveness Results (75 points)

Summarize your organization's key operational performance results that contribute to the achievement of organizational effectiveness. Segment your results by product groups and market segments, as appropriate. Include appropriate comparative data.

Provide data and information to answer the following questions:

a. Organizational Effectiveness Results
   1. What are your current levels and trends in key measures or indicators of the operational performance of your key value creation processes? Include productivity, cycle time, supplier and partner performance, and other appropriate measures of effectiveness and efficiency.
   2. What are your current levels and trends in key measures or indicators of the operational performance of your key support processes? Include productivity, cycle time, supplier and partner performance, and other appropriate measures of effectiveness and efficiency.
   3. What are your results for key measures or indicators of accomplishment of organizational strategy and action plans?

7.6 Governance and Social Responsibility Results (75 points)

Summarize your organization's key governance and social responsibility results, including evidence of fiscal accountability, ethical behavior, legal compliance, and organizational citizenship. Segment your results by business units, as appropriate. Include appropriate comparative data.

Provide data and information to answer the following questions:

a. Governance and Social Responsibility Results
   1. What are your key current findings and trends in key measures or indicators of fiscal accountability, both internal and external, as appropriate?
   2. What are your results for key measures or indicators of ethical behavior and of stakeholder trust in the governance of your organization?
   3. What are your results for key measures or indicators of regulatory and legal compliance?

4. What are your results for key measures or indicators of organizational citizenship in support of your key communities?

Note: This appendix is based on *Criteria for Performance Excellence for Business*. National Institutes of Standards and Technology. Baldrige National Quality Program. http://www.baldrige.nist.gov/Business_Criteria.htm.

Appendix F: The Feasibility Study and Cost–Benefit Analysis

A feasibility study is a detailed assessment of the need, value, and practicality of a proposed enterprise, such as systems development. Simply stated, it is used to prove that a project is either practical or impractical. The ultimate deliverable is a report that discusses the feasibility of a technical solution and provides evidence for the steering committee to decide whether it is worth going on with any of the suggestions.

What Is a Feasibility Study?

At the beginning of every project, it is often difficult to determine if the project will be successful, or if the cost of the project will be reasonable with respect to the requirements of building a certain software, or if it will be profitable in the long run.

In general, a feasibility study should include the following information:

1. Brief description of the proposed system and characteristics
2. Brief description of the business need for the proposed system
3. A cost–benefit analysis
4. Estimates, schedules, and reports

In developing the feasibility study there will be a need for considerable research into the business viability as well as technical viability of the proposed system.

Feasibility Study Components

There are actually three categories of feasibility.

Financial Feasibility

A systems development project should be economically feasible and provide good value to the organization. The benefits should outweigh the costs of completing the project. The financial feasibility also includes the time, budget, and staff resources used during all stages of the project through completion.

A feasibility study will determine if the proposed budget is enough to fund the project to completion. When finances are being discussed, time must also be a consideration. Saving time and user convenience have always been major concerns when companies develop products. Companies want to make sure that services rendered will be timely. No end user wants to wait for a long time to receive service or use a product, however good it is, if another product is immediately available.

Key risk issues:

1. The length of the project's payback. The shorter the payback is, the lower the risk.
2. The length of the project's development time. The shorter the development time is, the less likely objectives, users, and development personnel will change, consequently the lower the risk.
3. The smaller the differences are that people make in cost, benefit, and life-cycle estimates, the greater the confidence you will achieve the expected return.

Technical Feasibility

A computer system should be practical to develop and easy to maintain. It is important that the necessary expertise be available to analyze, design, code, install, operate, and maintain the system. Technical feasibility addresses the possibility and desirability of a computer solution in the problem area. Assessments can be made based on many factors, for example, knowledge of current and emerging technical solutions, availability of technical personnel on staff, working knowledge of technical staff, capacity of the proposed system to meet system requirements, and capacity of the proposed system to meet performance requirements.

Developing new technology will have to take into account the current technology. Will today's technology be able to sustain what we plan to develop? How realistic is the project? Do we have the knowledge and tools needed to accomplish the job? Emerging technology is getting more and more advanced with each passing day, and somehow we need to know if our objectives can be realized. It is not enough to note if the product in development is technologically feasible; we also have to make sure that it is at par with or more advanced than technology in use today.

Key risk issues:

1. Project staff skills and clarity of project design requirements. Technical risk is reduced where similar problems have been solved or where the design requirements are understandable to all project participants.
2. Proven and accepted equipment and software. Tried and tested hardware and software components carry lower risk. Projects that are novel or break new ground carry higher risk.
3. Project complexity. A project that requires a high degree of technical skills and experience will be a higher-risk undertaking than one that is not as sophisticated and can be handled by less specialized people.

Organizational or Operational Feasibility

A systems development project should meet the needs and expectations of the organization. It is important that the system be accepted by the user and be operational. The following requirements should be taken into consideration in determining if the system is operationally feasible: staff resistance or receptiveness to change, management support for a new system, nature or level of user involvement, direct and indirect impact of new system on current work practices, anticipated performance and outcome of the new system compared to the old system, and viability of development and implementation schedule. The following issues should also be addressed:

1. Does the organization for which the information system is to be supplied have a history of acceptance of information technology or has past introduction led to conflict?
2. Will personnel within the organization be able to cope with operating the new technology?
3. Is the organizational structure compatible with the proposed information system?

Key risk issues:

1. User acceptance. The more strongly the users support the project, the less risk there is of failure.
2. Changes to organizational policies and structure. The more a project influences changes to relationships within an organization or modifies existing policies, the greater the risk is.
3. Changes to method of operation, practices, and procedures. The more a project necessitates major changes or modifications to standard operating procedures in an organization, the greater the risk of failure.

Organizational feasibility, depending upon the scope of the software to be developed, might require the following analyses, particularly if the software being developed is a product that will be introduced to the marketplace:

Competitive analysis: Competitive analysis refers to the study of the current trends and different brand names available in today's market to enforce competitive advantage in product development.

New product development analysis: New product development is a key factor in feasibility studies; it studies the need and uniqueness of a product, justifying further study, development, and subsequent launching.

Performance tracking analysis: Performance tracking evaluates how well a product will perform technically, and financially in relation to its features and requirements.

Cost–Benefit Analysis

One of the major deliverables of the feasibility study is the cost–benefit analysis. In this document the organizational, financial, and technical aspects of creating the software are put into a dollars and cents format.

The purpose of this document is to determine whether the costs exceed the benefits of the new or modified system. Costs associated with a computer project can be categorized as follows:

1. Systems analysis and design
2. Purchase of hardware
3. Software costs
4. Training costs
5. Installation costs
6. Conversion and changeover costs
7. Redundancy costs
8. Operating costs including people costs

Many specific costs are subcategorized within these categories such as: analyst calculations of total cost of project, alternatives to purchasing hardware, the staff needed to train users, maintenance costs for hardware and software, costs of power and paper, and costs associated with personnel to operate the new system. A more detailed list follows:

Equipment: Disk drives, computers, telecommunications, tape drives, printers, facsimiles, voice and data networks, terminals, modems, data encryption devices, and physical firewalls (leased or purchased).

Software: Application programs, operating systems, diagnostic programs, utility programs, commercial off-the-shelf (COTS) software such as word processors and graphics programs, database management software, communications software, and server software (leased or purchased).

Commercial services: Teleprocessing, cell phones, voicemail, online processing, Internet access, packet switching, data entry, and legal services.

Support services: Systems analysis and design, programming, training, planning, project management, facilities management, and network support.

Supplies: CDs, tapes, paper, pens, pencils, CD-ROMs, and so on.

Personnel: The salary and benefits for all staff involved. Benefits are usually calculated at a rate of 30 percent of the base salary.

It is important that the benefits outweigh the costs. Some of the benefits cannot necessarily be measured, but nevertheless should be taken into consideration. Some of those benefits are intangible such as savings in labor costs, benefits due to faster processing, better decision making, better customer service, and error reduction. When dealing with both the benefits and the costs, it may be difficult to determine either in advance.

Cost information can be obtained from:

1. Experiences from the past: Old documents and information will be useful in getting some ideas about the cost of software, hardware, and each service. Invoices for expenses for resources purchased for prior projects are particularly useful.
2. Costs from market: It's also important to get the current market price for your software system.
3. Publishing: Business and trade publications and the Internet are other sources of price information, as well as product functionality.
4. Personal experience: End users and system staff might have relevant information on costs and product feature-sets.

Scheduling the Feasibility Study

Creating a schedule for the feasibility study is very important in that it puts into perspective the amount of time required, the people involved, potential consumers, and the competition that will provide the relevant information. Tasks include selecting a team, assigning appropriate tasks to each team member, and estimating the amount of time required to finish each task. Some of the scheduling tools that can be utilized are diagrams showing relevant work scheduling in relation to the tasks required to finish the feasibility study. Some of these use a table such as shown Table F.1, a Gantt chart (Figure F.1), or a PERT diagram (Figure F.2), which is represented by a network of nodes and arrows

Table F.1 Task List

Feasibility Study Tasks	Detailed Activity	Weeks Required
Data gathering	Conduct interviews	3
	Administer questionnaires	4
	Read company reports	4
	Introduce prototype	5
	Observe reactions to prototype	3
Data flow and decision analysis	Analyze data flow	8
Proposal preparation	Perform cost–benefit analysis	3
	Prepare proposal	2
	Present proposal	2

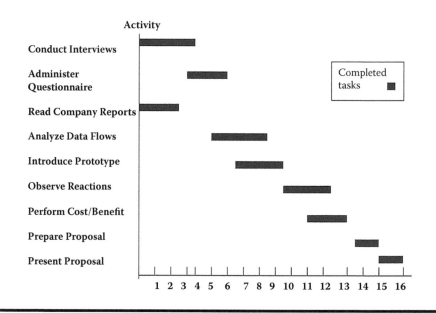

Figure F.1   Figuring the time schedule in relation to the related activity may also be accomplished using a two-dimensional Gantt chart.

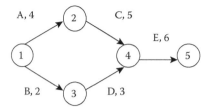

Figure F.2   A PERT diagram (program evaluation and review techniques).

that are evaluated to determine the project's critical activities. Precedence of activities is important in determining the length of the project when using a PERT diagram.

The Feasibility Study Process

There is a process that a feasibility study should follow. It should analyze the proposed project and produce a written description, define and document possible types of systems, and develop a statement of the probable types of systems. The feasibility study should analyze the costs of similar systems; produce a rough estimate of the system size, costs, and schedules; and define the benefits of the system. It should produce an estimate of the next stage of the life cycle. Analysis of the current system is necessary in order to establish feasibility of a future technical system. This will provide evidence for the functions that the new system will perform. Finally, a report should be written containing suggestions, findings, and necessary resources.

A feasibility report will be written and submitted to management containing all relevant information including financial expenses and expected benefits as shown in Figure F.3. Based on this report, management will make its determination about the future of the project. Much of the information will come from the analyst and the systems investigation. The report should include information on the feasibility of the project, the principal work areas for the project, any needs for specialist staff that may be required at later dates, possible improvements or potential savings, costs, and benefits as well as recommendations. Charts and diagrams relative to the project, such as Gantt and PERT charts, should be included in the feasibility report. Obviously, the project cannot proceed until the feasibility report has been accepted.

Determining Feasibility

A proposal may be regarded feasible if it satisfies the three criteria we've discussed at length: financial, technical, and operational. Scheduling and legal issues must also be considered. It is possible to proceed with the project even if one or more of

Int Rate	10.00%				
NPV	$1,450,582.94				
IRR	103%				
Payback	2.0yrs				
Payback manually calculated					

Assumptions	EXPENSES	YR1	YR2	YR3	YR4	YR5
	IT Related					
Initial Hardware plus additional yearly capacity	Hardware	$304,000	$50,000	$50,000	$50,000	$50,000
Solution Software and licensing costs for upgrades	Software	$111,000				
Project related design and implementation costs	People	$90,000				
Training, policies and procedures	Training/Materials	$250,000				
Costs associated with potential unknown factors	Variance	$75,000				
	User Related					
	Hardware					
	Software					
Human Resources for the Project	People	$300,000				
Training for developers on application rollback	Training/Materials	$10,000				
	Lost Opportunity					
	TOTAL	$1,140,000	$50,000	$50,000	$50,000	$50,000
	BENEFITS					
	IT Related					
Gains achieved from buying less servers	Hardware	$83,000	$83,000	$83,000	$83,000	$83,000
	Software	$0				
1 man less spent Managing Storage	People	$50,000	$50,000	$50,000	$50,000	$50,000
Gains from more efficient use of storage	Productivity Gains	$75,000	$100,000	$125,000	$150,000	$175,000
	User Related					
Improved development efficiency, based on company growth	Hardware	$0				
	Software	$0				
Improved profit margins on projects, based on company growth	People	$150,000	$175,000	$200,000	$225,000	$250,000
	Productivity Gains	$200,000	$225,000	$250,000	$275,000	$300,000
	TOTAL		$558,300	$633,300	$708,300	$783,300	$858,300
	TOTAL PMT	($581,700)	$583,300	$658,300	$733,300	$808,300

Figure F.3 Expected benefits compared to expenses.

these criteria fail to be met. For example, management may find that it is not possible to proceed with the project at one point in time but may find that the project can commence at a later date. Another option would be for management to make amendments to the proposed agenda and agree to proceed upon those conditions. Conversely, a project that may have been determined feasible may later be determined infeasible due to changes in circumstances.

Other Considerations

When dealing with many kinds of projects, costs and benefits are usually the main concerns. There are, however, other concerns that should be considered. Project timeframes should also be addressed in the feasibility study. Realistic estimates should be made detailing staff resources and time required to complete the different phases of the project.

In dealing with the project it is also important to consider all legal or regulatory issues that may occur throughout the feasibility or any stage of the project. It may be wise to conduct a preliminary investigation of any obligations or regulatory or legal issues prior to commencement of the initial project stages.

Stages of Feasibility Study

The stages of a feasibility study include, as shown in Figure F.4:

1. Define project scope
2. Activity analysis
3. Needs analysis
4. Conceptual modeling
5. Use case modeling
6. Identify nonfunctional requirements
7. Identify options
8. Select options
9. Plan acquisition strategy
10. Develop business case
11. Package feasibility study

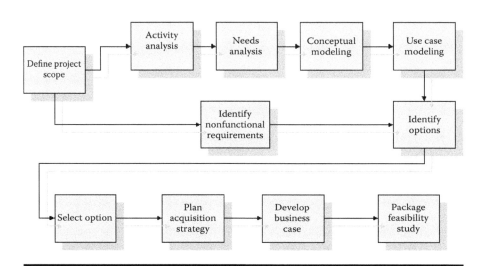

Figure F.4   The stages of a feasibility study.

Conclusion

The primary goal of the feasibility study is to evaluate the risks and benefits and the potential of a proposed project. We also know that the study should aid in producing a solid plan for the research stage and stages to follow so that the project will be given careful consideration and be properly funded. A feasibility study will help you make informed and transparent decisions at crucial points during the developmental process to determine whether it is operationally, economically, and technically realistic to proceed with a particular course of action. It should provide a means of minimizing risks, clarifying issues and expectations, and improving the decision-making process and the stages to follow.

Appendix G: Project Plan Outline: Project DeDS—The Dog e-Dating System ID – PRJ01

Approval Record

Department	Printed Name	Signature	Role	Date

August, 2007

Document Information

Document Name	Document Type	Doc. ID
Project DeDS - The Dog-eDating System.doc	Project Plan Outline	PRJ01

Document Creation Information

Date	Created By	Comments	Number of Pages
2007-08-07	SAMPLE	Document Creation	31

Document Revision History

Ver Number	Update Description	Updated by	Date
0.1	First Draft		07-08-07
0.2	Project Estimates		15-08-07
0.3	Project Schedule and Staff Organization		22-08-07
0.4	Risk Mitigation and Management Plan		28-08-07
0.5	Tracking and Control Mechanism		10-09-07

Table of Contents

G1 Goals And Objectives

G1.1 Project Name

This project plan serves as a coordinating tool, planning aid, and communication device to identify and convey the key elements of the DeDS project. The development effort will be performed entirely within the organization without the participation of outside parties.

> Project Title: DeDS—The Dog e-Dating System
> Sponsor: Sample
> Organization Name: Sample
> Email: email@domain.com
> Phone: +1

G1.2 Business Goals and Objectives

The primary business goal entails the company gaining a market share of 20 percent on the online Dog e-Dating System by the end of the first year, corresponding to a 32 percent increase on current yearly net revenue. Additionally it will serve as a promoting vehicle for partnership agreements and an advertisement medium for pet stores that will increase our net revenue by 8 percent by the end of the first year. The market share should rise to 30 percent by the end of the second year, representing 48 percent of yearly net revenue, and partnerships and advertisement revenues should represent 20 percent of our net revenue.

The goal of the project is to create a platform that enables the fulfillment of the business objectives, by creating an interactive online system which registers information from customers and potential customers that supports matching of eligible dogs for breeding based on different searchable criteria.

G1.3 Scope

The limited gene pool caused by continued inbreeding means that deleterious genes become widespread and the breed loses vigor. Apart from natural occurrences, most of the time this is due to lack of options or knowledge of the creator. The ultimate result of this continuous inbreeding is terminal lack of vigor and probable extinction as the gene pool contracts, fertility decreases, abnormalities increase (common examples in the bulldog and German shepherd), and mortality rates rise. On the other side, selective breeding also has risks inasmuch as a number of breeds now exhibit hereditary faults due to the overuse of a particular "typey" stud that was later found to carry a gene detrimental to health.

The Dog e-Dating System provides a secure and informative source for selective breeding allowing customers to preserve or improve breed purity. By subscribing to DeDS, users will provide their contact information and relevant dog information.

The system will perform an initial classification, analyze, and report potential matches based on client criteria or professional tips.

The system will promote business transactions among users, professional services, and products from our partners and a permission marketing database for personalized advertisement. These three areas will generate the revenue of the DeDS. The system will charge a 17 percent fee over the breed price on all business transactions between users, a monthly fee of $100 USD, an 8 percent fee on all products and services provided by partners, and a $300 USD for an advertisement e-mail service to selected customers based on dog, contact, purchased services and products, and transaction information.

G1.4 Time and Budget Constraints

We propose the following chronogram for the implementation of the DeDS:

Tasks/Week	1	2	3	4	5	6	7	8	9	10	11	12	13	14	15	16	17	18	19	20
Planning																				
Requirement Analysis																				
Specification																				
Construction																				
Test Scripts																				
System Tests																				
Configuration																				
Integration Tests																				
Training																				
Acceptance Tests																				
Production Roll Out																				
Technical Support																				
Project Management																				
Milestones	PPO			REQ SDP								TS				SDF SW			ACP	

PPO - Project Plan Outline
REQ - Requirements
SDP- Solution Design Draft
SDF-Solution Design Final
Doc-Manuals
SW- Software
TS- Test Specification
ACP- Aceptance

According to the budget defined for 2007, this project has a limited budget of $258,000 USD. This amount should be paid according to the following plan:

Phase	*Percentage*
Adjudication	30
After 4 Weeks	10
After 8 Weeks	10
After 12 Weeks	20
Acceptance Tests Deliver	20
Acceptance	10

G1.5 General and Technical Requirements

The DeDS should support the following general requirements:

- Web-based application allowing users easy access and use.
- The ability to create user accounts with contact and dog information.
- The ability to allow users to drop an existing account.
- The ability to authenticate users based on Login/Password.
- The ability to edit/delete contact and dog information.
- A mechanism to query and search the database based on definable criteria and filters.
- Support for secure e-payments.
- Creation of and participation in Online Forum and communities with e-mail forwarding.
- A mechanism for users to create alerts based on searchable criteria.
- Support for different currencies (four decimals).
- Support for e-mail broadcast based on predefined criteria.
- Support for banner advertisement based on user history and contact/dog information.
- Support for different tax rates.
- An external interface based on standard protocols such as Corba, APIs, Soap (XML), or Web services.
- Allowance of at least 500 simultaneous users with no visible performance bottlenecks.
- In machines with more than one CPU the system should be able to take advantage and run processes on different CPUs.
- System uptime should not be lower than 99 percent.
- Every authentication request and online payment should be based on the HTTPS protocol.

Currently the infrastructure is based on Solaris 10 and Linux AS4 Servers with Oracle 10g databases and Bea WebLogic 10 Application Server. All developments should be compatible with this requirement in order to avoid restrictions on technology migrations in the future.

According to our technological plan and system architecture, all systems should be based in an *N*-Tier layer with support of the following hardware:

- Database Server:
  - Platform: Solaris 10 64 bits
  - CPU: 4 × @ 850 MHz
  - RAM: 8 GB
  - Network Card: 1000 Mb
  - HD: 300 Gb
- Application Server
  - Platform: Solaris 10 64 bits
  - CPU: 4 × @1000 MHz
  - RAM: 16 GB
  - Network Card: 1000 Mb
  - HD: 100 Gb
- Presentation Layer
  - Platform: Windows XP SP2/Vista 32 or 64 Bits
  - CPU: Pentium III 700 MHz (minimum)
  - RAM: 256 MB SDRAM
- Graphics Card: AGP 4/8 MB SGRAM

G1.6 Training and Documentation

According to our standards all projects should deliver project and product documentation including but not limited to:

- Feasibility report
- Project plan
- System requirements specification
- Solution design
- System operator's policies and procedures
- User, support, and operations manuals
- Test specification

All training should be provided in specific courses with extensive use of real-case scenarios. All course, project and product documentation should be delivered both in paper and electronic format.

G1.7 Installation

Participation of one system administrator or DBA in all new software installations hosted in the datacenter is mandatory. For that reason, all installations should be signed by the IT manager and scheduled at least four days in advance with the datacenter manager.

G2 Project Estimates

G2.1 People Costs

G2.1.1 Historical or Researched Data

This project will be developed by our internal IT staff. There is no need to recruit new employees or outsources in order to finish this project. The team will be composed of eight IT resources and one business analyst from the business unit requirement team. The salaries of the resources involved in the project are shown in Table G.1.

G2.1.2 Salary Requirements

According to the figures in Table G.1, the average burdened labor rate is $57.70 USD per resource per hour based on the 40 percent salary per month

G2.2 Equipment Costs

G2.2.1 Hardware

According to Point 1.5 the project will be implemented in two different servers with Solaris OS 10. Oracle replied to our RFP with the following quotations:

- Application Server, $10,423 USD
- Database Server, $12,775 USD

Both servers include our partnership discount of 12 percent concerning market price.

G2.2.2 Software

The software will be developed in Java J2EE over the Bea Weblogic application server with Oracle 10g database. Our current agreement with Bea will be exceeded and we need to purchase four more licenses (one per CPU) of Bea Weblogic Integrator. According to their last proposal from June this year, each license costs $5,418 USD and a yearly support and maintenance fee of 20 percent over this value.

G2.3 Estimation Techniques

G2.3.1 COCOMO

According to historical data in similar projects the average number of lines of code per programmer per day in an object-oriented language is 120 with a 17 percent

Table G.1   Salary Requirements

Profession	Salary per Month (40%)	Average Salary per Month ($)
Program manager	140,80	10,057.14
Programmer 1	10,115	7,225.00
Programmer 2	9,875	7,053.57
Programmer 3	9,476	6,768.57
Quality and test 1	8,853	6,323.57
Quality and test 2	8,700	6,214.29
Web designer	9,563	6,830.71
Business analyst	7,718	5,512.86
Tecnhical manager	12,997	9,283.57

File   Edit   View   Parameters   Calibrate   Phase   Maintenance   Help

Project Name: Project DeDS

Scale Factor   Schedule

Development Model: Early Design

X	Module Name	Module Size	LABOR Rate ($/month)	EAF	NCM Effort DEV	EST Effort DEV	PROD	COST	INST COST	Staff	RISK
	Website Design	S : 2246	10032.00	1.00	8.2	8.2	275.0	81922.53	36.5	0.7	0.0
	System Administr	S : 702	10032.00	1.00	2.6	2.6	275.0	25605.35	36.5	0.2	0.0
	User Admisistrat	S : 561	10032.00	1.00	2.0	2.0	275.0	20462.40	36.5	0.2	0.0
	Search Engine	S : 421	10032.00	1.00	1.5	1.5	275.0	15355.92	36.5	0.1	0.0
	e-Payment	S : 1404	10032.00	1.00	5.1	5.1	275.0	51210.70	36.5	0.5	0.0
	Marketing	S : 1263	10032.00	1.00	4.6	4.6	275.0	46067.75	36.5	0.4	0.0
	Discussion Forum	S : 702	10032.00	1.00	2.6	2.6	275.0	25605.35	36.5	0.2	0.0
	Communications	S : 421	10032.00	1.00	1.5	1.5	275.0	15355.92	36.5	0.1	0.0
	Report	S : 421	10032.00	1.00	1.5	1.5	275.0	15355.92	36.5	0.1	0.0
	Authentication	S : 280	10032.00	1.00	1.0	1.0	275.0	10212.96	36.5	0.1	0.0

		Estimated	Effort	Sched	PROD	COST	INST	Staff	RISK
Total Lines of Code:	8421	Optimistic	20.5	9.6	410.5	205793.70	24.4	2.1	
		Most Likely	30.6	10.9	275.0	307154.78	36.5	2.8	0.0
		Pessimistic	45.9	12.4	183.4	460732.17	54.7	3.7	

Figure G.1   COCOMO cost estimation (SLOC method).

Brak. The estimation performed in COCOMO was based on the SLOC sizing method and considered the average burdened labor rate of $57.70 USD per resource per hour, provided by our budget expert. This corresponds to (57.7 × 8 × 22) $10,032 USD a month.

Because this was the first time that we are using COCOMO to estimate costs, the system was not calibrated with previous information.

The results of COCOMO show that the project will require 30.6 person-months of time to complete at cost of $307,154.78 USD.

G2.3.2 Process-Based

The team is composed of the elements in Table G.2. The team is composed of nine resources corresponding to [9(9 − 1)/2] 36 interfaces. The results of the process-based analysis (Figure G.2) show that the project will require 20.24 person-months of time to complete at cost of ($57.70 × 8 × 22 × 20.24) $205,541.24 USD.

G2.3.3 Triangulation

Both methods provide different values with a considerable difference. Process-based estimation requires 20.24 person-months of time and costs $205,541.24 USD. COCOMO shows that the project will require 30.6 person-months of time to complete at cost of $307,154.78 USD. Even though the optimistic figures of COCOMO match the process-based with a very small variance, there is a difference of nearly 34 percent. This is partly due to the process being in a very early stage, and the experience of the programmers both in this technology and in similar previous projects. The development pace will be very fast, and there is the possibility of adapting some code.

Table G.2 Resources and Allocation	
Resource	*Allocation (%)*
Program manager	20
Programmer 1	100
Programmer 2	100
Programmer 3	100
Quality and test 1	100
Quality and test 2	100
Web designer	100
Business analyst	100
Tecnhical manager	20

Activity	Cust. Comm	Planning	Risk Analysis	Engineering		Construction Release		Customer Eval.	Totals
Task				Analysis	Design	Code	Test		
Function									
Website Design	0.45	0.05	0.02	0.34	0.42	0.45	0.5	0.14	2.82
System Administration	0.2	0.08	0.1	0.35	0.37	0.35	0.25	0.10	2
User Administration	0.2	0.08	0.05	0.25	0.55	0.45	0.25	0.12	2.15
Search Engine	0.15	0.05	0.01	0.33	0.39	0.38	0.29	0.10	1.85
e-Payment	0.35	0.05	0.07	0.35	0.41	0.39	0.44	0.11	2.52
Marketing	0.25	0.08	0.07	0.35	0.42	0.45	0.41	0.15	2.43
Discussion Forum	0.1	0.02	0.01	0.19	0.25	0.38	0.41	0.10	1.56
Communication	0.05	0.02	0.01	0.27	0.28	0.44	0.37	0.11	1.6
Report	0.2	0.05	0.04	0.35	0.4	0.36	0.33	0.15	2.08
Authentication	0.05	0.05	0.02	0.05	0.25	0.38	0.23	0.15	1.23
Total	2	0.53	0.4	2.83	3.74	4.03	3.48	1.23	20.24
% effort	9.88	2.62	1.98	13.98	18.48	19.91	17.19	6.08	100

Figure G.2   Process-based estimation.

G3 Project Schedule

G3.1 Project Task List

Please see Table G.3 for the project task list.

Table G.3 Project Task List

Number	Tasks	Deliverable	Dates/ Days	Precedence	Milestone
T001	*Project kickoff*	*Agreement/ contact*	*15-08-2007*		
T999	*Project ends*	*Delivery*			*28-12-2007*
T010	Requirement definition and analysis	Elaborate plan	15-08-2007		24-10-2007
T011	Produce project plan	Deliver plan	3		22-08-2007
T012	Produce solution design	Define requirements	14	T010	
T013		Final solution design	25		22-10-2007
T014		Final project plan	1		24-10-2007
T020	Develop code	Web site	16		23-10-2007
T021		Modules	11		23-10-2007
T022	Create	Documentation	11		23-10-2007
T030	Design	Test plan	15	T013	14-11-2007
T031	Execute	System test	12	T030; T020; T021	14-11-2007
T032		Integration tests	8	T031	10-12-2007
T033	Prepare	Training	5	T022	05-12-2007
T034	Execute	Training	4	T033	05-12-2007
T035	Support	Acceptance tests	11	T034	21-12-2007
T036	Migrate	Software to production	5	T035	28-12-2007

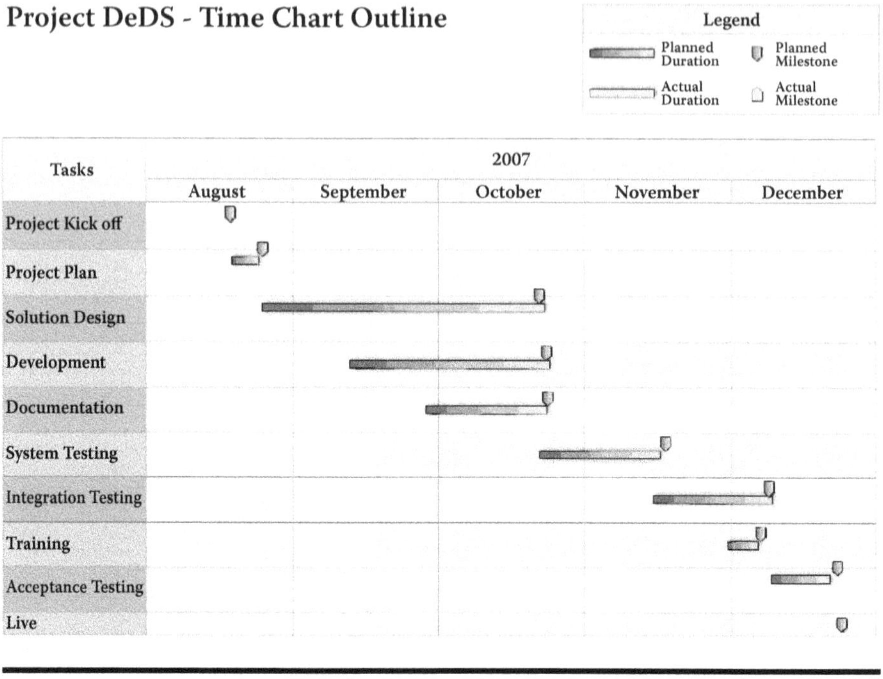

Project DeDS - Time Chart Outline

Figure G.3   Time chart.

G3.2 Timeline Chart

The timeline chart is shown in Figure G.3.

G4 Staff Organization

G4.1 Team Structure

The resources for this project are identified in Table G.4. Each resource is vital to this team and creates the necessary balance to achieve the project goals. This a functional structured team built in order to have all the skills and knowledge necessary for the success of the project.

According to the organization chart shown in Figure G.4, the project manager is supported by a business analyst and reports to the CIO.

G4.2 Management Reporting and Communication

Every week on Mondays, there will be a progress meeting with the program manager, quality manager, technical manager, and marketing manager to gain feedback on project performance. The program manager will report quarterly to the steering

Table G.4   Team Structure

Resource	Resource Role
Pedro	Program manager
Paul	Programmer
Kate	Programmer
John	Programmer
Bill	Quality and tests
Karl	Quality and tests
Roy	Web designer
Greg	Business analyst
Simon	Marketing manager
Jane	Technical manager

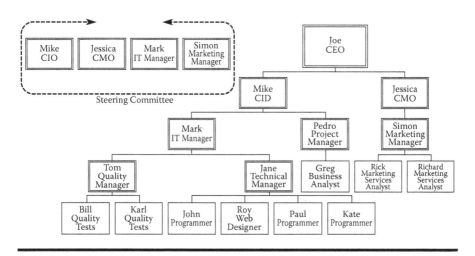

Figure G.4   Company organization chart.

committee on the project performance and major issues concerning project development. All change requests and new requirements will be approved in this forum. The program manager will present a revisited version of the project plan (Gantt chart) with the impact of the new requirements or changes for the evaluation of the steering committee.

G5 Risk Management

G5.1 Project Risks

This software will be running in our datacenter and exposed to the public network through port 80 and port 81 for authentication. It is necessary to ensure a private LAN to host this service and isolate it from the remaining applications hosted in the datacenter. Additionally it is necessary to implement the rules in the firewall between the red network (exposed to the outside world) and the green network (datacenter VLANS), in order to allow connectivity between the application and the database server.

It is imperative to perform stress tests in order to test the load balance Alteons and ensure that the failsafe solution based on cluster redundancy is working. A high volume of data is expected to be stored in the database. In order to avoid performance bottlenecks in the application it is necessary to guarantee that the DBAs suggest the necessary maintenance plans regarding reorganization of indexes and support activities in order to preserve the database performance as it grows.

According to the information uncovered in our analysis, we identified four risk areas:

1. Project risks: Budget, scheduling and resources
2. Technical risks: Solution design, application stress, failover, redundancy, data integrity
3. Business risks: Lack of senior support, marketing failure, miss time to market due to competitor's offer
4. Security risk: Secure customer information, online payments, outside world access to a server in our datacenter

These risks have been further expanded to the following categories:

- *Business Impact Risk (BU):* Product does not meet the customer requests or no longer meets the overall business strategy.
- *Financial (FI):* Budgetary requirements, creditor and debtor management, and general account management concerns.
- *Organizational (OI):* Internal requirements, cultural and structural issues.
- *Compliance/Legal (CL):* Legal requirements, regulation, standard codes, contractual requirements.
- *Equipment (EI):* Equipment utilized in the project (includes maintenance and upgrade).
- *Security (SI):* Overall security of the solution and information.

- *Customers Risk (CU):* Lack of customer involvement in the project.
- *Development Risks (DR):* Risks associated with bugs in the code and delays associated with development issues.
- *Staff Size and Experience Risk (ST):* The experience and knowledge of the people involved in the project as well as the amount of resources.
- *Technology Risks (TR):* The complexity associated with the design of the system

G5.2 Risk Table

Table G.5 lists the risks associated with the project according to the categories described in Section 5.1. Each risk has an estimated probability based on the team's previous experience and historical data and its impact on the development process.

Table G.5   Project Risks

Risk	Category	Probability (%)	Impact[a]
Change of requirements	OI	90	2
Lack of user involvement	CU	40	2
Lack of management involvement	CU	30	2
Poor acceptance by end users (product)	BU	15	2
Limited budget	FI	45	1
Inexperienced project team	ST	10	2
Fraud on payment server	SI	10	1
Customer information security hacked	SI	30	2
Delay in equipment delivery	EI	30	2
Poor estimation on load balance solution	TR	35	3
Datacenter security violated due to "pin holes"	SI	20	1
Not enough storage	EI	30	2
Staff leaving the project team	ST	10	2

[a] Impact values: 1, catastrophic; 2, critical; 3, marginal; 4, negligible.

G5.3 Risk Mitigation, Monitoring, Management Strategy

For each of the risk events there is a contingency plan associated in order to avoid, mitigate, accept, or transfer the risk.

Risk Event	Change of requirements
Risk ID	OI-1
Risk Response Action	Acceptance
Description	Customer will change requirements during the project life cycle, requesting the team to readapt already developed code, create new functionalities, and perform new system and integration tests. The project has a small buffer to accommodate change requests and new requirements. One of the programmers is just being used at 30 percent.
Assigned To	Pedro
Date	29/8/2007

Risk Event	Lack of user involvement
Risk ID	CU-1
Risk Response Action	Transfer
Description	Report lack of user involvement to the responsible functional manager and to project sponsors. Reflect the lack of participation on project schedules and stress that point in progress meetings.
Assigned To	Pedro
Date	29/8/2007

Risk Event	Lack of management involvement
Risk ID	CU-2
Risk Response Action	Mitigate
Description	Communicate the impact of AWOL project sponsors in the project success.
Assigned To	Pedro
Date	29/8/2007

Risk Event	Limited budget
Risk ID	FI-1
Risk Response Action	Avoid
Description	Any change that implies a budget change needs to be approved by the steering committee.
Assigned To	Pedro
Date	29/8/2007

Risk Event	Poor acceptance by the customers
Risk ID	BU-1
Risk Response Action	Mitigate
Description	Evaluate through user's feedback the reason for the poor acceptance. Depending on users' responses reformulate offer with marketing and if necessary design more features.
Assigned To	Simon
Date	29/8/2007

Risk Event	Inexperienced project team
Risk ID	ST-1
Risk Response Action	Avoid
Description	All managers assigned to this project have several years of experience allowing them to supervise more inexperienced resources and mitigate their lack of experience or knowledge.
Assigned To	Pedro
Date	29/8/2007

Risk Event	Fraud on payment server
Risk ID	SI-1
Risk Response Action	Avoid
Description	The secure payment server will be based in an out-sourced service with minimum development from our side. Before going live, our partner runs several tests in order to test compliance with their safety standards.
Assigned To	Pedro
Date	29/8/2007

Risk Event	Customer information security hacked
Risk ID	SI-2
Risk Response Action	Mitigate
Description	All customer information will be encrypted using a 256-bit AES key.
Assigned To	Jane
Date	29/8/2007

Risk Event	Delay in equipment delivery
Risk ID	EI-1
Risk Response Action	Mitigate
Description	A temporary server with similar capacity can be used for a period of one month.
Assigned To	Jane
Date	29/8/2007

Risk Event	Poor estimation on load balance
Risk ID	TR-1
Risk Response Action	Avoid
Description	Stress tests will be executed on the load balancers in order to test performance in several stress scenarios.
Assigned To	Jane
Date	29/8/2007

Risk Event	Datacenter security violated due to "pin holes"
Risk ID	SI-3
Risk Response Action	Mitigate
Description	A security team will be hired to find exploits in our system and recommend defensive measures. Additionally, system administrators will analyze machine logs for suspicious requests.
Assigned To	Pedro
Date	29/8/2007

Risk Event	Not enough storage
Risk ID	SI-3
Risk Response Action	Mitigate
Description	Storage was bought to cover marketing expectations for the first year plus 30 percent.
Assigned To	Jane
Date	29/8/2007

Risk Event	Staff leaving the project
Risk ID	SI-3
Risk Response Action	Mitigate
Description	The program manager will maintain a close relationship with every team member in order to spot alert signs that might indicate a desire to leave the project.
Assigned To	Pedro
Date	29/8/2007

G6 Tracking and Control Mechanisms

Control means comparing where we are to where we are supposed to be in order to employ corrective actions and correct deviations from target. In our project we will use a tracking Gantt chart in order to monitor planned project activities against actual performance. This process occurs every week on Mondays in the project team meeting. The first part of the meeting will review the issue log and establish priorities and corrective actions for each issue. All actions will be classified as Red, Yellow, or Green concerning the impact severity on the project plan. The second part of the meeting will focus on identifying and mitigating potential problems, reducing the probability of occurrence. If any impact on the original plan in terms of schedule, budget, or resources is identified and cannot be resolved with current reserves, it will be documented and a replanned version of the project made and submitted to the steering committee for approval. Replanning without impact on final constraints will be approved directly by the PM in project team meetings. All outputs of the project team meeting will be available to the relevant stakeholders through e-mail with the subject Project Review Week x. In order to avoid delays in solving issues, communication status of future actions or identification of new issues should be reported as soon as possible either formally or informally to the project manager.

G6.1 Quality Assurance and Control

Software quality assurance (SQA) is defined as a planned and systematic approach to the evaluation of the quality of and adherence to software product standards, processes, and procedures. It assures that standards and procedures are established and are followed throughout the project life cycle by monitoring and auditing agreed standards.

In the DeDS project the following standards and procedures will be adopted.

G6.1.1 Documentation

All the documentation respects the internal standards in their specific form and content. The approved standards are:

- IEEE 829: Software test documentation
- IEEE 1016: Recommended practice for software design descriptions
- IEEE 1063: Software user documentation
- BS ISO/IE 6592: Information technology guidelines for the documentation of computer-based applications systems

G6.1.2 Code Standards

This project will be developed using the Java programming language. All restrictions on the use of the language features, structures, style conventions, rules for data structures, interfaces, internal code documentation or comments, filenames, file organization, indentation, declarations, statements, naming conventions, and programming practices follow the Code Conventions for Java Programming Language recommended by Sun available at http://java.sun.com/docs/codeconv/.

G6.1.3 Procedures

The following procedures will be adopted:

- IEEE 1074: Standard for developing software life cycle processes
- ISO/IEC 12207: Information technology, software life cycle processes

G6.1.4 Software Quality Assurance Activities

The following activities will be audited by the QA team:

- Process monitoring, to ensure that all steps are carried out with the ones documented in the procedure
- Configuration management monitoring
- Baseline development and control
- Configuration control against associated documentation
- Software authentication
- Software performance against specification
- Approved changes to the baseline
- Test procedures (software requirements with test plans)
- Test reports are accurate and complete
- Regression testing to ensure that nonconformances have been corrected before delivery
- Adherence to design standards
- Ensuring that approved design is placed under configuration management
- Ensuring that approved design standards are followed
- Ensuring that allocated modules are included in the detail design
- Ensuring that all action items are solved
- Ensuring readiness for testing of all deliverables items
- Ensuring that all test reports are complete and correct
- Certifying that testing is complete and software documentation is ready for delivery
- Participation in the test readiness review and assuring all action items are completed

G6.2 Change Management and Control

The change management process is essential to proactively identify modifications in a project.

All change requests will be delivered by the requestor to the program manager. The program manager will keep a log of all requests received. All change requests will be tracked by the program manager through a change request log.

Appendix H: Project Management Glossary

A

Activity: An element of work performed during the course of a project. An activity normally has expected duration, cost, and resource requirements and results in a deliverable or handoff to another activity. In this way, the activity is tied back to the *Work Breakdown Structure*. Activities are often subdivided into tasks.

Activity-Based Budget: A budgeting concept based on the goods and services produced by an organization for its customers rather than the traditional cost-based budget based on requests from cost centers. Activities are processes that consume resources, such as time and money, to produce a given output.

Actual Cost (AC): Total costs incurred that must relate to whatever cost was budgeted within the planned value and earned value (which can sometimes be direct labor hours alone, direct costs alone, or all costs including indirect costs) in accomplishing work during a given time period. See also *Earned Value*.

Actual Cost of Work Performed (ACWP): This term has been replaced with the term *Actual Cost*.

Administrative Closure: Generating, gathering, and disseminating information to formalize phase or project completion.

Assumptions: Assumptions are factors that, for planning purposes, are considered to be true, real, or certain. Assumptions affect all aspects of project planning, and are part of the progressive elaboration of the project. Project teams frequently identify, document, and validate assumptions as part of their planning process. Assumptions generally involve a degree of risk.

B

Baseline: The original approved plan (for a project, a work package, or an activity), plus or minus approved scope changes. Usually used with a modifier (e.g., cost baseline, schedule baseline, performance measurement baseline). Also called *Baseline Plan.*

Budget at Completion (BAC): The sum of the total budgets for a project.

Budgeted Cost of Work Performed (BCWP): This term has been replaced with the term *Earned Value.*

Budgeted Cost of Work Scheduled (BCWS): This term has been replaced with the term *Planned Value.*

Business Case: Structured proposal for business improvement that functions as a decision package for organizational decision makers. It may contain the goals of the project and how those goals support the goals of the enterprise. Other sections may include a cost–benefit analysis, a requirement analysis, and a make or buy analysis. A business case usually includes a comprehensive fiscal analysis and estimate.

Business Requirements: (1) Requirements state those customer needs that the project output will satisfy. Requirements typically start with the phrase, "The system shall. ..." Business requirements refer to how the project will satisfy the business mission of the customer. (2) Business requirements refer to business functions of the project, such as project management, financial management, or change management.

Buy-In: Usually refers to securing a personal or organizational agreement with project goals or management methods. Buy-in from senior management or functional organizations may be necessary to accomplish many aspects of an enterprise project.

C

Capital Programming: An integrated process within a company for planning, budgeting, procurement, and management of the company's portfolio of capital assets to achieve company strategic goals and objectives with the lowest life-cycle cost and least risk.

Capital Project (Investment): The acquisition of a capital asset and the management of that asset through its life cycle after the initial acquisition. Capital projects (investments) may consist of several useful segments.

Change Control: The processes, procedures, and responsibilities for identifying, evaluating, and managing change. Integration is achieved by assessing a potential change's impact on all relevant aspects of a project, primarily scope, cost, schedule, risk, and quality. Change control involves implementing process change requests and the systematic tracking of change assessment and implementation.

Change Control Management Plan: See *Integrated Change Control Management Plan.*

Change Management: (1) The process of implementing change control. (2) The active involvement of project management in monitoring and controlling the change control process.

Closeout: The last phase of a project. Closeout involves closing contracts, archiving records, completing project administrative tasks, and conducting final project reviews.

Communications Management: See *Project Communications.*

Communications Management Plan: Describes how the various types of project information are distributed, reviewed, updated, and filed.

Concept Definition: A phase of a project where the initial business case (based on a business need) is tested and the viability of the proposed solution and approach are explored. During the *Concept Definition* phase the project is "initiated" or "chartered" and the project sponsor, business sponsor, or project manager is given authority to proceed with the project.

Configuration Management (CM): Any documented procedure used to apply technical and administrative direction and surveillance to identify and document the functional and physical characteristics of an item or system, control any changes to those characteristics, record and report the change and its implementation status, and audit the items and system to verify their conformance to requirements.

Constraint: Applicable restriction that will affect the performance of the project. Any factor that affects when an activity can be scheduled.

Contingencies: See *Reserve* and *Contingency Planning.*

Contingency Planning: The development of a management plan that identifies alternative strategies to be used to ensure project success if specified risk events occur.

Contingency Reserve: The amount of money or time needed above the estimate to reduce the risk of overruns of project objectives to a level acceptable to the organization.

Contract: A mutually binding agreement that obligates the seller to provide the specified product and obligates the buyer to pay for it.

Contract Administration: Managing the relationship with the seller.

Contract Closeout: Completion and settlement of the contract, including resolution of any open items.

Control: The process of comparing actual performance with planned performance, analyzing variances, evaluating possible alternatives, and taking appropriate corrective action as needed.

Control Charts: A graphic display of the results, over time and against established control limits, of a process. They are used to determine if the process is "in control" or in need of adjustment.

Corrective Action: Changes made to bring expected future performance of the project into line with the plan.

Cost Baseline: The process of freezing cost estimates and budget. When a baseline is established, the change control process is implemented and performance is measured against the baselined cost data.

Cost Budgeting: Allocating the overall cost estimates to individual project activities.

Cost Control: Controlling changes to the project budget.

Cost Estimating: Developing an approximation (estimate) of the cost of the resources needed to complete project activities.

Cost Management: The process of monitoring project cost data to determine performance and variance from the planned cost targets/estimates.

Cost Management Plan: Describes the process for implementing change control over cost estimates and the project time-phased cost baseline. The plan includes the steps taken when the performance measurement system identifies major or minor cost variances.

Cost of Quality: The costs incurred to ensure quality. The cost of quality includes quality planning, quality control, quality assurance, and rework.

Cost Performance Index (CPI): The cost efficiency ratio of earned value to actual costs (CPI = EV/AC). CPI is often used to predict the magnitude of a possible cost overrun using the following formula: BAC/CPI = projected cost at completion.

Cost Variance (CV): (1) Any difference between the budgeted cost of an activity and the actual cost of that activity. (2) In earned value (CV = EV − AC).

Crashing: Taking action to decrease the total project duration after analyzing a number of alternatives to determine how to get the maximum duration compression for the least cost.

Critical Activity: Any activity on a critical path. Most commonly determined by using the *Critical Path Method*. Although some activities are "critical," in the dictionary sense, without being on the *Critical Path*, this meaning is seldom used in the project context.

Critical Path: The series of activities that determines the duration of the project. In a deterministic model, the critical path is usually defined as those activities with *Float* less than or equal to a specified value, often zero. It is the longest path through the project. See *Critical Path Method*.

Critical Path Method (CPM): A network analysis technique used to predict project duration by analyzing which sequence of activities (which path) has the least amount of scheduling flexibility (the least amount of *Float*). Early dates are calculated by means of a forward pass using a specified start date. Late dates are calculated by means of a backward pass starting from a specified completion date (usually the forward pass' calculated project *Early Finish Date*).

Critical Success Factors: Defines how progress and outcomes will be measured on a project; sometimes called objectives. Some typical critical success factors include functionality, quality, time, and cost.

Current Finish Date: The current estimate of the point in time when an activity will be completed.

Current Start Date: The current estimate of the point in time when an activity will begin.

Customer: Generally the organization that receives and becomes the final owner of the output of the project. The customer can be either internal or external to the organization developing the project output.

Customer Approval: The formal process of receiving written acceptance of the project output.

Customer Requirements: Requirements enumerate and state the customer needs the project output will satisfy. Requirements typically start with phrase "The system shall . . . ."

D

Data Date (DD): The date at which, or up to which, the project's reporting system has provided actual status and accomplishments. Also called *as-of date.*

Deliverable: Any measurable, tangible, verifiable outcome, result, or item that must be produced to complete a project or part of a project. Often used more narrowly in reference to an external deliverable, which is a deliverable that is subject to approval by the project sponsor or customer.

Dependency: Logical relationship between and among tasks of a project's WBS, which can be graphically depicted on a network. May also refer to dependencies among projects.

Duration (DU): The number of work periods (not including holidays or other nonworking periods) required to complete an activity or other project element. Usually expressed as workdays or workweeks. Sometimes incorrectly equated with elapsed time. See also *Effort.*

Duration Compression: Shortening the project schedule without reducing the project scope. Duration compression is not always possible and often requires an increase in project cost.

E

Early Finish Date (EF): In the *Critical Path Method,* the earliest possible point in time in which the uncompleted portions of an *activity* (or the project) can finish based on the network logic and any schedule *Constraints*. Early finish dates can change as the project progresses and changes are made to the project plan.

Earned Value (EV): The physical work accomplished plus the authorized budget for this work. The sum of the approved cost estimates (may include overhead allocation) for activities (or portions of activities) completed during a given period (usually project-to-date). Previously called the budgeted cost of work performed (BCWP) for an activity or group of activities.

Earned Value Management (EVM): A method for integrating scope, schedule, and resources, and for measuring project performance. It compares the amount of work that was planned with what was actually earned with what was actually spent to determine if cost and schedule performance were as planned.

Effort: The number of labor units required to complete an activity or other project element. Usually expressed as staff hours, staff days, or staff weeks. Should not be confused with duration.

Element: One of the parts, substances, or principles that make up a compound or complex whole.

Estimate: An assessment of the likely quantitative result. Usually applied to project costs and durations and should always include some indication of accuracy (e.g., ± *X* percent). Usually used with a modifier (e.g., preliminary, conceptual, feasibility). Some application areas have specific modifiers that imply particular accuracy ranges (e.g., order-of-magnitude estimate, budget estimate, and definitive estimate in engineering and construction projects).

Estimate at Completion (EAC): The expected total cost of an activity, a group of activities, or of the project when the defined scope of work has been completed. Most techniques for forecasting EAC include some adjustment of the original cost estimate, based on project performance to date.

F

Final Performance Report: Developed during the closeout phase of the project to capture the final variance from baselined scope, cost, and schedule.

Finish Date: A point in time associated with an activity's completion. Usually qualified by one of the following: actual, planned, estimated, scheduled, early, late, baseline, target, or current.

Float: The amount of time that an activity may be delayed from its early start without delaying the project finish date. *Float* is a mathematical calculation, and can change as the project progresses and changes are made to the project plan. Also called slack, total float, and path float.

Functional Manager: A manager responsible for activities in a specialized department or function (e.g., engineering, manufacturing, marketing).

H

Human Resource Management: The processes employed to organize the efforts of personnel assigned to the project. Includes organizational planning, staff acquisition, and team development.

I

Impact Assessment: The process of evaluating project risks and performance variances to determine the effect on project disciplines such as scope, cost, and schedule.

Impact Probability Chart: Rates risks on the cost effect a risk occurrence will generate on the project budget. Can be stated as a percentage or also as a statement such as: very high (above 81 percent), high (60 to 80 percent), probable (40 to 79 percent), low (20 to 39 percent), and very low (below 19 percent).

Information Collection and Distribution: Making needed information available to project shareholders.

Initiation: Approving the project sponsor, business sponsor, or project manager to begin the next phase in the project life cycle.

Integrated Change Control: Coordinating changes across the entire project.

Integrated Change Control Management Plan: Establishes the processes, procedures, and responsibilities for identifying, evaluating, and managing change. Integration is achieved by assessing a potential change's impact to all relevant aspects of a project, primarily scope, cost, schedule, risk, and quality.

Integrated Project Team (IPT): A multidisciplinary team led by a project manager responsible and accountable for planning, budgeting, procurement, and life-cycle management of the investment to achieve its cost, schedule, and performance goals. Team skills include: budgetary, financial, capital planning, procurement, user, program, value management, earned value management, and other staff as appropriate.

L

Lessons Learned: The documented learning gained from the process of performing the project. Lessons learned may be identified at any point. Also considered a project record.

Life Cycle: The entire useful life of a product or service, usually divided into sequential phases that include initiation, development, execution, operation, maintenance, and disposal or termination.

Life-Cycle Costing: The concept of including acquisition, operating, and disposal costs when evaluating various alternatives.

Life-Cycle Costs: The overall estimated cost for a particular program alternative over the time period corresponding to the life of the program, including direct and indirect initial investment (nonrecurring) costs plus any periodic or continuing (recurring) costs of operation and maintenance.

M

Major Acquisition: A capital project (investment) that requires special management attention because of its: (1) importance to a company's mission; (2) high development, operating, or maintenance costs; (3) high risk; (4) high return; or (5) significant role in the administration of a company's programs, finances, property, or other resources.

Management Plan: See also *Project Management Plan.*

Master Schedule: A summary-level schedule that identifies the major activities and key *Milestones.*

Milestone: A significant event in the project, usually completion of a major *Deliverable.*

Milestone Reviews: Decision points in the life cycle where the project or system is presented to stakeholders and approved (or disapproved) to move forward to the next step in the process.

Mitigation: See *Risk Mitigation.*

Monitoring: The capture, analysis, and reporting of project performance, usually as compared to plan.

N

Network Analysis: The process of identifying early and late start and finish dates for the incomplete portions of project activities. See also *Critical Path Method*, and *Program Evaluation and Review Technique.*

O

Operational (Steady State): An asset or part of an asset that has been delivered and is performing the mission.

Organizational Breakdown Structure (OBS): A depiction of the project organization arranged so as to relate *Work Packages* to organizational units.

Organizational Planning: Identifying, documenting, and assigning project roles, responsibilities, and reporting relationships.

P

Performance Criteria: Various standards used to evaluate variances from the scope, schedule, and cost baselines. Examples could include schedule activities that are one week late, cost increases that exceed ten percent of budget, or the addition of a work breakdown structure work package

Performance Reporting: Collecting and disseminating performance information. This includes status reporting, progress measurement, and forecasting.

PERT Chart: The term is commonly used to refer to a project network diagram. See *Program Evaluation and Review Technique* for the traditional definition of PERT.

Planned Value (PV): The cumulative budgeted value of the project for work scheduled to date. PV is calculated by applying the scheduled percentage of completion against the cost budget.

Planning: Preparing, developing, or acquiring the information used to design the investment; assess the benefits, risks, and risk-adjusted life-cycle costs of alternative solutions; and establish realistic cost, schedule, and performance goals, for the selected alternative, before either proceeding to full acquisition of the capital project (investment) or useful segment or terminating the investment. Planning must progress to the point where you are ready to commit to achieving specific goals for the completion of the acquisition before proceeding to the acquisition phase. Information-gathering activities may include market research of available solutions, architectural drawings, geological studies, engineering and design studies, and prototypes. Planning is a useful segment of a capital project (investment). Depending on the nature of the investment, one or more planning segments may be necessary.

PMBOK: *The Project Management Institute's Guide to the Project Management Body of Knowledge.* This document represents project management best practices.

PMBOK Map/Mapping: Coordinating organizational project management functions to the functional processes and knowledge area activities described in the PMBOK.

Policy and Governance: Formal written standards that control the operational functions of a major enterprise organization.

Post-Implementation Report: Documents project status and performance as a result of the *Post-Implementation Review.*

Post-Implementation Review: The last of the IT milestone reviews. Conducted at a time when an assessment of the operation of the project output is practical. Determines open project activities and ensures major project requirements are satisfied.

Procurement Management: See *Project Procurement Management.*

Procurement Management Plan: Describes the project procurement processes such as: solicitation planning, solicitation, source selection, and contract administration. Includes the tools, techniques, and output from each procurement process.

Program: A group of related projects managed in a coordinated way. Programs usually include an element of ongoing work.

Program Evaluation and Review Technique (PERT): An event-oriented network analysis technique used to estimate project duration when there is uncertainty in the individual activity duration estimates. PERT applies the critical path method using durations that are computed by a weighted average of optimistic, pessimistic, and most likely duration estimates. PERT computes the standard deviation of the completion date from those of the path's activity durations.

Project: A temporary endeavor undertaken to create a unique product, service, or result.

Project Assumptions: See *Assumptions.*

Project Authority: Generally a senior organizational executive who approves project mission and cost planning. In some cases the project authority and project sponsor may be the same executive.

Project Budget: The estimated costs, over time, for each project *Work Breakdown Structure* element.

Project Charter: A document issued by senior management that formally authorizes the existence of a project. It provides the *Project Manager* with the authority to apply organizational resources to project activities.

Project Closeout: See *Closeout.*

Project Constraints: See *Constraints.*

Project Control: The act of monitoring and measuring variances from the project plan. Implementation of the integrated change control process establishes control over project activities.

Project Communications: The process that ensures the generation, collection, dissemination, and storage of project information. Project communications includes communications planning, information distribution, performance reporting, and administrative closure.

Project Initiation: See *Initiation.*

Project Life Cycle: A collection of generally sequential project phases whose name and number are determined by the control needs of the organization or organizations involved in the project.

Project Management: The application of knowledge, skills, tools, and techniques to project activities in order to meet the project requirements.

Project Management Information System (PMIS): A system that facilitates project information flow within an organization.

Project Management Office (PMO): The organization, either at the enterprise, administration, or project level that aids *Project Managers* with standards, tools, and techniques. The PMO maintains project metrics and in most cases monitors and consolidates project cost reporting

Project Management Plan: A formal approved document used to guide both project execution and project control. The primary uses of the project plan are to document planning assumptions and decisions, facilitate communication among stakeholders, and document approved scope, cost, and schedule *Baselines*. It gives the essentials of a project in terms of its objectives, justification, and how the objectives are to be achieved. It describes how major activities of the project management function are to be accomplished (project execution), and describes the methods of overall project control. The project management plan includes the subsidiary plans covering the project management knowledge areas.

Project Management Plan Development: Integrating and coordinating all project plans to create a consistent coherent document.

Project Management Plan Execution: Carrying out the project plan by performing the activities included therein.

Project Management Process: Overlapping activities occurring at varying intensities throughout each phase of the project.

Project Management Software: A class of computer applications specifically designed to aid with planning and controlling project costs and schedules.

Project Management Team: The members of the project team who are directly involved in project management activities. On some smaller projects, the project management team may include virtually all of the project team members.

Project Manager (PM): The individual responsible for managing a project.

Project Master Schedule: A detailed schedule, based on project milestones and deliverables, that integrates all aspects of the project. The project master schedule uses the *Work Breakdown Structure (WBS)*.

Project Performance Reports: See *Performance Reporting*.

Project Phase: A collection of logically related project activities, usually culminating in the completion of a major *Deliverable*.

Project Planning: The development and maintenance of the project plan.

Project Procurement Management: A subset of project management that includes the processes required to acquire goods and services to attain project scope from outside the performing organization. It consists of procurement planning, solicitation planning, solicitation, source selection, contract administration, and contract closeout.

Project Procurement Management Plan: See *Procurement Management Plan*.

Project Quality Management: A subset of project management that includes the processes required to ensure that the project will satisfy the needs for which it was undertaken. It consists of quality planning, quality assurance, and quality control.

Project Schedule: The planned dates for performing activities and the planned dates for meeting *Milestones*.

Project Scope: The work that must be done to deliver a product with the specified features and functions.

Project Scope Management: A subset of project management that includes the processes required to ensure that the project includes all of the work required, and only the work required, to complete the project successfully. It consists of initiation, scope planning, scope definition, scope verification, and scope change control.

Project Sponsor: Executive-level person or organization that champions the project goals. In some cases, but not all, the project sponsor may control the financial resources for the project.

Project Status Report: Details the current and upcoming activities on the project. Also can report on performance related to project scope, schedule, and cost.

Project Team Members: The people who report either directly or indirectly to the *Project Manager.*

Project Team Resources: Generally refers to personnel assigned to the project team. May include skill descriptions and availability.

Project Time Management: A subset of *Project Management* that includes the processes required to ensure timely completion of the project. It consists of activity definition, activity sequencing, activity duration estimating, schedule development, and schedule control.

Q

Qualitative Risk Analysis: Performing qualitative analysis of risks and conditions to prioritize their effects on the project objectives. It involves assessing the probability and impact of project risks and using methods such as the probability and impact matrix to classify risks into categories of high, moderate, and low for prioritized risk response planning.

Quality Assurance (QA): (1) The process of evaluating overall project performance on a regular basis to provide confidence that the project will satisfy the relevant quality standards. (2) The organizational unit that is assigned responsibility for quality assurance.

Quality Control (QC): (1) The process of monitoring specific project results to determine if they comply with relevant quality standards and identifying ways to eliminate causes of unsatisfactory performance. (2) The organizational unit that is assigned responsibility for quality control.

Quality Management: A collection of quality policies, plans, procedures, specifications, and requirements is attained through *Quality Assurance* (managerial) and *Quality Control* (technical).

Quality Management Plan: Addresses what will be measured, how it will be measured, the responsibility for those activities, and how quality improvement will be implemented during the course of the project.

Quality Planning: Identifying which quality standards are relevant to the project, and determining how to satisfy them.

Quantitative Risk Analysis: Measuring the probability and consequences of risks and estimating their implications for project objectives. Risks are characterized by probability distributions of possible outcomes. This process uses quantitative techniques such as simulation and decision tree analysis.

R

Reserve: A provision in the project plan to mitigate cost or schedule risk. Often used with a modifier (e.g., management reserve, contingency reserve) to provide further detail on what types of risk are meant to be mitigated. The specific meaning of the modified term varies by application area.

Resource: People, equipment, or materials used to accomplish activities.

Rework: Action taken to bring a defective or nonconforming item into compliance with requirements or specifications.

Risk: An uncertain event or condition that, if it occurs, has a positive or negative effect on a project's objectives.

Risk Category: A source of potential risk reflecting technical, project management, organizational, or external sources.

Risk Containment Plan: A document detailing all identified risks, including description, cause, probability of occurring, impact(s) on objectives, proposed responses, owners, and current status. Also referred to as *Risk Response Plan*.

Risk Event: A discrete occurrence that may affect the project for better or worse.

Risk Identification: Determining which risk events might affect the project and documenting their characteristics.

Risk Management: The art and science of identifying, analyzing, and responding to risk factors throughout the life of a project and in the best interests of its objectives.

Risk Management Plan: Documents how risk processes will be carried out during the project. This is an output of risk management planning.

Risk Mitigation: Risk mitigation seeks to reduce the probability or impact of a risk to below an acceptable threshold.

Risk Monitoring and Control: Monitoring residual risks, identifying new risks, executing risk reduction plans, and evaluating their effectiveness throughout the project life cycle.

Risk Response Plan: See *Risk Containment Plan*.

S

Schedule Baseline: See *Baseline*.

Schedule Control: Controlling changes to the schedule.

Schedule Critical Path: Activities or tasks in a project schedule that, if the duration changes, will either shorten or lengthen the total duration of the project.

Schedule Dependency: The linking of tasks in a project schedule in order of execution or implementation. Example: Task A must be completed before task B.

Schedule Development: Analyzing activity sequences, activity durations, and resource requirements to create the project schedule.

Schedule Management: Updating the project master schedule and comparing progress with the baseline schedule. Changes to the project schedule are managed through the *Integrated Change Control Management Plan*.

Schedule Performance: Comparing the project master schedule with the baseline schedule to determine slippage or changes in scope.

Schedule Performance Index (SPI): The schedule efficiency ratio of *Earned Value* accomplished against the planned value. The SPI describes what portion of the planned schedule was actually accomplished. SPI is calculated as (SPI = EV/PV).

Schedule Variance (SV): (1) Any difference between the scheduled completion of an activity and the actual completion of that activity. (2) In *Earned Value*, (SV = EV – PV).

Scope: The sum of the products and services to be provided as a project. See *Project Scope*.

Scope Change: Any change to the *Project Scope*. A scope change almost always requires an adjustment to the project cost or schedule.

Scope Change Control: Controlling changes to *Project Scope*.

Scope Creep: Any change to the *Project Scope* (products and services described by the project) that happens incrementally and is subtle in recognition.

Scope Definition: Subdividing the major *Deliverables* into smaller, more manageable components to provide better control.

Scope Management: See *Integrated Change Control*.

Scope Planning: The process of progressively elaborating the work of the project, which includes developing a written scope statement that includes the project justification, the major deliverables, and the project objectives.

Scope Statement: The scope statement provides a documented basis for making future project decisions and for confirming or developing common understanding of project scope among the stakeholders. As the project progresses, the scope statement may need to be revised or refined to reflect approved changes to the scope of the project.

Scope Verification: Formalizing acceptance of the *Project Scope*.

Simulation: A simulation uses a project model that translates the uncertainties specified at a detailed level into their potential impact on objectives that are expressed at the level of the total project. Project simulations use computer models (e.g., Monte Carlo technique) and estimates of risk at a detailed level.

Solicitation: Obtaining quotations, bids, offers, or proposals as appropriate.

Source Selection: Choosing from among potential sellers.

Sponsor: See *Project Sponsor.*

Staff Acquisition: Getting needed human resources assigned to and working on the project.

Stakeholders: Individuals and organizations that are actively involved in the project, or whose interests may be positively or negatively affected as a result of project execution or project completion. They may also exert influence over the project and its results.

Start Date: A point in time associated with an activity's start, usually qualified by one of the following: actual, planned, estimated, scheduled, early, late, target, baseline, or current.

Statement of Work (SOW): A narrative description of products or services to be supplied under contract.

System Development: A project life-cycle phase encompassing the design, integration, and demonstration of the project output. Generally follows the planning phase and is usually accomplished in conjunction with the execution and control process groups.

System Development Life Cycle: Varies by project output. For example, in the construction of the system development life cycle it could be described as feasibility, planning, design, construction, and turnover. For software development a spiral (the life cycle repeats until complete) process is employed: requirements identification, system design, build and rebuild, and evaluation.

System Development Methodology: The type of methodology to be used in a system development project, such as rational unified process, spiral development, iterative development, system development methodology, information engineering methodology, or rapid application development methodology.

System Operation: The phase in the system life cycle where the system is in use and ongoing activities such as regular maintenance and improvement are underway.

System Prototype: A development model that is used for testing in an operational environment. Typically built to be modified into the production model.

T

Task: A generic term for work that is not included in the work breakdown structure, but potentially could be a further decomposition of work by the individuals responsible for that work. Also, lowest level of effort on a project.

Triggers: Triggers, sometimes called risk symptoms or warning signs, are indications that a risk has occurred or is about to occur. Triggers may be discovered in the risk identification process and watched in the risk monitoring and control process.

U

User: Usually a member of the customer's organization. Person or organization that will operate the project's output.

V

Variance: Divergence from plan. For example, if the schedule falls behind it is said to have negative variance. A variance is typically expressed in explicit terms such as a $200,000 overrun. Variance can also be expressed as an index, in which case a schedule performance index of .89 would mean the schedule is 11 percent behind the baseline plan (schedule).

W

Work Activities: Sometimes called *Tasks*. Generally project events or efforts that make up a schedule. Activities have a duration (time), consume resources, and in most cases are dependent on or result from other activities.

Work Activity Durations: The amount of time it takes to accomplish the work. Can be expressed in hours, day, weeks, or months.

Work Breakdown Structure (WBS): A deliverable-oriented grouping of project elements that organizes and defines the total scope of the project. Each descending level represents an increasingly detailed definition of a project work.

Work Breakdown Structure (WBS) Baseline: The process of freezing the WBS to measure the effect of change. When the WBS is baselined, change control is applied and change is assessed against other aspects of the project, such as cost and schedule.

Work Package: A deliverable at the lowest level of the *Work Breakdown Structure*, when that deliverable may be assigned to another *Project Manager* to plan and execute. This may be accomplished through the use of a subproject where the work package may be further decomposed into activities.

Note: Adapted from *VA IT Project Management Handbook*. Retrieved from http://www.ocio.usda.gov/p_mgnt/.

Appendix I: Staff Competency Survey

Directions: Please rate your perception of your abilities on a scale of 1 to 5 with 1 being the lowest and 5 being the highest. In addition, please use the same scale to rate the importance of this trait in your current work environment.

Communications

1. Professionals must communicate in a variety of settings using oral, written, and multimedia techniques:

Your self rating:
Low   High
1   2   3   4   5
Importance of this trait to your organization:
Low   High
1   2   3   4   5

Problem Solving

2. Professionals must be able to choose from a variety of different problem-solving methodologies to analytically formulate a solution.

Your self rating:
Low   High
1   2   3   4   5
Importance of this trait to your organization:
Low   High
1   2   3   4   5

3. Professionals must think creatively in solving problems.

Your self rating:

Low   High

1   2   3   4   5

Importance of this trait to your organization:

Low   High

1   2   3   4   5

4. Professionals must be able to work on project teams and use group methods to define and solve problems.

Your self rating:

Low   High

1   2   3   4   5

Importance of this trait to your organization:

Low   High

1   2   3   4   5

Organization

5. Professionals must have sufficient background to understand the functioning of organizations because the product or service must be congruent with, and supportive of the strategy, principles, goals, and objectives of the organization.

Your self rating:

Low   High

1   2   3   4   5

Importance of this trait to your organization:

Low   High

1   2   3   4   5

6. Professionals must understand and be able to function in the multinational and global context of today's information dependent organizations.

Your self rating:

Low   High

1   2   3   4   5

Importance of this trait to your organization:

Low   High

1   2   3   4   5

Quality

7. Professionals must understand quality planning steps in the continuous improvement process as it relates to the enterprise, and tools to facilitate quality development.

Your self rating:

Low   High

1   2   3   4   5

Importance of this trait to your organization:

Low   High

1   2   3   4   5

8. Error control, risk management, process measurement, and auditing are areas that professionals must understand and apply.

Your self rating:

Low   High

1   2   3   4   5

Importance of this trait to your organization:

Low   High

1   2   3   4   5

9. Professionals must possess a tolerance for change and skills for managing the process of change.

Your self rating:

Low   High

1   2   3   4   5

Importance of this trait to your organization:

Low   High

1   2   3   4   5

10. Education must be continuous.

Your self rating:

Low   High

1   2   3   4   5

Importance of this trait to your organization:

Low   High

1   2   3   4   5

Groups

11. Professionals must understand mission-directed, principle-centered mechanisms to facilitate aligning group as well as individual missions with organizational missions.

Your self rating:

Low				High
1	2	3	4	5

Importance of this trait to your organization:

Low				High
1	2	3	4	5

12. Professionals must interact with diverse user groups in team and project activities.

Your self rating:

Low				High
1	2	3	4	5

Importance of this trait to your organization:

Low				High
1	2	3	4	5

13. Professionals must possess communication and facilitation skills with team meetings and other related activities.

Your self rating:

Low				High
1	2	3	4	5

Importance of this trait to your organization:

Low				High
1	2	3	4	5

14. Professionals must understand the concept of empathetic listening and utilize it proactively to solicit synergistic solutions in which all parties to an agreement can benefit.

Your self rating:

Low				High
1	2	3	4	5

Importance of this trait to your organization:

Low				High
1	2	3	4	5

15. Professionals must be able to communicate effectively with a changing workforce.

Your self rating:
Low   High
1   2   3   4   5
Importance of this trait to your organization:
Low   High
1   2   3   4   5

Appendix J: Behavioral Competencies

Companies interesting in stimulating learning and growth among employees will be interested in this list of behavioral competencies for employees and managers.

For Employees

Communicates Effectively

1. Listens to others in a patient, empathetic, and nonjudgmental way; acknowledges their ideas in a respectful manner; questions appropriately
2. Is straightforward and direct; behavior is consistent with words
3. Discusses concerns and conflict directly and constructively
4. Communicates in a timely fashion

Promotes Teamwork

1. Networks with other employees within and outside of own area; makes internal referrals to connect people with each other
2. Readily volunteers to be on teams
3. Is a participating and equal partner on teams; has the same purpose as the team; encourages cohesion and trust
4. Is receptive to and solicits other team members' advice and ideas
5. Keeps supervisor/team informed of status of work so that surprises are minimized
6. Verbally and nonverbally supports established decisions and actions; represents the collective stance

Presents Effectively

1. Understands the makeup of the audience and is sensitive to their values, backgrounds, and needs
2. Presents ideas clearly so that others can easily understand their meaning
3. Delivers presentations with the appropriate level of expression and confidence
4. Incorporates humor when appropriate and in good taste

Makes Sound Decisions

1. Knows when a decision is necessary and makes decisions in a timely manner
2. Connects decisions to strategic plans; separates essential from nonessential information, considering all logical alternatives when generating conclusions
3. Seeks and considers input from others who are close to the situation before establishing a course of action
4. Considers the relevance and impact of decisions on others prior to making decisions

Uses Resources Wisely

1. Considers need and cost prior to making resource-related requests and decisions
2. Makes maximum use of available resources through the efficient and creative use of people, time, material, and equipment
3. Reduces waste, reuses materials, and recycles appropriate materials
4. Functions within the budget

Takes Initiative and Accepts Accountability

1. Is proactive; plans ahead; sees things that need to be done and accomplishes them on own initiative and on time
2. Accepts responsibility and consequences for his or her decisions and actions
3. Follows through on commitments; does what he says he will do, the first time
4. Acknowledges, accepts, and learns from mistakes

Lives Company's Values

1. Demonstrates the organizational and professional code of ethics including honesty, respect, dignity, caring, and confidentiality
2. Demonstrates and consistently applies organizational principles, policies, and values to all employees and situations

3. Respects and operates within the boundaries established for her job and personal boundaries set by others
4. Promotes a positive work environment

Demonstrates a Customer First Approach (Internal Partners and External Customers)

1. Anticipates customers' needs; facilitates customers in expressing their needs; listens to customers and hears what they say
2. Promptly attends to customers' needs (e.g., answers phone and returns phone calls within a reasonable amount of time)
3. Treats customers with respect, politeness, and dignity while maintaining appropriate boundaries
4. When appropriate, provides customers with options for action in response to their needs

Generates New Ideas

1. Generates imaginative and original ideas that will bring about positive change
2. Seizes opportunities to expand on other people's ideas to create something new and add value
3. Encourages others to create new ideas, products, or solutions that will add value to the organization

Demonstrates Flexibility

1. Adapts to and accepts changing work schedules, priorities, challenges, and unpredictable events in a positive manner
2. Is visible and accessible; is approachable even when interruptions are inconvenient
3. Is receptive to new ideas that are different from own ideas
4. Offers to help others when circumstances necessitate sharing the workload

Demonstrates a Professional Demeanor

1. Demonstrates acceptable hygiene and grooming; dresses appropriately for the job
2. Uses proper verbal and nonverbal communications and tone with internal partners and external customers
3. Places work responsibilities and priorities before personal needs while at work

4. Maximizes positive and professional communication with internal partners and external customers; minimizes complaining and nonfactual communication

Stimulates and Adapts to Change

1. Stimulates positive attitudes about change; pushes the change process along
2. Takes personal responsibility for adapting to and coping with change
3. Commits quickly when change reshapes own area of work
4. Accepts ambiguity and uncertainty; is able to improvise and still add value

Continually Improves Processes

1. Anticipates and looks for opportunities to improve steps in the development and delivery of products or services; takes logical risks that may lead to improvement and change
2. Examines work for conformance to predetermined plans, specifications, and standards
3. Freely shares and promotes new ideas that may lead to improvement and positive change, even when the idea may be unpopular
4. Seeks input from others who are closest to the situation in making improvements

For Managers

Organizational Acumen

1. Demonstrates thorough knowledge of the company model, organizational history, and values
2. Applies knowledge of services, products, and processes to understand key issues within own division and work unit
3. Demonstrates understanding of and ability to influence organizational culture, norms, and expectations
4. Contributes to, fosters, and supports changes resulting from organizational decisions and initiatives

Strategic Direction

1. Integrates own work and that of her work unit with the organization's mission, values, and objectives
2. Analyzes and utilizes customer, industry, and stakeholder inputs in strategic and operating plan processes

3. Establishes work group priorities to support strategic objectives
4. Gathers input from internal and external resources to analyze business unit needs
5. Promotes and embraces innovation and creativity to achieve organizational and work unit goals
6. Develops work unit plans and measures that are aligned with division and organization strategic objectives
7. Defines operational goals for work unit
8. Integrates strategies and plans with other areas
9. Promotes and supports the use of corporate and cross-functional teams
10. Ensures customer and employee confidentiality through monitoring access to information to individuals who have need, reason, and permission for such access

Systems Improvement

1. Demonstrates understanding of the "big picture": interrelationships of divisions, departments, and work units
2. Incorporates a broad range of internal and external factors in problem solving and decision making
3. Solicits and incorporates customer and stakeholder needs and expectations into work unit planning
4. Applies and encourages the use of process improvement methods and tools
5. Encourages and supports innovative and creative problem solving by others
6. Integrates process thinking into management of daily operations to enhance quality, efficiency, and ethical standards
7. Utilizes data in decision making and managing work units

Communication

1. Communicates the mission, values, structure, and systems to individuals, groups, and larger audiences
2. Provides leadership in communicating up, down, and across the organization
3. Reinforces organization's key messages
4. Creates a work environment for and models open expression of ideas and diverse opinions
5. Routinely includes a communications plan in work and project planning
6. Applies, communicates, and educates others about organizational policies and procedures
7. Keeps employees informed of industry trends and implications
8. Understands, communicates, and administers compensation and benefits to employees

Employee and Team Direction

1. Anticipates and assesses staffing needs
2. Maintains and updates staff job descriptions, linking employee job descriptions and projects to unit, division, and corporate strategies
3. Recruits, selects, and retains high-performing individuals
4. Provides information, resources, and coaching to support individual/team professional and career development
5. Applies knowledge of team dynamics to enhance group communication, synergy, creativity, conflict resolution, and decision making
6. Ensures staff has training to fully utilize technological tools necessary for job performance
7. Delegates responsibilities; coaches and mentors employees to develop their capabilities
8. Involves staff in planning and reporting to assure integration with operational activities and priorities
9. Coaches employees by providing both positive and constructive feedback and an overall realistic picture of their performance
10. Ensures that core functions in areas of responsibility can be continued in the absence of staff members, either short-term or long-term
11. Recognizes and acknowledges successes and achievements of others

Financial Literacy

1. Partners with financial specialists in planning and problem solving
2. Develops and meets financial goals using standard budgeting and reporting processes
3. Continually finds ways to improve revenue, reduce costs, and leverage assets in keeping with the organization's strategic direction and objectives
4. Uses financial and quantitative information in work unit management
5. Communicates unit budget expectations and status to employees
6. Coaches employees on financial implications of work processes

Professional Development

1. Keeps up to date with external environment through professional associations, conferences, journals, and the like
2. Nurtures and maintains working relationships with colleagues across the organization
3. Demonstrates commitment to professional development, aligning that development with current and future needs of the organization whenever possible
4. Models self-development and healthy work/life balance for employees

Appendix K: Balanced Scorecard Best Practice Metrics for Projects

All metrics are accompanied by targets. For the most part, these are percentages that will be ascertained via a calculation based on data entry of raw data. Some targets have the word "Baseline" encoded. Baseline indicates that the metric is informational; for example, only the raw value will be displayed (i.e., aggregated by the specified period: weekly, monthly, etc.). The targets should be set to default (or 0 in the case of base-lined targets). The entirety of metrics provided is greater than the "norm" for a typical balanced scorecard, which usually has just a few key metrics per perspective.

Financial

Objectives	Measures	Targets	KPI
Optimize cost efficiency of purchasing	Cost to spend ratio [1]	<1 percent	F1
	Negotiated cost savings [2]	>=20 percent	F2
	Costs avoided/total costs [3]	>=10 percent	F3
	Percentage of goods and services obtained through competitive procurement practices [4]	>=19 percent	F4
Control costs	Dollar amount under budget	Baseline	F5

Objectives	Measures	Targets	KPI
	Dollar amount over budget	Baseline	F6
	Budget as a percentage of revenue	<=30 percent	F7
	Expenses per employee	<=$35,000	F8
	Cost of acquired technology/ technology developed in house	<=50 percent	F9
	Percentage new products/ services where break-even point is within one year	80 percent	F10
	Total cost of ownership [5]	<=$6,000 per device per year	F11
	Overtime ratio [6]	<=25 percent	F12
	Cost performance index [7]	>=1	F13
	Average break-even point [8]	<=1.5 years	F14
	Schedule performance index [9]	>=1	F15
	Total cost reductions due to use of technology	>=33 percent	F16
	Workforce reduction due to use of new products	>=10 percent	F17
	Contractor utilization [10]	<=35 percent	F18
Increase business value	Revenue from new products or services [11]	Baseline	F19
	Average ROI [12]	>=1	F20
	Percentage resources devoted to strategic projects	>=55 percent	F21
	Percentage favorable rating of project management by top management	>=93 percent	F22
	Average cost–benefit ratio	>=22 percent	F23
	Net present value [13]	>=1	F24

Objectives	Measures	Targets	KPI
	Assets per employee	Baseline	F25
	Revenues per employee	Baseline	F26
	Profits per employee	Baseline	F27
Improve technology acquisition process	Total expenditures	Baseline	F28
	Total expenditures/industry average expenditures	>=1	F29
	Amount of new technology acquired through M&A	Baseline	F30

[1] Operational costs/purchasing obligations (goods and services purchased).

[2] Cost savings compared to total costs.

[3] Costs avoided compared to total costs. You can avoid costs by reusing hardware or software, utilizing a partner, and so on.

[4] Difference between average qualified bid and the cost of the successful bid. The sum of each calculation is aggregated into a new savings ratio for all transactions.

[5] Additional capital costs: Software, IT support software and network infrastructure.

Technical support costs: Hardware and software deployment, help desk staffing, system maintenance.

Administration costs: Financing, procurement, vendor management, user training, asset management.

End-user operations costs: The costs incurred from downtime and in some cases, end users supporting other end users as opposed to help desk technicians supporting them.

[6] Overtime hours/regular hours worked.

[7] Ratio of earned value to actual cost. EV, often called the budgeted cost of work performed, is an estimate of the value of work actually completed. It is based on the original planned costs of a project.

[8] Break-even analysis. All projects have associated costs. All projects will also have associated benefits. At the outset of a project, costs will far exceed benefits. However, at some point the benefits will start outweighing the costs. This is called the break-even point. The analysis that is done to figure out when this break-even point will occur is called break-even analysis.

[9] SPI is the ratio of earned value to planned value and is used to determine whether the project is on target. (See Cost Performance Index for a definition of earned value, EV).

[10] Cost of external contractors/cost of internal resources.

[11] Use real dollars if systems are external customer facing. Use internal budget dollars if these are internal customer-facing systems.

[12] Return on investment. Most organizations select projects that have a positive return on investment. The return on investment, or ROI as it is most commonly known, is the additional amount earned after costs are earned back.

The formula for ROI is:

ROI = (Benefit − Cost)/Cost

Organizations want ROI to be positive.

[13] NPV is a method of calculating the expected monetary gain or loss by discounting all expected future cash inflows and outflows to the present point in time. If financial value is a key criterion, organizations should only consider projects with a positive NPV. This is because the positive NPV means the return from the project exceeds the cost of capital, the return available by investing elsewhere. Higher NPVs are more desirable than lower NPVs.

Formula for NPV:

NPV = −II + (Sum of) [OCF/(1 + R(r))t] + TCF/(1 + R(r))n]

Where:

II = Initial investment

OFC = operating cash flows in year t

t = year

n = life span (in years) of the project

R(r) = project required rate of return

from http://www.mtholyoke.edu/~aahirsch/howvalueproject.html

[14] Use research from a company such as Infotech (http://www.infotech.com/)

Customer

Objectives	Measures	Targets	KPI
Increase customer satisfaction	Percentage of customers satisfied with system timeliness (speed)	>=92 percent	C1
	Percentage of customers satisfied with responsiveness to questions	>=92 percent	C2
	Percentage of customers satisfied with quality	>=92 percent	C3

Objectives	Measures	Targets	KPI
	Percentage of customers satisfied with sales/customer service representatives	>=92 percent	C4
	Length of time to resolve disputes	<=4 hours	C5
Conformance with customer requests	Percentage of baselined projects with a plan	>=90 percent	C6
	Percentage of customer requests satisfied	>=90 percent	C7
Increase customer base	Customer lifetime value ($)	Baseline	C8
	Share of wallet (percentage) [1]	>=25 percent	C9
	Retention percentage	>=80 percent	C10
	Win-back percentage	>=85 percent	C11
	New acquisitions/current number of customers	>=10 percent	C12
	Rate of defection	<=3 percent	C13
Enhance customer-facing systems	Average number of searches per order/query	Baseline	C14
	Average number of support calls per order/query	Baseline	C15
	Average elapsed time to select product and select an order	Baseline	C16
	Average elapsed time to search Web site	Baseline	C17
	Number of steps required to select and purchase	Baseline	C18
	Average time to answer incoming phone call	Baseline	C19
	Percentage availability of customer-facing applications	>=98 percent	C20
	Average cost to service each customer's transaction	Baseline	C21

Objectives	Measures	Targets	KPI
Support internal customers	Percentage better decisions	>=90 percent	C22
	Percentage time reduction in making decisions	>=90 percent	C23
	Average time to answer a support phone call	Baseline	C24

[1] Compare to competition using service such as http://www.lexisnexis.com/marketintelligence/

Internal Business Processes

Objectives	Measures	Targets	KPI
Improve data quality	Forms input	Baseline	I1
	Data entry error rate	<=3 percent	I2
	Age of current data	Baseline	I3
	Percentage of employees who have up-to-date data	>=98 percent	I4
Improve balance between technical and strategic activities	Percentage of time devoted to maintenance	<=20	I5
	Strategic project counts	Baseline	I6
	Percentage of time devoted to ad hoc activities	<=15 percent	I7
Increase product quality and reliability	Percentage reduction in demand for customer support	>=25 percent	I8
	Number of end-user queries handled	Baseline	I9
	Average time to address an end-user problem	<=4 hours	I10
	Equipment downtime	<=1 percent	I11

Objectives	Measures	Targets	KPI
	Mean time to failure	<=1,000 hours	I12
	Percentage remaining known product faults	<=5 percent	I13
	Percentage of projects with lessons learned in database	>=95 percent	I14
	Fault density [1]	<=3 percent	I15
	Defect density [2]	<=3 percent	I16
	Cumulative failure [3]	Baseline	I17
	Fault days number [4]	<=1	I18
	Functional test coverage [5]	>=95 percent	I19
	Requirements traceability [6]	>=98 percent	I20
	Maturity index [7]	>=1	I21
	Percentage of conflicting requirements	<=5 percent	I22
	Test coverage [8]	>=92 percent	I23
	Cyclomatic complexity [9]	<=20	I24
	Percentage of project time allocated to quality testing	>=15 percent	I25
Reduce risk	Percentage of definitional uncertainty risk [10]	<=10 percent	I26
	Percentage technological risk [11]	<=45 percent	I27
	Percentage developmental risk [12]	<10 percent	I28
	Percentage nonalignment risk [13]	<=4 percent	I29
	Percentage service delivery risk [14]	<=5 percent	I30
	Number of fraudulent transactions	<=1 percent	I31

Objectives	Measures	Targets	KPI
	Percentage of systems with risk contingency plans	>=95 percent	I32
	Percentage of systems assessed for security breaches	>=95 percent	I33
Improve processes	Percentage resources devoted to planning and review of product development activities	>=25 percent	I34
	Percentage resources devoted to R&D	Baseline	I35
	Average time required to develop a new product/ service	Baseline	I36
	Person-months of effort/ project	Baseline	I37
	Percentage of requirements fulfilled	>=90 percent	I38
	Pages of documentation	Baseline	I39
	Percentage of on-time implementations	>=97 percent	I40
	Percentage expected features delivered	>98 percent	I41
	Average time to provide feedback to the project team	<=1 day	I42
	Project development time	>=50 percent	I43
	Percentage of project backlog	<=10 percent	I44
	Percentage of project cancellation rate	<=20 percent	I45
	Support personnel to development personnel ratio	>=35 percent	I56
Enhance resource planning	Number of supplier relationships	Baseline	I47

Objectives	Measures	Targets	KPI
	Decision speed	<5 days	I48
	Paperwork reduction	>=10 percent	I49
Monitor change management	Number of change requests per month	Baseline	I50
	Percentage change to customer environment	Baseline	I51
	Changes released per month	Baseline	I52
Enhance applications portfolio	Age distribution of projects	Baseline	I53
	Technical performance of project portfolio [15]	Baseline	I54
	Rate of product acceptance	>=95 percent	I55

[1] Faults of a specific severity/thousand.

[2] Total number of unique defects detected.

[3] Failures per period.

[4] Number of days that faults spend in the system from their creation to their removal.

[5] Number of requirements for which test cases have been completed/total number of functional requirements.

[6] Number of requirements met /number of original requirements.

[7] Number of functions in current delivery – (adds + changes + deletes)/number of functions in current delivery.

[8] (implemented capabilites/required capabilities)*(capabilities tested)/total capabilities)*100 percent.

[9] Cyclomatic complexity equals the number of decisions plus one. Cyclomatic complexity, also known as V(G) or the graph-theoretic number, is calculated by simply counting the number of decision statements. A high cyclomatic complexity denotes a complex procedure that's hard to understand, test, and maintain. There's a relationship between cyclomatic complexity and the risk in a procedure

[10] Low degree of project specification. Rate risk probability from 0 to 100 percent.

[11] Use of bleeding-edge technology. Rate risk probability from 0 to 100 percent.

[12] Lack of development skillsets.

[13] Resistance of employees or end users to change. Rate probability of risk from 0 to 100 percent.

[14] Problems with delivering system, for example, interface difficulties. Rate risk probability from 0 to 100 percent.

[15] Rate on a scale of 1 to 2 with 1 being unsatisfactory and 2 being satisfactory

Learning and Growth

Objectives	Measures	Targets	KPI
Create a quality workforce	Percentage of employees meeting mandatory qualification standards	>=95 percent	L1
	Percentage of voluntary separations	>=98 percent	L2
	Percentage of leader's time devoted to mentoring	>=45 percent	L3
	Percentage of employees with certifications	>=54 percent	L4
	Percentage of employees with degrees	>=75 percent	L5
	Percentage of employees with three or more years of experience	>=75 percent	L6
	Average appraisal rating	Baseline	L7
	Number of employee suggestions	Baseline	L8
	Percentage expert in currently used technologies	>=95 percent	L9
	Rookie ratio [1]	<=10 percent	L10
	Percentage expert in emerging technologies	>=75 percent	L11
	Proportion of support staff	>=35 percent	L12
	Availability of strategic information	>=100 percent	L13
	Intranet searches	Baseline	L14
	Average years of experience with team	Baseline	L15
	Average years of experience with language	Baseline	L16
	Average years of experience with software	Baseline	L17
	Percentage of employees whose performance evaluation plans are aligned with organizational goals and objectives	>=98 percent	L18

Objectives	Measures	Targets	KPI
	Percentage conformity with HR roadmap as a basis for resource allocation	>=95 percent	L19
	Percentage of critical positions with current competency profiles and succession plans in place	>=98 percent	L20
	Percentage number of net meetings	>=20 percent	L21
	Number of new templates, procedures tools to increase productivity	Baseline	L22
Increase employee satisfaction	Percentage of employees satisfied with the work environment	>=98 percent	L23
	Percentage of employees satisfied with the professionalism, culture, values, and empowerment	>=98 percent	L24
	Employee overtime	Baseline	L25
	Employee absenteeism	Baseline	L26
	Discrimination charges	Baseline	L27
	Employee grievances	Baseline	L28
	Tardiness	Baseline	L29
	Number of employee suggestions implemented	Baseline	L30
	Percentage in-house promotions	>=90 percent	L31
Enhance employee training	Percentage of technical training goals met	>=90 percent	L32
	Number of training sessions attended per employee	Baseline	L33
	Training budget as a percentage of overall budget	>=20 percent	L34
	Frequency of use of new skills	>=85 percent	L35
Enhance R&D	Research budget as a percentage of budget	>=35 percent	L36

Objectives	Measures	Targets	KPI
	Number of quality improvements	Baseline	L37
	Number of innovative processes deployed	Baseline	L38
	Percentage of R&D directly in line with business strategy	>=98 percent	L39
	Number of technologies owned or possessed by company	Baseline	L40
	Number of new patents generated by R&D	Baseline	L41
	Number of patentable innovations not yet patented	Baseline	L42
	Number of patents protecting the core of a specific technology or business area	Baseline	L43
	Number of entrepreneurs in company [2]	Baseline	L44
	Percentage of workforce currently dedicated to innovation projects	>=5 percent	L45
	Number of new products, services, and businesses launched	Baseline	L46
	Percentage of employees who have received training in innovation	>=5 percent	L47

[1] Rookie means new, inexperienced, or untrained personnel.

[2] Number of individuals who previously started a business.

Appendix L: Benchmarking Data Collection Techniques

Without proper information it is difficult, if not impossible, to initiate a proper benchmarking effort. Information gathered in this process—called data collection or requirements elicitation by planners—will enable the project manager to develop valid measures against which the project should be measured.

Interviewing

The most common method of gathering information is by interviewing people. Interviewing can serve two purposes at the same time. The first is a fact-finding mission to discover what each person's goals and objectives are with respect to the project, and the second is to begin a communications process that enables one to set realistic expectations for the project.

There are a wide variety of stakeholders that can and should be interviewed. Stakeholders are those who have an interest in seeing this project successfully completed; that is, they have a "stake" in the project. Stakeholders include employees, management, clients, and benchmarking partners.

Employees

Interviews have some major obstacles to overcome. Interviewees may resist giving information out of fear, they may relate their perception of how things should be done rather than how they really do them, or they may have difficulty in expressing themselves. On the other hand, the analyst's own mindset may also act as a filter. The interviewer sometimes has to set aside his own technical orientation and make the best effort that he can to put himself in the same position as the interviewee. This requires that the analyst develop a certain amount of empathy.

An interview outline should contain the following information:

1. Name of interviewee
2. Name of interviewer
3. Date and time
4. Objectives of interview, that is, what areas you are going to explore and what data you are going to collect
5. General observations
6. Unresolved issues and topics not covered
7. Agenda, that is, introduction, questions, summary of major points, closing

Recommended guidelines for handling the employee interview process include:

1. Determine the process type to be analyzed (tactical, strategic, hybrid).
2. Make a list of departments involved in the process.
3. For each department, either request or develop an organization chart that shows the departmental breakdown along with the name, extension, and list of responsibilities of each employee.
4. Meet with the department head to request recommendations and then formulate a plan that details which employees are the best interview prospects. The "best" employees to interview are those: (a) who are very experienced (i.e., senior) in performing their job function; (b) who may have come from a competing company and, thus, have a unique perspective; (c) who have had a variety of positions within the department or company.
5. Plan to meet with employees from all units of the department. In some cases, you may find that interviewing several employees at a time is more effective than dealing with a single employee, as interviewing a group of employees permits them to bounce ideas off each other.
6. If there are many employees within a departmental unit it is not optimum to interview every one. It would be wrong to assume that the more people in a department the higher the number of interviewees. Instead, sampling should be used. Sampling is used to (a) contain costs, (b) improve effectiveness, (c) speed up the data gathering process, and (d) reduce bias. Systems analysts often use a random sample. However, calculating a sample size based on population size and your desired confidence interval is more accurate. Rather than provide a formula and instructions on how to calculate sample size, I direct the reader to the sample size calculator located at http://www.surveysystem.com/sscalc.htm.

7. Carefully plan your interview sessions. Prepare your interview questions in advance. Be familiar with any technical vocabulary your interview subjects might use.
8. No meeting should last longer than an hour. A half hour is optimum. There is a point of diminishing returns with the interview process. Your interviewees are busy and usually easily distracted. Keep in mind that some of your interviewees may be doing this against their will.

Customers

Customers often have experiences with other vendors or suppliers and can offer insight into the processes that other companies use or that they have experienced.

Guidelines for interviewing customers include:

1. Work with the sales or marketing departments to select knowledgeable and cooperative customers.
2. Prepare an adequate sample size as discussed in the prior section.
3. Carefully plan your interview sessions. Prepare your interview questions in advance.

Companies and Consultants

Another source of potentially valuable information is from other companies in the industry and consultants who specialize in the process areas being examined. Although consultants can be easily located and paid for their expert advice, it is wise to tread slowly when working with other companies who are current or potential competitors.

Guidelines for interviewing other companies include:

1. Work with senior management and marketing to create a list of potential companies to interview. This list should contain the names of trading partners, vendors (companies that your company buys from), and competitors.
2. Attend industry trade shows to meet and mingle with competitor employees and listen to speeches made by competitive companies.
3. Attend trade association meetings; sit on policy and standards committees.

Suppliers

Suppliers of the products you are considering are also an important source of ideas. These suppliers know a great deal about how their products are being used in the processes you are examining.

Types of Questions

When interviewing anyone it is important to be aware of how to ask questions properly. Open-ended questions are the best for gaining the most information because they do not limit the individuals to predefined answers. Other benefits of using open-ended questions include: puts the interviewee at ease, provides more detail, induces spontaneity, and it's far more interesting for the interviewee. Open-ended questions require more than a yes or no answer. An example of an open-ended question is, "What types of problems do you see on a daily basis with the current process?" These questions allow individuals to elaborate on the topics and potentially uncover the hidden problems at hand that might not be discoverable with a question that requires a yes or no answer.

One disadvantage of open-ended questions is that they create lengthier interviews. Another disadvantage is that it is easy for the interview to get off track and it takes an interviewer with skill to maintain the interview in an efficient manner.

Closed-ended questions are, by far, the most common questions in interviewing. They are questions that have yes and no answers and are utilized to elicit definitive responses.

Past-performance questions can be useful to determine past experiences with similar problems and issues. An example of how a past-performance question is used is, "In your past job how did you deal with these processes?"

Reflexive questions are appropriate for closing a conversation or moving it forward to a new topic. Reflexive questions are created with a statement of confirmation and adding a phrase such as: don't you, couldn't you, or wouldn't you.

Mirror questions form a subtle form of probing and are useful in obtaining additional detail on a subject. After the interviewee makes a statement, pause and repeat the statement back with an additional or leading question: "So, when this problem occurs, you simply move on to more pressing issues?"

Often answers do not give the interviewer enough detail so one follows the question with additional questions to prod the interviewee to divulge more details on the subject. For example:

1. Can you give some more details on that?
2. What did you learn from that experience?

Another, more subtle, prodding technique can be used by merely sitting back and saying nothing. The silence will feel uncomfortable causing the interviewee to expand on his or her last statement.

Questionnaires/Surveys

If there are large numbers of people to interview, one might start with a questionnaire and then follow up with certain individuals who present unusual ideas or issues in the questionnaires. Survey development and implementation is composed of the following tasks, according to Creative Research Systems, makers of a software solution for survey creation (surveysolutions.com):

1. Establish the goals of the project: What you want to learn.
2. Determine your sample: Whom you will interview.
3. Choose interviewing methodology: How you will interview.
4. Create your questionnaire: What you will ask.
5. Pre-test the questionnaire, if practical: Test the questions.
6. Conduct interviews and enter data: Ask the questions.
7. Analyze the data: Produce the reports.

Similar to interviews, questionnaires may contain closed- or open-ended questions or a hybrid, a combination of the two.

Survey creation is quite an art form. Guidelines for creation of a survey include:

1. Provide an introduction to the survey. Explain why it's important they respond to it. Thank them for their time and effort.
2. Put all important questions first. It is rare that all questions will be responded to. Those filling out the survey often become tired or bored with the process.
3. Use plenty of "white space." Use an appropriate font (e.g., Arial), font size (i.e., at least 12), and do skip lines.
4. Use nominal scales if you wish to classify things (e.g., What make is your computer? 1 = Dell, 2 = Gateway, 3 = IBM).
5. Use ordinal scales to imply rank (e.g., How helpful was this class? 3 = Not helpful at all, 2 = Moderately helpful, 1 = Very helpful).
6. Use interval scales when you want to perform some mathematical calculations on the results (e.g., How helpful was this class?

   Not useful at all   Very useful
     1   2   3   4   5

Survey questions must be carefully worded. Ask yourself the following questions when reviewing each question:

1. Will the words be uniformly understood? In general, use words that are part of the commonly shared vocabulary of the customers. For example:
   a. (Poor) Rate the proficiencies of the personnel.
   b. (Better) Are personnel knowledgeable?
2. Do the questions contain abbreviations or unconventional phrases? Avoid these to the extent possible, unless they are understood by everyone and are the common way of referring to something. For example:
   a. (Poor) Rate our walk-in desk.

      b. (Better) Are personnel at our front desk friendly?

3. Are the questions too vague? Survey items should be clear and unambiguous. If they aren't, the outcome is difficult to interpret. Make sure you ask something that can truly be measured. For example:

      a. (Poor) Should this library change its procedures?

      b. (Better) Did you receive the information you needed?

4. Are the questions too precise? Sometimes the attempt to avoid vagueness results in items being too precise and customers may be unable to answer them. For example:

      a. (Poor) Each time you visit the library, is the waiting line long?

      b. (Better) Generally, is the waiting line in the library long?

5. Are the questions biased? Biased questions influence the customer to respond in a manner that does not correctly reflect her opinion. For example:

      a. (Poor) How much do you like our library?

      b. (Better) Would you recommend our library to a friend?

6. Are the questions objectionable? Usually this problem can be overcome by asking the question in less direct way. For example:

      a. (Poor) Are you living with someone?

      b. (Better) How many people, including yourself, are in your household?

7. Are the questions double-barreled? Two separate questions are sometimes combined into one. The customer is forced to give a single response and this, of course, would be ambiguous. For example:

      a. (Poor) Is the library attractive and well-maintained?

      b. (Better) Is the library attractive?

8. Are the answer choices mutually exclusive? The answer categories must be mutually exclusive and the respondent should not feel forced to choose more than one. For example:

      a. (Poor) Scale range: 1, 2–5, 5–9, 9–13, 13 or over

      b. (Better) Scale range: 0, 1–5, 6–10, 11–15, 16 or over

9. Are the answer choices mutually exhaustive? The response categories provided should be exhaustive. They should include all the possible responses that might be expected. For example:

      a. (Poor) Scale range: 1–5, 6–10, 11–15, 16–20

      b. (Better) Scale range: 0, 1–5, 6–10, 11–15, 16 or over

Tallying the responses will provide a "score" which assists in making a decision that requires the use of quantifiable information. When using interval scales keep in mind that not all questions will carry the same weight. Hence, it is a good idea to use a weighted average formula during calculation. To do this, assign a "weight" or level of importance to each question. For example, question 9 might be assigned a weight of 5 on a scale of 1 to 5 meaning that this is a very important question. On the other hand, a question such as: "Was the training center comfortable?" might carry a weight of only 3. The weighted average is calculated by multiplying the weight by the score ($w \times s$) to get the final score. Thus the formula is $s_{new} = w \times s$.

There are several problems that might result in a poorly constructed questionnaire. Leniency is caused by respondents who grade nonsubjectively, in other words, too easily. Central tendency occurs when respondents rate everything as average. The halo effect occurs when the respondent carries his good or bad impression from one question to the next.

There are several methods that can be used to successfully deploy a survey. The easiest and most accurate is to gather all respondents in a conference room and hand out the survey. For the most part, this is not realistic, so other approaches would be more appropriate. E-mail and traditional mail are two methodologies that work well, although you often have to supply an incentive (i.e., prize) to get respondents to fill out those surveys on a timely basis. Web-based surveys (Internet and intranet) are becoming increasingly popular as they enable the inclusion of demos, audio, and video. For example, a Web-based survey on what type of user interface is preferable could have hyperlinks to demos or screenshots of the choices.

Observation

Observation is an important tool that can provide a wealth of information. There are several forms of observation including silent and directed. In silent observation, the analyst merely sits on the sidelines with pen and pad, and observes what is happening. If it is suitable, a tape recorder or video recorder can record what is being observed. However, this is not recommended if the net result will be several hours of random footage.

Silent observation is best used to capture the spontaneous nature of a particular process or procedure. For example:

1. When customers will be interacting with staff
2. During group meetings
3. On the manufacturing floor
4. In the field

Directed observation provides the analyst with a chance to micro-control a process or procedure so that it is broken down into its observable parts. At one accounting firm a tax system was being developed. The analysts requested that several senior tax accountants be paired with a junior staff member. The group was given a problem as well as all of the manuals and materials they needed. The junior accountant sat at one end of the table with the pile of manuals and forms while the senior tax accountants sat at the other end. A tough tax problem was posed. The senior tax accountants were directed to think through the process and then direct the junior member to follow through on their directions to solve this problem. The catch was that the senior members could not walk over to the junior person nor touch any of the reference guides. This whole exercise had to be verbal and use just memories and expertise. The entire process was videotaped. The net result was that the analyst had a complete record of how to perform one of the critical functions of the new system.

Participation

The flip side of observation is participation. Actually becoming a member of the staff, and thereby learning exactly what it is that the staff does so that it might be automated, is an invaluable experience.

Documentation

It is logical to assume that there will be a wide variety of documentation available to the analyst. This includes, but is not limited to the following:

1. Documentation from existing systems. This includes requirements and design specifications, program documentation, user manuals, and help files. This also includes whatever "wish lists" have been developed for the existing system.
2. Archival information.
3. Policy and procedure manuals.
4. Reports.
5. Memos.
6. Standards.
7. E-mail.
8. Minutes from meetings.
9. Government and other regulatory guidelines and regulations.
10. Industry or association manuals, guidelines, and standards (e.g., accountants are guided not only by in-house rules and regulations but by industry and other rules and regulations).

Brainstorming

In a brainstorming session you gather together a group of people, create a stimulating and focused atmosphere, and let people come up with ideas without risk of being ridiculed. Even seemingly stupid ideas may turn out to be "golden."

Focus Groups

Focus groups are derived from marketing. These are structured sessions where a group of stakeholders is presented with a solution to a problem and then closely questioned on their views about that solution.

Index

Milton Keynes UK
Ingram Content Group UK Ltd.
UKHW031139141024
449569UK00024B/1219